KNOWLEDGE-IN-PRACTICE
IN THE CARING PROFESSIONS

Knowledge-in-Practice in the Caring Professions
Multidisciplinary Perspectives

Edited by

HEATHER D'CRUZ
Deakin University, Australia
STRUAN JACOBS
Deakin University, Australia
ADRIAN SCHOO
Greater Green Triangle
University Department of Rural Health
(Deakin and Flinders Universities), Australia

ASHGATE

Published by
Ashgate Publishing Limited
Wey Court East
Union Road
Farnham
Surrey, GU9 7PT
England

Ashgate Publishing Company
Suite 420
101 Cherry Street
Burlington
VT 05401-4405
USA

www.ashgate.com

British Library Cataloguing in Publication Data
Knowledge-in-practice in the caring professions: multi-disciplinary perspectives.
1. Social service--Practice. 2. Medicine--Practice.
I. D'Cruz, Heather. II. Jacobs, Struan. III. Schoo, Adrian.
362.1-dc22

Library of Congress Cataloging-in-Publication Data
Knowledge-in-practice in the caring professions : multidisciplinary perspectives / [edited] by Heather D'Cruz, Struan Jacobs, and Adrian Schoo.
    p.cm.
  Includes bibliographical references and index.
  ISBN 978-0-7546-7282-1 (hardback) -- ISBN 978-0-7546-7284-5 (pbk) 1. Clinical competence. 2. Medical personnel--Psychology. I. D'Cruz, Heather. II. Jacobs, Struan. III. Schoo, Adrian M. M.
  [DNLM: 1. Health Knowledge, Attitudes, Practice. 2. Clinical Competence. 3. Health Personnel--psychology. W 21 K73 2009]
  RA399.A1K566 2009
  610.69--dc22

                                                                    2009031151

ISBN 978-0-7546-7282-1 (hbk)
ISBN 978-0-7546-7284-5 (pbk)
ISBN 978-0-7546-9063-4 (ebk)

Mixed Sources
Product group from well-managed forests and other controlled sources
www.fsc.org Cert no. SA-COC-1565
© 1996 Forest Stewardship Council
FSC

Printed and bound in Great Britain by
MPG Books Group, UK

Contents

List of Tables

Contributors

Malcolm Battersby is Director, Flinders Human Behaviour and Health Research Unit, Flinders University Medical Centre, Adelaide, Australia.

Tracey Bucknall is Professor, Deakin University Head, Cabrini-Deakin Centre for Nursing Research, Cabrini Institute, Melbourne, Australia.

Jennifer Cameron is Lecturer, Graduate School for Health Practice, Charles Darwin University, Darwin, Australia.

Lisa Chaffey is a Lecturer in Occupational Science and Therapy, Deakin University. She is a PhD candidate at LaTrobe University, and has the qualifications Grad.Cert (Hlth Prom), B.OccTHy (Hons).

Heather D'Cruz is a Senior Lecturer in Social Work, School of Health and Social Development, Faculty of Health, Medicine, Nursing, and Behavioural Sciences, Deakin University, Waterfront campus, Geelong, Australia.

Peter Greenberg is Physician, General Medicine and Principal Fellow, Dept of Medicine, Project Director, Evidence Based Practice, Clinical Epidemiology and Health Care Evaluation Unit, Dept of General Medicine, The Royal Melbourne Hospital, Melbourne, Australia.

Alex Holmes is Senior Lecturer, Department of Psychiatry, Royal Melbourne Hospital, University of Melbourne, Melbourne, Australia.

Alison Hutchinson is Postdoctoral Fellow, Knowledge Utilization Program, Faculty of Nursing, University of Alberta, Edmonton, Canada.

Struan Jacobs is Senior Lecturer in the Faculty of Arts-Education, Deakin University, Geelong, Australia.

Sharon Lawn is Course Coordinator, Graduate Program in Chronic Condition Management and Self-Management, Flinders University Medical Centre , Adelaide, Australia.

Sylvie Meyer is Professeure, filière ergothérapie, Ecole d'études sociales et pédagogiques, Lausanne Haute école de travail social et de la santé, EESP Vaud, Lausanne, Switzerland.

Peter Miller is NHMRC Howard Florey Fellow, School of Psychology, Faculty of Health, Medicine, Nursing, and Behavioural Sciences, Deakin University, Waterfront campus, Geelong, Australia.

Joy Norton in private practice in Melbourne, has worked as an analytical psychologist for over thirty years.

Frances Sheean is Lecturer in Nursing, Division of Nursing and Midwifery, La Trobe University, Bendigo, Australia

Megan Smith is Senior Lecturer, Course Co-ordinator Physiotherapy Program, School of Community Health, Charles Sturt University, Albury, Australia.

Adrian Schoo is Associate Professor, Director Workforce Development, Greater Green Triangle University Department of Rural Health (Flinders University and Deakin University), Hamilton, Australia.

Karen Stagnitti is Associate Professor, Deakin University, Occupational Science and Therapy, Faculty of Health, Medicine, Nursing and Behavioural Sciences, Geelong, Australia.

Introduction

Heather D'Cruz, Struan Jacobs and Adrian Schoo

In most countries there is a trend for government departments and funding agencies to favour interprofessional (or multidisciplinary) models of care. The intention underlying this trend is to provide a holistic approach to understanding service users' problems and needs, which are usually multifaceted and multi-causal, and which therefore may benefit from multidisciplinary knowledge. Examples include services to prevent and intervene in cases of elder abuse (National Committee for the Prevention of Elder Abuse); cancer research (Cancer Research, UK); acute healthcare (Atwal and Caldwell 2006); psychiatric services (Salmon 1994); and palliative care (Corner 2003). However, while many health and human service organizations recognize the desirability of multidisciplinary teams, primarily to promote coordinated services, to minimize problems of 'gaps' in services to clients and problems of service duplication and waste of resources (e.g. the National Committee for Prevention of Elder Abuse, Cancer Research, UK), there is less appreciation of how such interprofessional relationships work in practice with actual service users and their particular needs and problems. These largely unrecognized, yet complex, features of interdisciplinary group dynamics that go beyond 'teamwork' have been critiqued based on personal experience by individual professionals (e.g. Salmon 1994), as well as those seeking to develop organizational and professional practice (e.g. Corner 2003, van Norman 1998, Davis 1997). To achieve such an appreciation, it would be essential to understand both the differences and similarities between professions, rather than taking for granted that professional goodwill alone will achieve desired outcomes for service users. Furthermore, while each professional education programme aims to inculcate graduates into prescribed ways of knowing and doing as representative of that profession, demarcated from 'other' professions, individual practitioners may not strictly adhere to professional prescriptions for a variety of reasons, including personal beliefs and values, exposure to alternative knowledge and value bases, and the particular demands of practice (Davis 1997). Thus while interprofessional practice as an abstraction is a laudable aim, there are also contextual issues that need to be understood so that the strengths of such practice can be maximized, while attending to the features that may limit its effectiveness. This book begins to address some of these underlying features of professional practice, for example, different professional knowledge bases and different organizational roles and responsibilities. The title *Knowledge-in-Practice in the Caring Professions*: *Multidisciplinary Perspectives*, refers to two themes.

The first theme, related to knowledge-in-practice in the caring professions, explores a common preoccupation for all professions, that of the complicated relationship between 'knowledge' and 'practice', which involves at least four strands. The first strand is that 'practice' may be informed by or apply 'knowledge' (hence talk of applied science and applied social science [Beck 1959: 18]). A second strand is that 'knowledge' as theoretical abstractions must be negotiated and translated 'in practice' with actual people in their life circumstances (Benner 2004). A third strand is that 'knowledge' exists in 'the practice', sometimes described as 'practice wisdom'. Finally, practice may give rise to new knowledge and understanding (Diwan et al. 1997). Moreover, as an accredited and accomplished agent, each professional is expected to work autonomously, even if he or she is engaged in a multidisciplinary team.

The aim of this book is to seek for answers to related questions. How do professionals understand knowledge that they apply to, or that is incorporated in, their practice? What does it mean to talk of knowledge-in-practice? How do professionals, engaged in problem-solving activities with or on behalf of service users, 'know how' to exercise skill, judgement, discernment and discretion? And, how do they apply theory in practice, in a variety of contexts? How much of their knowledge is akin to that in 'craft traditions' in which procedures, maxims and rules have been found useful in the past and have been handed down from accredited practitioners to the younger generation? Is this knowledge, of which practitioners themselves may not be fully aware, systematically interconnected, or is it weak in structure (see Nash 1963: 63–4)? Encapsulating these questions, this book explores the important but insufficiently understood topic of professional knowledge expressed in and through practice as involving agents exercising their judgement and discretion, which is embodied in their skilled activities.

The book's second thematic strand – a counterpoint to the first – involves recognizing and acknowledging differences between and within professions. The idea of difference underpins most discussions of professional perspectives and practice approaches, even when professionals may be working in the same field of practice, for example, child and family welfare, or mental health.

The most salient differences between professions relate to the substantive disciplines and knowledge informing professional education. These disciplines are, broadly, the natural sciences (including biology) and the social sciences (including the humanities). Further differences include concepts, theories and practices that are peculiar to a profession; the extent to which professionals use technology as part of their helping repertoire; and the degree of visibility afforded to the interventions offered, for example through medication or testing, as opposed to counselling or 'talk' therapies. Differences between professions may also relate to the rigour with which their claims about the efficacy of interventions – problem, intervention, outcome – can be assessed empirically. Thus differences between professions may also relate to the claims that can be made for the efficacy of interventions that depend on the ability to make correlations or see causal relationships between problem, intervention and outcome. The ability of some professions to claim greater efficacy for their interventions may be both a cause and an effect of increasing demands for 'evidence-based practice', which tend to rely only or primarily on 'evidence' that has been produced through experimental science models that include random control trials. The increasing tendency to gauge professional efficacy according to the principles of experimental science models has generated significant professional and scholarly debate about what is to count as evidence, and how different forms of 'evidence' are to be graded in different research and practice paradigms (Roberts et al. 2004). The ethical and political issues, not to mention funding allocations, that arise from particular understandings of efficacious practice can pose considerable difficulties for professions that do not or cannot work in such ways in performing their helping role, or practitioners within professions who may find just one model of knowledge and practice extremely limiting in understanding and responding to clients' needs and problems (Camilleri 1999, Bainbridge 1999, Powell 2001). Thus, in addition to differences between professions, we also consider differences within each profession: that is, despite professional education and accreditation of practitioners, no profession can claim to work from a single perspective because different client groups, fields of practice and organizational contexts affect their practice. We also recognize that professions change over time and place and may seek to include new responses to emerging problems that require innovative knowledge, theories and practice approaches (Toulmin 1972).

It can be argued that scholars have addressed these aspects of knowledge-in-practice in the caring professions, either practitioners within one profession, for example, social work (Fook 1996, Fook et al. 2000), nursing (Mallik et al. 2004) and physiotherapy (Donaghy and Morss 2000), or from multidisciplinary perspectives, especially in the health professions, for example, physiotherapy, occupational therapy, medicine and nursing (Higgs et al. 2001, 2004). The scholarship indicates important points. First, there is the common interest in understanding the translation of formal, abstract knowledge, in daily practice, with and on behalf of service users. Secondly, as a counterpoint to the commonality of discretionary practice, there are differences between professions that have consequences for what 'knowledge' and 'practice' may mean, and how the connections between 'knowledge' and 'practice' are made. Finally, professions are not homogeneous monoliths; contextual and idiosyncratic forms of knowledge-in-practice extend professional boundaries and generate demarcation disputes ('turf wars'), as between obstetricians and midwives (Boxall and Flitcroft 2007); nurses and social workers; clinical psychologists and psychiatrists (Salmon 1994); physiotherapists and orthopaedic surgeons or sports medicine physicians; and occupational therapists and social workers.

We have canvassed the options for adequately addressing these complexities involving similarities and differences between professions especially as they present conceptual and practical problems. Most fundamental is the problem that individuals (for example, educators) and professional groups (for example, accrediting and regulatory bodies) espouse the importance of multidisciplinary practice but tend to focus on the knowledge generated by and about their own profession. Furthermore, entrenched professional paradigms can encourage power struggles over the perceived 'superiority' of some disciplinary paradigms over others, including disagreements about epistemology and its relationship to problem definition, interventions and team members' roles (Davis 1997). Perceived epistemological differences between, and hierarchies involving, 'different ways of knowing' can lead to inequalities between team members and their contributions to team decision-making processes and outcomes (Salmon 1994, Davis 1997, Corner 2003). Additionally, van Norman (1998) identifies the ethical and legal issues of professional authority and responsibility that team decision making may not address when individuals may be held ethically and legally liable as 'team leaders'.

These factors serve to underscore a practical problem that attends a text that has chapters by different professionals/academics. There are those who would reject the text as unmarketable, because professionals and educators will only read the chapter(s) 'relevant to their profession'. We view this practical problem as being closely connected to the conceptual problem for moving beyond the position of mere *multidisciplinarity* (the existence of a range of professions whose 'members work in parallel or sequentially from a specific disciplinary base to address a common problem' (Rosenfield 1992, in Corner 2003: 11, Soklaridis et al. 2007). The very fact that different disciplines are represented within one organization and may even practice under the same roof does not necessarily mean they are able to achieve *interdisciplinarity* ('working jointly but still from a disciplinary base to address a common problem') or the more desirable, *transdisciplinarity*, where there is a shared conceptual framework, drawing together disciplinary-specific theories, concepts and approaches to address a common problem (Rosenfield 1992, in Corner 2003: 11). In many cases, professionals may even accept (transdisciplinary) task substitution between disciplines as a means of working more efficiently and effectively (Kessel and Rosenfield 2008).

As one way of exploring knowledge-in-practice, we might have invited representatives of a single profession to contribute their ideas on the topic. This approach appealed in that we expected it would be relatively easy to coordinate. We rejected it, however, on the grounds that rather than cross disciplinary boundaries – the aim we envisaged for the book – it would only serve to confine analysis within a profession and solidify demarcations between professions. The stance we have taken has been to foster multidisciplinary perspectives for the potential enrichment of professional knowledge and practice. This made it reasonable to ask representatives of different professions to each contribute their interpretation of what knowledge-in-practice means to them. Our approach is not designed to produce definitive, all-encompassing claims about multidisciplinary knowledge-in-practice, but we are confident that it will offer fresh insights into these differences and stimulate discussion that can only be beneficial for scholarly engagement and professional practice. Just such an approach has been enthusiastically proposed by Davis (1997) writing about interdisciplinary curriculum development and teaching.

The challenge for interdisciplinarity that our approach foregrounds is how to encourage an audience of professional educators and practitioners to read chapters other than those that relate to their own profession. Problems of interdisciplinarity in understanding and in practice are evident in the very structure and approach of our book. Transcending differences between disciplines and professions to improve professional practice is an ongoing project (Corner 2003). One is reminded of the debate concerning science's incommensurable theories, methods and classes of objects (ontologies) in, and out of, the physical sciences to which Kuhn drew attention in his *Structure of Scientific Revolutions* (1962) and Feyerabend in *Against Method* (1975) (Harris 2005). Readers of this book will find that it foregrounds professional, organizational and practical imperatives that justify the continued development of cross-professional and cross-disciplinary knowledge and justify the improvement of professional education and practice in multidisciplinary settings.

Complementing existing texts, the book casts light on how expertise is understood differently between (and within) various disciplines and professions.

The book rests on sociological assumptions, among the more important of which are that knowledge is, in a significant sense, socially constructed; social interaction involves interpretive processes; and between knowledge and practice there is an implicit relation, which can be represented as knowledge-in-practice.

In approaching potential authors, we sought scholarly professionals (not necessarily academics) who had an ability to reflect on aspects of professional practice. We did not prescribe a particular approach to authors in regard to the topic of knowledge-in-practice. Nor did we expect to establish that the same issues pervade knowledge-in-practice in each caring profession. We asked each author to write on the topic from his or her particular professional perspective. Each author has been encouraged to stand back from his or her practice to reflect on and analyze that practice. Authors were invited to give an account of the knowledge that they take to be embodied in their professional practice, paying particular attention to what is distinctive about practical knowledge and the problems to which that knowledge is applied in their field. Emphasis, it was suggested, should be given to *practical* over theoretical knowledge ('knowing *how*' over 'knowing *that*', according to the distinction as drawn by the philosopher Gilbert Ryle), without in any way excluding the author from providing theoretical insights into that practice. It was expected by the editors that the writing of chapters would vary as to the degree of self-awareness according to authors' personal tastes and interests. Contributors to the book were specifically asked to pitch their discussion at a level accessible to a wide audience, comprising intelligent laypeople, undergraduate students in the arts and the social sciences, and students of and practitioners in the caring professions.

The recognition of professional differences that we have outlined above – differences within and between caring professions – provides an argument for the emergent and non-prescriptive approach we have taken. At the same time, however, the issue of how knowledge-in-practice is understood by members of different professions constitutes the unifying theme and focus of our book. This feature is central to the dialogue between professions. We hope that the insights gained from reading the contributions to this book will illuminate and enhance multidisciplinary and interprofessional practice, with its blurring of professional boundaries. The book contributes a credible alternative to contemporary organizational understandings and expectations of professional practice that tend to minimize professional discretion and the ways in which knowledge-in-practice can contribute to effective practice. In order to address more effectively the range of social, psychological and health problems facing contemporary societies, professionals need to engage in cooperative models of practice. This book will give an additional impetus to that engagement.

In Chapter 1, Struan Jacobs theorizes knowledge-in-practice. He draws from the history of ideas and from philosophy to survey different understandings of relations between knowledge and practice and, more pertinently to the subject of this book, knowledge-in-practice. Particular attention is paid to the ideas of Michael Polanyi, arguably the most influential of all writers on the subject. Historically, Polanyi explains, agriculture and major industries, including brewing, smelting, tanning, dyeing, weaving and potting, relied upon operatives who possessed considerable skill but had very little formulated knowledge about how to proceed. Craftwork is Polanyi's historical analogy for explaining forms of practice in modern society: doctors making diagnoses, judges reaching verdicts, and – Polanyi's principal interest – scientists conducting research as the primary way of discovering more about reality. The art of science, as envisaged by Polanyi, relies upon scientists conforming to rules that are embodied in their practice. Polanyi argues that scientists assimilate these rules as part of their broad 'practical knowledge' of the art of research, while the practice itself 'cannot be specified in detail'. The knowledge of scientific research is representative of skilled practice in being largely unspecifiable, which excludes the possibility of this knowledge being set down in textbooks and requires that it be learned through an apprenticeship, the apprentice carefully observing his 'master' and endeavouring to emulate the master's 'efforts in the presence of his example'.

Subsequent chapters are by professionals who are practitioners and/or academics in universities involved in professional education. Each of these authors explores the nature and role of knowledge in the practical work of his or her profession, writing from particular professional perspectives, and from their particular interpretation of the overall theme and aims of this book.

Having indicated earlier in this Introduction that 'evidence-based practice' is a common contemporary issue for professionals, with reference to claims about efficacy and effectiveness of practices, it is apposite that Chapter 2, by Peter Greenberg, begins with an account 'of the history and evolution of "evidence-based practice", and its strengths and limitations'. Greenberg's discussion is from his perspective in medicine. Under the title of 'Information, Knowledge and Wisdom in Medical Practice', Greenberg's chapter analyzes different kinds of 'evidence'. Inquiring as to how scientific and other forms of evidence are 'translated into practice', he pays close attention to how medical practitioners deal with 'uncertainty' and to the place of heuristics, diagnosis and practice. Greenberg describes how the uncertainties of medical practice arise in a context, the elements of which include influences on clinical decision making, changing consumers' expectations, 'medicalization' and 'disease mongering'.

A second issue that needs to be addressed in relation to the caring professions is how abstract (theoretical) knowledge is applied in practice where actual problems are presented to professionals by clients. This process, known variously as 'applying theory to practice' (Tuckett 2005), 'clinical decision making' (Hardy and Smith 2008), and professional discretion

(Baker 2005), is common to all caring professions and must be taught as part of professional education. Chapter 3, by Alex Holmes, considers how the practice of the psychiatrist is largely invisible in the pages of the discipline's textbooks and journals, each trainee gaining mastery by means 'of an arduous clinical apprenticeship' that is augmented by accredited and 'documented' knowledge, the process being overseen and guided by the professional 'guild'.

Another common issue for caring professions discussed above is the importance of the contexts in which abstract knowledge as 'theories' influence and enter practice, for example the organizational context and the field of practice, as well as the particularities of each client's needs and problems (Whiteford and Wright St-Clair 2004). In Chapter 4, 'Social Work Knowledge-in-Practice', Heather D'Cruz explores how she has interpreted social work knowledge-in-practice as research, and the broader implications of such interpretive processes for professional knowledge-in-practice. Chapters 2 to 4 attend to professional issues explored through the particular professional lenses of medicine, psychiatry and social work. The next two chapters consider the connections between personal experiences and professional knowledge-in-practice.

In Chapter 5, 'Disability: A Personal Approach', Lisa Chaffey explores factors involved in the approach that the healthcare worker brings to bear when dealing with clients with disabilities. The approach of the health professional is envisaged by Chaffey as a unique personal blend of thinking in action, described as 'clinical reasoning'. Examining 'the biomedical and social models of disability', she provides an account of the ways in which these models affect the practice of the health professional whose focus is on disability.

In Chapter 6, 'Psychotherapeutic Practice', Joy Norton, a Jungian analyst, looks at strands that exist between professionals' and clients' perspectives on knowledge in psychotherapy. Noting that 'knowledge and clinical practice are always mediated and informed by the experience of the client', Norton identifies a 'process of co-creation unfolding in the work'. Using detailed case material and drawing on three schools of analytical psychology – archetypal, classical and developmental – Norton amplifies the 'moments where practice meets knowledge'. Theory is detrimental to the practice of analysis when it has the determining role. As argued by Norton in regard to her profession, for theoretical knowledge to be of value, it 'needs to emerge in the practice of analysis and not be predetermined by existing, formalized, thinking'.

Chapter 7, 'Knowledge to Action in the Practice of Nursing', Tracey Bucknall and Alison Hutchinson discuss the significance of knowledge utilization in nursing and provide models to describe the knowledge utilization process. They extend their analysis to include what constitutes evidence for nurses and how nursing knowledge is constructed. Evidence is shown to be integrated and blended with other forms of knowledge (expertise, patient preference and knowledge of available resources) to inform evidence-based clinical decision making in nursing.

The remaining four chapters indicate different approaches to multidisciplinary, interdisciplinary and transdisciplinary knowledge-in-practice. Chapter 8, 'The Risky Business of Birth' is an exploration of the boundaries between obstetricians and midwives, with contested knowledge being considered in relation to caring for pregnant women. The authors, Frances Sheean and Jennifer Cameron, provide an historical survey of the changing institutional boundaries of professional knowledge, roles and responsibilities in the care of pregnant women and trace out implications for professional power and expertise as practice-based knowledge. Risk is a prominent theme in this chapter.

In Chapter 9, 'Skills for Person-Centred Care: Health Professionals Supporting Chronic Condition Prevention and Self-Management', Sharon Lawn and Malcolm Battersby discuss collaborative approaches between providers and consumers of health services for more effectively dealing with 'the growing burden of chronic conditions'. They argue that the problem calls for approaches that circumvent 'traditional turf sensitivities between professionals', and that counteract 'structural boundaries between services'. For Lawn and Battersby, the voice of the consumer, along with 'core skills of engagement and person-centred care', needs to be at the centre of strategies for responding to the challenges posed by chronic illness. 'The focus is on the needs, concerns, beliefs and goals of the person rather than the needs of the systems or professionals.'

Another example of interdisciplinarity and effective professional development is discussed by Megan Smith, Sylvie Meyer, Karen Stagnitti and Adrian Schoo in Chapter 10, 'Knowledge and Reasoning in Practice: An Example from Physiotherapy and Occupational Therapy'. The authors give an account of the knowledge that physiotherapists and occupational therapists use in their clinical practice, and the sources from which that knowledge derives. They discuss knowledge in conjunction with clinical reasoning, reflecting on the intimate relation between knowledge and reasoning in clinical reasoning. The thematic argument of the chapter is illustrated in relation to the care given by physiotherapists and occupational therapists to clients following a stroke. The authors conclude 'that the knowledge and reasoning processes used by these professions include shared and distinctive elements reflecting a close relationship between two professions who maintain defined and separate roles in health practice'.

The final chapter of the book sees Peter Miller explicating the 'truly pan-disciplinary nature' of 'working with alcohol and other drug problems'.

In Miller's account, the complexities of alcohol and other drug (AOD) problems are shown to require a multidimensional understanding. This is a sphere, according to Miller, in which economic, political, sociological, psychological, physiological, psychopharmacological and neuropsychological considerations generate extensive debates about what constitutes valuable knowledge and about appropriate policy responses. These multidimensional features of essential knowledge for effective practice are seen to be embodied in disputes about who constitutes 'an AOD professional'.

This perusal of the chapters of the book points to three salient features that connect them. The first noticeable feature of the contributions is the *range of professions* represented, in which knowledge-in-practice is a major consideration, from medicine and psychiatry, to analytical psychology, allied health (physiotherapy, occupational therapy, nursing, midwifery) and social work; and to professional care for alcohol and other drug users. Second, the authors represent *diverse fields of practice*, from primary, secondary and tertiary care of physical, mental and emotional health across a range of populations, disability, alcohol and other drug problems, midwifery, and social welfare. Third, the authors interpret the *meaning* of professional knowledge-in-practice in various ways. Some authors (Greenberg, Holmes and D'Cruz) have approached this conceptually, appraising the meanings of 'knowledge', 'practice' and 'knowledge-in-practice' from their professional perspectives. They have done this in ways that have significant resonances for other 'caring' professions. The book includes exploration of connections between the personal and the professional – as in Norton's account of knowledge-in-practice being a process and an outcome. There are studies of actual interprofessional relationships, some of which concern conflict and disputes about the legitimacy of 'practice knowledge' (Sheean and Cameron, Miller), with others involving consensual, effective, interprofessional processes and outcomes in allied health settings (Lawn and Battersby, Smith, Meyer, Stagnitti and Schoo).

References

Atwal, A. and Caldwell, K. 2006. Nurses' perceptions of multidisciplinary team work in acute health-care. *International Journal of Nursing Practice*, 12(6), 359–65.

Bainbridge, L. 1999. Competing paradigms in mental health practice and education, in *Transforming Social Work Practice: Postmodern Critical Perspectives*, edited by B. Pease and J. Fook. St Leonards: Allen and Unwin, 179–94.

Baker, K. 2005. Assessment in youth justice. *Youth Justice*, 5(2), 106–22.

Beck, S. 1959. *The Simplicity of Science*. New York: Doubleday.

Benner, P. 2004. Using the Dreyfus model of skill acquisition to describe and interpret skill acquisition and clinical judgment in nursing practice and education. *Bulletin of Science, Technology and Society*, 44(8), 1221–8.

Boxall, A. and Flitcroft, K. 2007. From little things, big things grow: a local approach to system-wide maternity services reform in the absence of definitive evidence. *Australia and New Zealand Health Policy*, 4, 1–6. Available at: http://www.pubmedcentral.nih.gov/articlerender.fcgi?artid=2067755.

Camilleri, P. 1999. Social work and its search for meaning: theories, narrative and practices, in *Transforming Social Work Practice: Postmodern Critical Perspectives*, edited by B. Pease and J. Fook. St Leonards: Allen and Unwin, 25–39.

Cancer Research, UK, *Multi-disciplinary Team*. Available at: http://www.cancerhelp.org.uk/help/default.asp?page=19243.

Corner, J. 2003. The multidisciplinary team – fact or fiction? *European Journal of Palliative Care*, 10(2), 10–13.

Davis, J.R. 1997. Chapter 3. Structuring and delivering interdisciplinary courses: approximating the ideal, in *Interdisciplinary Courses and Team Teaching*. American Council on Education. Phoenix: Oryx Press. Available at: http://www.ntlf.com/html/lib/ictt_xrpt.htm.

Diwan, V.K., Sachs, L. and Wahlström, R. 1997. Practice-knowledge-attitudes-practice. *Social Science and Medicine*, 44(8), 1221–8.

Donaghy, M.E. and Morss, K. 2000. Guided reflection: a framework to facilitate and assess reflective practice within the discipline of physiotherapy. *Journal of Physiotherapy Theory and Practice*, 16(1), 3–14.

Feyerabend, P. 1975. *Against Method*. London: New Left Books.

Fook, J. (ed.) 1996. *The Reflective Researcher*. St Leonards: Allen and Unwin.

Fook, J., Ryan, M. and Hawkins, L. 2000. *Professional Expertise: Practice, Theory and Education for Working with Uncertainty*. London: Whiting and Birch.

Hardy, D. and Smith, B. 2008. Decision making in clinical practice. *British Journal of Anaesthetic and Recovery Nursing*, 9(1), 19–21.

Harris, R. (ed.) 2005. *Rhetoric and Incommensurability*. West Lafayette: Parlor Press.

Higgs, J. and Titchen, A. (eds) 2001. *Practice Knowledge and Expertise in the Health Professions*. London: Butterworth-Heinemann.

Higgs, J., Richardson, B. and Abrandt Dahlgren, M. (eds) 2004. *Developing Practice Knowledge for Health Professionals*. London: Butterworth-Heinemann.

Kessel, F. and Rosenfield, P.L. 2008. Toward transdisciplinary research: historical and contemporary perspectives. *American Journal of Preventive Medicine*, 35(2), 225–34.

Kuhn, T. 1962. *The Structure of Scientific Revolutions*. Chicago: University of Chicago Press.

Mallik, M., Hall, C. and Howard, D. 2004. *Nursing Knowledge and Practice*, 2nd Edition. Oxford: Elsevier.

Nash, L. 1963. *The Nature of the Natural Sciences*. Boston: Little, Brown.

National Committee for the Prevention of Elder Abuse. *Multidisciplinary Teams*. Available at: http://www.preventelderabuse.org/communities/mdt.html [accessed 14 December 2007].

Powell, F. 2001. *The Politics of Social Work*. London: Sage.

Roberts, A.R. and Yeager, K.R. (eds) 2004. *Evidence-based Practice Manual: Research and Outcome Measures in Health and Human Services*. New York: Oxford University Press.

Rosenfield, P. 1992. The potential of transdisciplinary research for sustaining and extending linkages between the health and social sciences. *Social Science and Medicine*, 35(11), 1343–57.

Salmon, G. 1994. Personal view: working in a multidisciplinary team: need it be so difficult? *British Medical Journal*, 309, 1520.

Soklaridis, S., Oandasan, I. and Kimpton, S. 2007. Family health teams: can health professionals learn to work together? *Canadian Family Physician*, 53(7), 1198–9.

Toulmin, S. 1972. *Human Understanding*. Princeton: Princeton University Press.

Tuckett, A. 2005. Applying thematic analysis theory to practice: a researcher's experience. *Contemporary Nurse*, 19, 1–2. Available at: http://www.contemporarynurse.com/archives/vol/19/issue/1-2/.

Whiteford, G. and Wright-St Clair, V. (eds) 2004. *Occupation and Practice in Context*. Oxford: Churchill Livingstone.

Van Norman, G. 1998. Interdisciplinary team issues. *Ethical Topics in Medicine*, University of Washington. Available at: http://depts.washington.edu/bioethx/topics/team.html.

1   Ideas of knowledge in practice

Struan Jacobs

The specialized practice of caring professionals comprises several cognitive dimensions. The most obvious of the dimensions consists in theories, understandings, experiences, facts, advisory rules, stipulations and other such items as have been expressed as *formulated* knowledge, this knowledge serving as a resource from which agents draw in guiding their practice. The concept of formulated knowledge points to a broad distinction between *theory* and *practice*, which has been drawn from the time of ancient Greek philosophy (Lobkowicz 1967). Textbooks are the obvious bearers of formulated knowledge in the training of the professional. Some of the formulated knowledge that she acquired in her professional training may eventually disappear from the practitioner's view, perhaps on account of its having become obsolete, second nature, or having fallen into disuse. Articles in journals and papers at conferences are sources of formulated knowledge with which the professional can supplement her textbook knowledge, inform her practice and keep herself up to date. Theorists have lavished attention over many years on the topic of formulated knowledge and its involvement in professional practice. Relatively little will be said about knowledge of this type in this chapter, one theory being noted to illustrate how such knowledge may come to be produced and used.

The philosopher Karl Popper (1902–1994) advanced a metaphysical theory of three worlds: the physical and the psychological (subjective) – worlds one and two, respectively – and the world of objective products, including language, and knowledge which is formulated in language as affirmations (or denials) of facts and theories and prescriptions of rules and values (Popper 1972: 118).

Complementing his three worlds view, Popper presented a theory the skeleton of which is rendered as PP1→TT→EE→PP2, signifying that the human agent is constantly having to solve problems of one sort or another (for example, technical difficulties, practical issues, explanatory

13

questions) (PP1), by conceiving of theories, framing policies and devising innovative courses of action (designated as TT).[1] As explained by Popper, criticizing (EE) a tentative solution (TT) to one problem might expose it as unsatisfactory, which produces a new problem, question or difficulty (PP2) and a further sequence (TT2→EE→P3). Chiefly interested in knowledge that is formulated and objective, Popper envisaged it as an external resource that is produced by scientific researchers, of which the caring professional avails himself in his problem-solving work, seeking, in the words of Schön (1983: 147), to transform 'the situation from what it is to something he likes better'. The problems that professionals encounter in their practice are of different degrees of difficulty, their solutions calling for more or less inventiveness. New problems may be encountered and preexisting solutions may have to be applied in unusual circumstances.

More directly relevant to the theme of this book is the *unformulated* knowledge that professional practice *embodies*. To better understand this rather remote subject, it will be helpful to view it from different vantage points, bringing its more important features into clearer focus. Three theories of embodied knowledge receive pride of place in this chapter, theories that, having exerted a lasting and pervasive influence, deserve the honorific adjective, 'classical'. They are summarized in Table 1.1

Table 1.1   Theories of embodied knowledge

Theorist	Distinctions between:
Gilbert Ryle	Knowing how (to perform a task) and knowing that (… is the case).
Michael Oakeshott	Technique or technical knowledge (formulated knowledge assisting agents to perform tasks) and practical or traditional knowledge (unformulated knowledge of practices).
Michael Polanyi	(i) Tacit knowledge (knowledge that is unformulated) and express (formulated) knowledge, either of which may concern facts, procedures, values. (ii) Focal (directed) awareness, and objects of which an agent's awareness is subsidiary (unspecifiable). (iii) Personal knowledge (the product of an agent's interpretation, intuition and other such skills) and impersonal knowledge (achievement and use of which is mechanical rather that skilful).

---

1   Popper extended his schema to all animate life.

We should note that the term 'practice' is ambiguous *between,* on the one hand, the activity of *individual agents* and, on the other, *inclusive social processes* comprising the activities and culture (language, knowledge, traditions, presuppositions) of social groups. The second notion of practice is represented by Michel Foucault (1991) who envisaged practices of medicine, jailing, psychiatry and nursing as disciplining members of modern society: people's bodily demeanours and dispositions, vocabularies and worldviews, perceptions and understandings. The two concepts of practice complement each other, but this chapter principally studies the practice of *individuals* as that which is more directly relevant to the subject of this book. (The more inclusive concept of practice – found also in the tradition of Emile Durkheim, and in the writings of Pierre Bourdieu – is well discussed by Schatzki et al. 2001, see also Filmer 1998: 230–33.)

Knowing how

A distinction has been drawn in the philosophical literature between *knowing that* (indicative knowledge) and *knowing how* (practical knowledge). The idea of knowing how appeared in Greek philosophy, and the Chinese Taoist philosopher, Chuang Tzu (399–295 BC), expressed it when he quoted a wheelwright who appreciated that his work needed to be done at 'the right pace, neither slow nor fast' and this, he observed, 'cannot get into the hand unless it comes from the heart. It is a thing that cannot be put into words … there is an art in it that I cannot explain to my son' (quoted by Oakeshott 1991: 14, n.7). Practical knowledge has been analyzed by American pragmatist philosophers, including William James (1842–1910) and John Dewey (1859–1952), with Smith observing (1988: 15, n.2) that it probably was Dewey who explicitly introduced the opposition between knowing how and knowing that into the modern philosophical literature. Thus in his *Human Nature and Conduct* (1922: 178) Dewey identifies knowing how with habitual and instinctive knowledge, to be contrasted with knowing that things are thus and so, which 'involves reflection and conscious appreciation'.

The knowing that/knowing how distinction was most famously explicated in the twentieth century by the Oxford philosopher Gilbert Ryle (1900–1976), in his book *The Concept of Mind* (1949). Ryle's overriding aim was to show that, when using mental adjectives (for example, 'efficient', 'competent', 'skilful', 'committed', 'ignorant', 'erratic', 'slipshod' and 'unskilled'), we are referring not to what occurs in the consciousness of people, to processes taking place in some special entity or 'organ' 'in the head', but to public actions (Ryle 1949: 40, 50–51, 61). Explained Ryle (1949: 51, also 50, 54, 58), we are describing, not 'occult causes' but *dispositions* that people have, exercise and manifest by way of their conduct. Bodily performances 'are not clues to the workings of minds; they are those workings. Boswell described [the workings of] Dr Johnson's mind when he described how he wrote, talked, ate, fidgeted and fumed' (Ryle 1949: 58).

Ryle considered that the common view of mental activity gave pride and place to cognition and to problem solving. This type of activity, described by Ryle (1949: 26) as 'theorizing' is, in the common view, designed to achieve 'knowledge of true propositions or facts', as exemplified by knowledge in mathematics and the natural sciences. 'Theorizing' is commonly construed as a 'private, silent or internal operation' (Ryle 1949: 27).

Paying disproportionate attention to analyzing the sources, nature, and validation of theoretical knowledge, philosophers have, Ryle suggested (1949: 28, emphasis added), insufficiently explored 'what it is for someone to *know how* to perform tasks', this knowledge consisting in people's talents, competences, abilities and skills. In Ryle's interpretation (1949: 28, 41), to state that a person knows how to perform a task of a particular type implies that she performs it 'correctly or efficiently or successfully', the agent regulating her performance by observing relevant rules ('bans', 'permissions') and applying correct standards. There is an 'intellectualist legend', rejected by Ryle, according to which intelligent conduct is preceded by a thoughtful consideration of how best to proceed, what rule to follow. Argued Ryle (1949: 32),

> 'thinking what I am doing' does not connote 'both thinking what to do and doing it'. When I do something intelligently, i.e. thinking what I am doing, I am doing one thing and not two. My performance has a special procedure or manner, not special antecedents.

The performance is skilful, and a skill is 'not an act', nor an event, but a *disposition* (tendency) on the part of a person to conduct herself in a certain way in situations of a given sort (Ryle 1949: 33, 40). A disposition is, for Ryle (1949: 34), an agent's 'mind at work'.

Ryle noticed different ways in which a skill can be acquired, including explicit instruction in the rules that govern it. Having mastered the rules of the skill by rote, an agent may be able to express them upon request. But in complying with the rules of the activity, Ryle believed, an agent typically follows the rules without thinking *of them* (although she does think *about what* it is that she happens to be doing).

A trainee can also 'pick up the art' of *how* to perform a task by observing conduct that is exemplary of it without 'hearing or reading the rules at all', the acquisition of rudiments 'of grammar and logic' being a case in point (Ryle 1949: 41). The agent has to *practise* the repertoire if she is to master the conduct and the rules it incorporates. Ryle wrote (1949, 41), 'we learn *how* by practice, schooled ... by criticism and example, but often quite unaided by any lessons' in a corresponding theory or rules. Graduated tasks are set for the student; each set of tasks being achievable by her but challenging her more than the last. The training may involve repetitive drill, but since the aim is to have her incrementally improve her performance, the trainee will be encouraged to extend her thinking and to sharpen her judgement (Ryle 1949: 42–3). Subjected to criticism (and self-criticism), each task 'performed is itself a new lesson to him how to perform better' (Ryle 1949: 43). The test of whether Ryle's trainee has acquired the knowledge of how to perform some kind of task consists not in her being able to formulate and express the guiding rules but in her conforming to them in competently enacting the task. An agent's knowing how to perform a task is not to say she can give a detailed verbal description of the performance. In much of her activity the social worker, psychotherapist or other caring professional conforms to rules and uses criteria without being conscious that she does so (Ryle 1949: 48).

Some of the competent practice of caring professionals may become habitual, which is to say blind and repetitive. Usually, however, their practice involves a disposition to exercise an 'intelligent capacity', meaning that an agent gives thought to her task. It is a characteristic feature 'of intelligent practices that one performance is modified by its predecessors'; the agent continues to learn and aims to do better (Ryle 1949: 42, also 48). The caring professional, for example, is called on to handle 'emergencies', to carry out 'tests and experiments', to interpret new or unusual evidence, and to make new connections between experiences. She has to innovate and adapt. Exercising 'skill and judgement', Ryle's agent (1949: 42) aims to avoid making mistakes, and wishes to learn from any that she does make. In Ryle's words (1949: 49), 'A man knowing little or nothing of medical science could not be a good surgeon, but excellence at surgery is not the same thing as knowledge of medical science; nor is it a simple product of it'. Besides having been taught the formulated knowledge of his profession, a surgeon 'must have learned by practice a great number of aptitudes'. In the practice of the caring professional, rules have to be applied, and 'putting the prescriptions into practice' calls for intelligence of a *different kind* from that which is involved in learning and understanding the formulated prescriptions.

Knowing how is, Ryle noticed, relative (whereas knowing that – say, that Jupiter has 63 moons or that the British settled in Sydney in 1788 – is absolute) in the sense that cases of it occur across a spectrum, ranging from ignorance to complete knowledge. No caring professional acquits herself perfectly (with complete knowledge of both kinds) in any of her professional activities.

Technical and practical knowledge

Inquiring into modern rationalism as a style of political thinking, in a 1947 essay, 'Rationalism in Politics', the British political theorist Michael Oakeshott (1901–1990) envisaged knowledge as a part of each and every activity (the sciences, and the arts, among others). Although his essay appeared after Ryle's first published investigation in 1946 of the distinction between knowing how and knowing that, Oakeshott made no mention of, and may not have seen, Ryle's discussion. Among the few authors Oakeshott cited in 'Rationalism in Politics' was Michael Polanyi, whose ideas we will consider shortly.

Oakeshott (1991: 12) separated out two types of knowledge involved in human activity, while recognizing that in any 'concrete human activity' the types occur inseparably intertwined. Oakeshott described one of the types as '*technical* knowledge or knowledge *of technique*' or simply as '*technique*' (1991: 12 emphasis added). He considered that knowledge of this type lends itself to being formulated in propositions ('rules, principles, directions, maxims') that agents can study, recall and apply (1991: 14). His examples of formulated technique range from the homely (knowledge expressed in cookery books), to the esoteric (rules of research in science and in history). Oakeshott (1991: 12) designated the second type of knowledge as '*practical*', otherwise referring to it as 'traditional knowledge'. This knowledge, Oakeshott argued (1991: 15), is expressed 'in a customary or traditional way of doing things' (a 'practice'), and in discriminations of 'taste or connoisseurship' that agents make in their enactment of a practice. In Oakeshott's account, no skill or practice is acquirable without a dimension of traditional/practical knowledge, and no task can be performed by an agent who has a command of relevant technique and of formulated rules but is without the practical knowledge of the tradition.

Oakeshott (1991: 15) looked on each form of knowledge as transmitted and received in its own way. Technical knowledge is conveyed in textbooks and lectures, being 'taught and learned' (1991: 15), whereas practical knowledge exists only in the activities that actualize a practice and it cannot be verbally transmitted. Because it is unformulated, Oakeshott reasoned (1991: 15) that practical knowledge must be 'imparted and acquired', each generation of practitioners having to be trained as apprentices to 'master[s]', observing and emulating the skill of accredited craftsmen, acquiring practical knowledge and technique together. In regard to the 'human arts', which have people 'as their plastic material', it is, Oakeshott suggested (1991: 13 emphasis added), a mistake to imagine that *technique* indicates '*what*' the midwife, or doctor, psychologist, nurse, or social worker is to do, and to assume that *practice* guides her on '*how*' to proceed. 'Even in the *what*' (for example, the diagnosis of a condition, the classification of a behaviour, deciding on the best treatment or the appropriate response), the 'dualism of technique and practice' is already present (Oakeshott 1991: 13). There is, according to this view (1991: 14–15), *no* knowledge that is devoid of 'know how'. Would a Gilbert Ryle have agreed with this generalization of Oakeshott? Given that Ryle distinguished between 'knowing that' and 'knowing how', there has to be, in his view, some appreciable difference between them. He might have allowed that the distinction is artificial in as much as each instance of an agent *knowing that*, in some concrete discipline or practice, incorporates an element of *knowing how* (if only subordinately). For example, a proficient chemist who knows *that* Boyle's gas law is PV=k also knows *how to* do the calculations that are needed to apply the law. Nonetheless, Ryle would probably have disagreed with Oakeshott, arguing that, in real concrete disciplines and in situations in which professionals act, knowing *that* differs in its emphasis and purpose from knowing how, including more of indicative (descriptive or explanatory) knowledge and less of practical knowledge (of how to proceed). Conversely, for Ryle, knowing *how* differs in its emphasis and purpose from knowing that, being primarily practical knowledge (about the way in which an agent needs to proceed in her execution of a particular task), with indicative knowledge in a subordinate role. In this manner, one surmises, Ryle would have considered Oakeshott's 'all knowledge is "know how"' to be a confused and confusing statement.

At around the time of the appearance of these works by Ryle and Oakeshott, Ludwig Wittgenstein (1889–1951), a professor of philosophy at Cambridge University in the 1940s, was formulating ideas of a similar nature to theirs. In the posthumously published work *On Certainty* (1974), Wittgenstein argued that, as members of 'a community which is bound together by science and education' (1974: § 298), our cultural endowment includes a 'picture of the world' (*Weltbild*) (1974: § 94). The world picture is not an object of thought and examination for members of a community, their thinking being *embedded* in, and impossible without, this usually unformulated picture.

In another of his posthumously published writings, *Philosophical Investigations* (1953), Wittgenstein made a point about *rules* that bears on our topic of knowledge-in-practice: even when they are explicit, rules *never determine* people's conduct, but leave space for interpretation (and misinterpretation). Wittgenstein observed (1953: § 85) that,

> A rule stands there like a sign-post. Does the sign-post leave no doubt open about the way I have to go? Does it shew which direction I am to take when I have passed it; whether along the road or the footpath or cross-country? But where is it said which way I am to follow it; whether in the direction of its finger or (e.g.) in the opposite one? – And if there were, not a single sign-post, but a chain of adjacent ones or of chalk marks on the ground – is there only one way of interpreting them?

Tacit knowledge[2]

Oakeshott mentioned Michael Polanyi (1891–1976) in his 'Rationalism' essay, citing Polanyi's book, *Science, Faith and Society* (first published in 1946). There Polanyi argued (1964: 42, also 71) that scientific research, like any other 'major intellectual process', depends on unformulated 'premisses'. Illustrating this analogically, Polanyi (1964: 42) wrote that, in coming 'to think' in naturalistic terms, children receive *no* '*explicit* knowledge of the principles of causation. They learn to regard events in terms of what we call natural causes and by practicing such interpretations day by day they are eventually confirmed in the premisses underlying them'. The distinction between *explicit* and *tacit* (unformulated) knowledge proved to be pivotal in Polanyi's mature thought. This differs from, and may have been developed independently of, Ryle's knowing how/knowing that distinction. Polanyi's distinction cuts across that of Ryle: whether it be explicit or tacit, knowledge may concern either '*that* which is' or '*how* to proceed'.

Far and away Polanyi's most important work is *Personal Knowledge* (1958), in which the reader is presented with a detailed analysis of knowledge-in-practice. Polanyi was particularly interested in creative practices, whose agents strive to achieve original results, with scientific research as his chief exemplar. After training in medicine and practising it for a short time, Polanyi completed a PhD in physical chemistry and spent over 20 years as a researcher in this field. His account of scientific research has been widely approved of, having resonances, for example, in Thomas Kuhn's celebrated study, *The Structure of Scientific Revolutions* (1962: 47), which depicts paradigms – exemplary problems-and-solutions – as objects of scientists' unformulated knowledge. Writes one commentator (Zammito 2004: 57): Kuhn 'insists on the essential role of the implicit or, in the terminology of Michael Polanyi, the "tacit" … It is here, perhaps more than anywhere else, that Kuhn's work has effected a long-term shift of inquiry in the philosophy of science: from logic to practice'. The activities of caring professionals are, as a rule, not intended to create new knowledge or new modes of practice, although they may be creative as an unintended consequence. We will abstract ideas from Polanyi's account as seem best able to illuminate the knowledge-in-practice of caring professionals.

Polanyian practice (1958: 53–4) is characterized by skill ('art') and is mastered through training. It is learning by (but not only by) doing. Polanyi drew a distinction between skilled doing ('craftsmanship') and skilled knowing ('connoisseurship'). Skills of each sort blend in different proportion from one practice to the next. In visual perception, for example,

---

2 Certain passages in this section paraphrase some of Jacobs (2004) with the kind permission of the editors of the journal, *Discipline Folosofiche*.

the proportion of skilful doing – controlling eye muscles, adjusting pupils and lenses, and so on – exceeds that of skilful knowing (Polanyi 1969: 126–7). It might be said that in the practice of social work the proportion of skilful *knowing* (trained perception, assessment of the situation, use of evidence to support a recommendation) exceeds the proportion of skilful *doing*. In midwifery and nursing, the greater proportion of skill may often consist in practitioners' conduct and techniques (doing). In medical examination and diagnosis, Polanyi suggested in a later writing (1969: 126), the skills of knowing and of doing balance each other. 'To percuss a lung is as much a muscular feat as a delicate discrimination of the sounds thus elicited. The palpation of a spleen or a kidney combines a skilful kneading of the region with a trained sense for the particular feel of the organ's resistance'.

Polanyi regarded an agent participating in a skilled practice (1958: 49) as following rules, many of which are *unknown* by her, for example the rules that regulate respiration during swimming, or those a cyclist must follow to maintain her balance. Some rules of a practice can be formulated and knowledge of these may assist a student to learn, and assist the accredited agent to participate more effectively, in the practice of her profession. But knowledge of formulated rules represents only a small part of the 'practical knowledge' that an agent requires for her practice. Many rules and particulars of the 'practical knowledge' of a profession are, for Polanyi, *unspecifiable*. They are objects of what we have seen him refer to as *tacit knowledge*, an everyday example being knowledge of the rules of grammar, which we avail ourselves of in speaking and writing without being conscious of the rules we happen to be obeying. Agents in caring professions draw on unspecifiable particulars in their activities of diagnosing, analyzing, appraising, judging, classifying, prescribing and treating. No skilled practice, and probably none of its strands, can be determined by formulated rules. Jere Moorman (2008) has specifically referred to nursing in this light:

> The tacit dimension of nursing – the realm that cannot be fully discovered with recipe books, rules, charts, maxims, sacred texts …microscopes … and other formal processes – is a richer and often under-appreciated dimension of the comprehensive picture of patient care … Nursing involves … recognizing and defining problems; this is a tacit activity, and …cannot be adequately learned by reading about it … Much of nursing involves a knowing under pressure, involving rapid, intuitive and imaginative understanding or response.

Polanyi's emphasis stands in contrast to a tradition in the theory of science and knowledge that probably originated in ancient Greek philosophy, definitely had prominent advocates (for example, Bacon, Descartes, Galileo, Newton) during the Scientific Revolution of the seventeenth century, and remained important well into the twentieth century. Contributors to this tradition formulated rules of scientific method with the object of assisting scientists to proceed more efficiently in their work. A notable later exemplar in the tradition of explicit prescription is Popper's book *The Logic of Scientific Discovery* (1959), the first edition of which had appeared in German as *Logik der Forschung* (1935). Popper explained (1959: 49) that his decision to enunciate 'suitable rules for what I call the "empirical method" is closely connected with my criterion of demarcation: I propose to adopt such rules as will ensure the testability of scientific statements; which is to say, their falsifiability'. In essence, Popper's method rules for scientific researchers included: 'Prefer falsifiable to unfalsifiable theories', 'Prefer theories of greater, to ones of lesser, falsifiability', and 'Test highly falsifiable theories using those of their predictions that are most likely to lead to falsification of the theories'. Polanyi on the other hand issued no rules of method to scientists; the rules of research are, for him, *embodied (and largely concealed) in* its practice.

Polanyi argued (1958: 50) that skilled practice cannot be fully described 'in terms of [its] … particulars', and cannot be mastered by any agent who attempts to learn its activities and its knowledge one particular at a time. The fact that a skilled practice cannot be specified in its details meant, for Polanyi, that it cannot be taught in the classroom. This is, at any rate, true of highly skilled practices. To be sure, practices call for different degrees of skill, and can be envisaged as situated at points along a continuum, between the extreme of practice that is devoid of skill and that of practice which is replete with skill, these opposite limits being theoretical possibilities (exemplifying what the German sociologist, Max Weber, referred to as 'ideal types'). Polanyi paid special attention to elucidating the highly skilled and creative practice of scientific research and to the way in which its skills come to be acquired. He was less interested in analyzing the education of the undergraduate scientist, much of which occurs in lecture theatres and in the solving of standard problems in laboratories. Most caring professionals received an undergraduate education that combined classroom instruction with 'on site' observation and experience (the latter being comparable to training under an 'apprenticeship'), and the debate that perennially flares up and dies down is whether nurses, social workers, psychologists, teachers and others ought to receive more 'on site' training and less instruction at universities (or vice versa).

The highly skilled craftsmanship of scientific research and of other such practices has to be transmitted by a master to her apprentice by the direct contact of 'on site' training. For this reason, Polanyi believed (1958: 53), skilled practice or craftsmanship typically occurs 'in closely circumscribed local traditions' and, if a traditional craft comes to be practised in another country, it is likely to be on account of craftsmen having migrated, and recommenced their practice, there. In Polanyian skilled practice, learnt by an apprentice as she emulates the example of an accredited practitioner, the apprentice submits to the craftsman's *authority*. 'You follow your master because you trust his manner of doing things even when you cannot analyse and account in detail for its effectiveness' (Polanyi 1958: 53). Observing the practice of the master, emulating his practice 'in the presence of his example, the apprentice unconsciously' acquires the rules of the art, embodying them in his craftsmanship. The skilled practice of craftsmen participates in the *tradition* of their occupation, the practice being informed by, at the same time as it sustains, the tradition. The profession's rules of method and its standards of sound practice and of valuable results permeate current professional knowledge, approved techniques and the activities of members of the profession. Knowledge of the standards and of how to apply them is tacit.

Polanyi drew a further distinction, between *focal* and *subsidiary* forms of *awareness*. An agent using a hammer has, in Polanyi's interpretation (1958: 55), subsidiary awareness 'of the feeling in the palm of ... [his] hand', and focal (directed) awareness of the head of the hammer as he guides it in clouting a nail.[3] Subsidiary awareness of a tool or instrument consists, for Polanyi (1958: 59, cf. Kettle 1999: 192), in our making it 'form a part of our own body ... While we rely on a tool or a probe, these are not handled as external objects'. The object of focal awareness for the pianist is not the keyboard but the structure/gestalt of the score. Should the pianist divert 'his attention from the piece he is playing to' the movement of his fingers on the keys of his piano (of which particulars, to this point, he had only been subsidiarily aware), he destroys the gestalt, and becomes confused, to the detriment of his performance (Polanyi 1958: 56). Successful musical performance depends on its detailed particulars remaining as unspecifiable objects of tacit knowledge in the agent's subsidiary awareness, while her focal awareness is of the score and performance as a whole (Polanyi 1958: 56). The idea of practice as enacted by agents who are only subsidiarily aware of its particulars (its tacitly known rules, pitfalls, standards, responses) applies to most, and probably all, social practices, Polanyi (1958: 62) citing 'manners, laws and ... the many different arts which man knows how to use, comply with, enjoy or live by, without specifiably knowing their contents'.

Complementing his theory of tacit knowledge, Polanyi paid careful attention to understanding knowledge as a *personal* achievement. Left with latitude by her profession's knowledge, rules of procedure, standards and values, the practitioner brings her own unique qualities, intuitions, interpretations and judgements to bear in her practice. All Polanyian practices are creative, some more so than others. Personal knowledge was traced by Polanyi (1958: 60) to a combination of 'our focal awareness

---

3   In a similar vein to Polanyi, Tallis (2003, 172) refers to 'the (tool-amplified) power of the hand' and 'the (tool-enhanced) precision of the fingers'.

of [select] external objects' and 'our subsidiary awareness of our body'. Subsidiary awareness extending to particulars outside our bodies is also included in personal knowledge. Tools form a 'part of ourselves' as the users of them. 'We pour ourselves out into … [tools and objects] and assimilate them as parts of our own existence. We accept them existentially by *dwelling in them*'. *'Indwelling' in particulars*, through our subsidiary awareness of them, was recognized by Polanyi as occurring in all forms of knowledge and practice. Personal knowledge of any 'object arises out of the bodily, linguistic, cultural, and historical indwelling of the person' (Apczynski 2003: 4 emphasis added). Deciding on a course of action as being appropriate in the circumstances, or deciding to accept an idea as worthy of credence, the caring professional is taken by Polanyi to be affirming many particulars in which she indwells, including the background assumptions, facts, beliefs, concepts and so on, against which her decision makes sense to her as, she expects, it will to her colleagues.

The practice of each profession is grounded on unformulated presuppositions. These were assimilated by the student as she learned the profession's vocabulary and about the world that the vocabulary described. Indwelling her profession's presuppositional framework, the agent has invested her faith in it. Polanyi followed St Augustine in arguing that, having chosen a framework of knowledge, logically a person cannot set about questioning it. Polanyi wrote (1958: 60) that to accept 'a certain set of presuppositions and [to] use them as our interpretative framework, we … dwell in them as we do in our own body'. We 'live in' the framework much as though it were 'the garment of our own skin' (1958: 64). The framework enables the Polanyian professional to use her profession's formulated and unformulated knowledge, to perceive and describe her community's world of objects and properties, and to participate in its activities.

Timeliness and *mētis*

Recent discussions of the topic of practice and its knowledge chime with the arguments of the thinkers whom we have covered. Stephen Toulmin (1922–), for example, finds a fundamental difference between forms of knowledge. One form is exemplified by theoretical physics which aims to reveal 'general features of the world', expressing its knowledge in theories and generalizations that are abstracted from time and place (Toulmin 2001, 108–9). As depicted by Toulmin (2001: 111), the theoretician bases 'rational computations' and 'rational deductions' on 'mathematically formulated theories'. Toulmin's other main form of knowledge concerns 'practical fields', including medicine, engineering, economics navigation, law, accountancy, and psychotherapy (2001: 109). The approach that is adopted and the knowledge gained in these fields Toulmin describes as '*clinical*' (2001: 109, 111), with practitioners aiming not to infer new truths from proven knowledge but to support *reasonable* judgements with *reasonable* arguments. In clinical practice, emphasis is placed on decision taking that is *timely*, and on the exercise of *skills* that have been acquired through experience and honed in practice. Toulmin (2001: 109) illustrates these points as follows:

> A sailor or a doctor may face rapid changes or unforeseen developments, and the need to act 'as the occasion requires' puts the timeliness of his decisions squarely in the picture. The helmsman experienced in navigating the Aegean, for example, gains the skills that are needed when sailing in close waters. Standing at the helm of a boat, he will look for a way to steer between two close-by headlands against the wind, and he continually glances from side to side to judge variations in the wind or the depth of the water in order to recognize when the water is shoaling so rapidly that he must change tack.

Among the contents of Toulmin's (2001: 109–11) clinical knowledge are general statements, facts, and procedures of science. 'Craft activity' and 'day-to-day arts' figure prominently in clinical practice, Toulmin (110–12 emphasis added) referring to medicine and to kindred disciplines as '*clinical arts*'. He cites a case in which clinicians carried out diagnostic tests on a patient to determine the cause of the recent onset of blackouts. The tests had negative results, leaving the physicians stumped until one of them took it upon himself to *ask the patient* to describe the circumstances in which she suffered her first blackout. The patient recalled that it coincided with the sudden death of her mother. Without suggesting the other physicians were remiss or incompetent, Toulmin writes that (2001: 114), wearing 'professional blinders', they had forgotten about 'the role of *timeliness* in medical history', and had probably assumed that the history of the patient 'was irrelevant to a proper diagnosis'. For Toulmin, clinical arts call for skills of the kind that Aristotle described as *phronesis* (practical wisdom), the root of our word 'prudence'.

Another concept of Greek philosophy, related to that of *phronesis*, is *mētis*, and it has been interestingly used by Michel de Certeau (1984), and by James Scott in his book *Seeing Like a State* (1998). In his *The Practice of Everyday Life*, de Certeau (1984: xix) envisages 'everyday practices' and 'ways of operating' as involving tactics, tricks, opportunistic improvizations and other such ploys which the Greeks regarded as various forms of *mētis*. De Certeau (1984: 1) discusses the trend in modern life of singularity succumbing to standardization, with rationalizing techniques engendering the 'masses', then affecting 'managers … technicians' and the professions.

Scott's interest – the dysfunctionality of so many governmental efforts at 'modernizing' social reconstruction – appears to be remote from the subject of the present book, but certain points that he makes are pertinent to our analysis. Scott (1998: 311) argues that politicians and officials in our era of 'high modernism' have been quick to deprecate 'the practical skills that underwrite any complex activity'. Many of them have gone out of their way to replace 'local knowledge' of 'vernacular' character with knowledge that is 'general, [and] abstract'; the scientific (and, perhaps, the pseudo-scientific) being preferred to the traditional.

Mētis, for Scott (1996: 313), signifies the practical skills and practical knowledge that agents use in trying to deal effectively with social situations and in responding to physical challenges. He understands *mētis* as occurring in all human activities. Perhaps the routines and repetitions of a clerk or an assembly line worker have only slight traces of it. But riding a bicycle or driving a car is replete with *mētis*, being embodied in 'hand–eye coordination[s]', the interpretation of changing conditions along the path or the road ahead, and in the 'appropriate adjustments' that continuously have to be made (Scott 1998: 313). The more of *mētis* that there is in activities, Scott explains (1998: 313), the more that students rely on practice in their training, so as to acquire the '"feel"' of their 'continual, nearly imperceptible adjustments'. 'Explicit instructions' will not suffice for the person learning to drive a car. 'No wonder that most crafts and trades requiring a touch or feel for implements and materials have traditionally been taught by long apprenticeships to master craftsmen', writes Scott (1998: 314). He describes *mētis* (1998: 314) as infusing the work of paramedics, nurses, doctors, police and firemen, most notably when they are called on to 'respond quickly and decisively' to 'emergencies'. These people received 'rules of thumb' in their training, rules on which they continue to rely, but each emergency is 'unique' and 'unpredictable', including the problems, needs and contexts of each client or patient. 'Half the battle is knowing which rules of thumb to apply in which order and when to throw the book away and improvise' (Scott 1998: 314).

Conclusion

We have viewed the subject of knowledge-in-practice through several theoretical lenses. The theories are overlapping, but each has specific concepts, with a particular angle on the subject. Two major theories studied have been those of Ryle and Polanyi, respectively illuminating the 'know how' of performances and their embodiment of 'tacit knowledge', Polanyi emphasizing that much of the knowledge with which agents act is unknown to, and perhaps unknowable by them. The concept of Oakeshott that is of particular relevance to our discussion is 'practical knowledge', which he envisaged as an essential element of traditions of taste, discernment and skilled conduct. Such knowledge, for Oakeshott, does not exist other than in the practice of agents. In Wittgenstein's account of rule-following, implicit interpretation is always called for. Polanyi's distinction between explicit and tacit knowledge, between the expressed and the unexpressed, cross-cuts the 'knowing how' and 'knowing that' distinction of Ryle. The subject material of tacit knowledge may be either process/procedure (appropriate conduct) or substantive fact (that which is affirmed as being so). Similar themes to these have, we noted, been addressed in recent years by Scott, and de Certeau, with reference to activity which the ancient Greeks described as *mētis*, and by Toulmin with reference to *phronesis*.

References

Apczynski, J. 2003. *The Discovery of Meaning through Scientific and Religious Forms of Indwelling*, The Polanyi Society Annual Meeting. Available at: http://www.missouriwestern.edu/orgs/polanyi/.

de Certeau, M. 1984. *The Practice of Everyday Life*. Berkeley: University of California Press.

Dewey, J. 1922. *Human Nature and Conduct*. London: George Allen and Unwin.

Filmer, P. 1998. Theory/practice, in *Core Sociological Dichotomies*, edited by Chris Jenks. London: Sage, 227–45.

Foucault, M. 1991. *Discipline and Punish*. Harmondsworth: Penguin Books.

Jacobs, S. 2004. Abilita artigianale, conoscenza tacita e altri elementi della practica. *Discipline Folosofiche*, xiv(1), 101–18.

Kettle, D. 1999. On the primacy of indwelling. *Appraisal*, 2(4), 191–7.

Kuhn, T. 1962. *The Structure of Scientific Revolutions*. Chicago: University of Chicago Press.

Lobkowicz, N. 1967. *Theory and Practice*. Notre Dame: University of Notre Dame Press.

Moorman, J. 2008. *Polanyian and Nursing: (Pedigogical* [sic.] *Resources)*. Available at: polanyi_list@yahoogroups.com [posted: 11 April 2008].

Oakeshott, M. 1991 [1947]. Rationalism in politics, in *Rationalism in Politics and Other Essays*, edited by T. Fuller. Indianapolis: Liberty Press, 5–42.

Polanyi, M. 1958 [1947]. *Personal Knowledge*. London: Routledge and Kegan Paul.

Polanyi, M. 1964. *Science, Faith and Society*. Chicago: University of Chicago Press.

Polanyi, M. 1969. *Knowing and Being*. Chicago: University of Chicago Press.

Popper, K. 1935. *Logik der Forschung*. Vienna: Julius Springer Verlag, translated in 1959 as *The Logic of Scientific Discovery*. London: Hutchinson.

Popper, K. 1972. *Objective Knowledge*. Oxford: Clarendon Press.

Ryle, G. 1949. *The Concept of Mind*. London: Hutchinson.

Ryle, G. 1971 [1946]. Knowing how and knowing that, in *Collected Essays*, vol. 2. London: Hutchinson, 212–25.

Schatzki, T.R., Knorr-Cetina, K. and von Savigny, E. (eds) 2001. *The Practice Turn in Contemporary Theory*. London: Routledge.

Schön, D. 1983. *The Reflective Practitioner*. New York: Basic Books.

Scott, W. 1998. *Seeing Like a State*. New Haven: Yale University Press.

Smith, B. 1988. Knowing how vs. knowing that, in *Practical Knowledge*, edited by J. Nyiri and B. Smith. London: Croom Helm, 1–16.

Tallis, R. 2003. *The Hand*. Edinburgh: Edinburgh University Press.

Toulmin, S. 2001. *Return to Reason*. Cambridge, Mass.: Harvard University Press.

Wittgenstein, L. 1953. *Philosophical Investigations*. Oxford: Basil Blackwell.

Wittgenstein, L. 1974. *On Certainty*. Oxford: Basil Blackwell.

Zammito, J. 2004. *A Nice Derangement of Epistemes*. Chicago: University of Chicago Press.

2 Information, knowledge and wisdom in medical practice

P.B. Greenberg

There has never been more healthcare information available to consumers, medical practitioners and other clinicians. 'The modern practitioner swims in a river of clinical research evidence that is unprecedented in its depth, velocity and turbulence' (Naylor 2002). Some of it is incorporated into healthcare decisions, frequently by consumers alone, but more usually after consumers have considered the advice they have sought, and to the extent that they choose, from trusted clinicians (NHMRC 2006). T.S. Eliot (1934) wrote 'Where is the wisdom we have lost in knowledge? Where is the knowledge we have lost in information?', and in this context he may well have considered that there is an overabundance of information, as only some of this 'information' has been distilled into 'knowledge'.

'Knowledge', 'knowledge transfer', 'knowledge uptake', 'knowledge management' and 'knowledge translation' replaced the 1980s buzzwords 'information technology' in the late 1990s. The modern era of epistemology had arrived. From now on, not only philosophers were interested in the sources and nature of knowledge. The UK National Health Service (NHS) established a 'National Knowledge Service', with a mission 'to support the delivery of high quality information to patients and staff' (NHS 2002). One responsibility of the NHS Chief Knowledge Officer (CKO) is to ensure that the knowledge derived from research, called 'evidence', is integrated with that derived from the analysis of routinely collected and audit data, and with knowledge arising from the experiences of both clinicians and consumers. The subtitle of a recent review of NHS health library services is 'From knowledge to health in the 21st century' (Hill 2008). One of its recommendations is that every NHS organization should have a CKO. Only some of this 'knowledge', however, has been transformed by, in the words of the eighteenth-century poet Cowper, 'smoothing, squaring and fitting', to become the 'wisdom' that healthcare consumers increasingly expect from medical practitioners.

29

Evidence-based clinical practice (EBP) is discussed here in the context of the historical evolution of Western medicine. Examples of its strengths and weaknesses are presented, as well as responses to some criticism it has attracted. Its potential to possibly provide the framework for the elusive wisdom that is needed for clinical decisions is also considered. Many of the issues considered here are also relevant to those in other chapters in this book where knowledge in other caring professions is addressed.

A short history

Skulls showing circular trephinations in cranial bones date from the New Stone Age (~9000–2000 BC), but whether these were early surgical efforts to cure disease still remains unclear. Scanty information about Egyptian (~1500 BC) medical practices derives from details preserved on the few retrieved papyri, and from mummies. Mesopotamian practices, from a similar era, were recorded as cuneiform signs on soft clay tablets. As in Egypt, medicine in Mesopotamia was magico-religious, with three classes of priests addressing diseases: diviners, exorcists and physicians. The latter performed procedures and prescribed medications, fumigations, inhalations and applications.

Greek medicine was derived from Egyptian, Mesopotamian and Minoan sources. The Hippocratic medical school on the island of Cos in ~400–300 BC blended these earlier approaches with Sicilian, Athenian, Alexandrian, Indian and Persian thoughts and practices. Perhaps the main contribution of the ancient Greeks was a more systematic approach to understanding disease and illness, underpinned by evolving philosophical approaches, which to some extent replaced the religious notions of the time (Singer 1962). Another of their key contributions was that Greek physicians focused on the 'whole' person, while Herodotus (484–425 BC) reported that their Egyptian counterparts, in contrast, tended to specialize in particular areas (Herodotus 1996: 114).

Clinical decisions in medical practice are often based on answers to questions of diagnosis, cause (aetiology), prognosis (for those with particular conditions or diseases), risk (for those without a specified condition or disease) and therapy. Assessment of the validity of the answers to such clinical questions depends largely on the kind of evidence that is considered to be most acceptable by those making the judgement at the time. As there is no unique, universally accepted, 'evidence base' underpinning competing types of evidence, the merits of these different types of evidence still largely remain a matter of opinion.

Evidence

The relative value of evidence derived from observations compared to that derived from thoughts has been debated extensively in different times and settings for the last ~2,500 years.

According to Bertrand Russell (1961: 53), Pythagoras (~500 BC) regarded mathematical knowledge, obtained through mere thought, without the need for observation, as 'certain, exact, and applicable to the real world: moreover it was obtained by mere thinking, without the need for observation'. At that time, thought and the intuitive evidence subsequently derived from it were considered superior to empirical evidence based on observation. On the other hand, Russell (1961: 110) also reports how specific strategies for progressing thoughts and ideas, such as the dialectic method for seeking knowledge through questioning and answering, although suitable for some questions, proved quite unsuitable for others. In valuing evidence derived from thought alone, however, a dilemma arose. The assumptions of Aristotelian physics were shown to be incompatible with the subsequent observations of Galileo, and hence with Newton's first Law of Motion, which was formulated from these (Russell 1961: 217).

Francis Bacon (1561–1626) emphasized the value of both observation and experience on the one hand, and thought on the other. He compared observation and experience to the behaviour of the ant, which collects and uses, in contrast to the spider, which forms webs from its own being, resembling conceptual understanding through thoughts alone (Bacon 1620). His aphorism was extended to the bee, which combines these roles by transforming pollen gathered from flowers into an entirely new product, thus combining the processes of observation and thought.

The observations versus thoughts ('dogma') controversy was considered so important in the late eighteenth century that Edinburgh students were lectured about it at the start of their medical course (Cullen 1987). In our era, the relative weighting given to these two broad forms of evidence depends on who is expressing an opinion or making the decision at the time and, to some extent, the issue in question. The proposition, 'Of the two main sources of knowledge, the rational has traditionally been held in the higher respect; but where there is conflict, the empirical has had the last say' (Murphy 1976: 162) is not universally supported, so unresolved disagreements persist. Much emotion has been generated over the centuries as zealots defend the type of 'evidence' they support. The disagreements continue. Consumers as well as clinicians become involved and confused in the debate.

The first question in evaluating evidence-based clinical practice is therefore to consider what the term 'evidence' means. There is no simple answer. Evidence may mean entirely different things to different individuals and groups, and in different contexts. The consequence is that different but equally 'valid' conclusions result when equally rational and logical processes shape concepts arising from discrete and different evidence bases.

Types of evidence, which, depending on the assessors' perspective, might be considered to be equally valid, include:

- fundamental evidence: based on rigid adherence to unchallengeable beliefs
- rational evidence: based exclusively on logical thought
- empirical evidence: based exclusively on observations
- experimental evidence: empirical evidence following deliberate interventions
- legal evidence: information, deemed acceptable in specified settings, which supports or refutes assertions
- post-modern evidence: based on personal experience.

In contrast to the situation in ancient Greece discussed above, EBP overtly values empirical evidence more than evidence that is based on thought alone. This value judgement is further emphasized by allocating higher 'levels of evidence'(LOE) to empirical evidence derived from specific study designs, such as randomized controlled clinical trials (RCTs) or systematic reviews of RCTs (NHMRC 2000). Studies with these designs are understandably considered less likely to be 'biased' in comparison with those with other designs. Studies based on personal accounts or on anecdotes of cases or exclusively on thought, for example, are allocated a lower LOE. This is in spite of the LOE being only one parameter of the net quality of a study, meaning that there are very poor quality systematic reviews and RCTs, which, because of their design, have a high LOE.

Evidence-based clinical practice

The term 'evidence-based medicine' (EBM) was first used at McMaster University, Ontario, Canada in the late 1980s (Haynes 2002). At least three factors contributed to the concept. The increasing rate and volume of research publications meant that it was no longer possible for medical practitioners to keep informed by perusing biomedical journals and texts systematically. Another factor was the novel possibility of clinicians becoming able to rapidly access research publications through advancing computer and e-web technologies. In addition, the development of EBM was a response to the criticism of answering key clinical questions by making assumptions, for example, about the theoretical benefits of a treatment, based only on pathological and physiological considerations, however sound these might be (EBM Working Group 1992). Verification with 'hard' empirical data was now expected. EBM became a MEDLINE medical subject (MeSH) term in 1997. By March 2008 there were ~28,000 citations in MEDLINE using this MeSH term, with ~2,100 citations including 'evidence-based medicine' in the title, of which ~940 had been published within the last five years and ~150 in the last year.

The definition of EBM became more precise over time. It was seen as a tripod, which topples over with fewer than three pillars. EBM is now defined as 'the integration of best research evidence, with clinical expertise and patients' unique values and circumstances' (Straus et al. 2005). It could be argued, in part at least, that it is the 'integration' which indicates a shift from mere information, to knowledge and possibly to wisdom. The term 'evidence based practice' (EBP), which is seen as less clinician-specific, has replaced the term EBM to some extent in recent years, as it embraces other clinical professions like nursing, allied health and dentistry (Dawes et al. 2005).

Both the process and teaching of EBP are often described in terms of the 'steps' of EBM (Straus et al. 2005). The steps are:

- asking highly structured patient- (or group-) specific questions
- seeking the answers to questions by searching published data
- critically appraising the data retrieved for its validity and relevance
- applying results of studies to individuals (or groups).

Each of these 'steps' can be learned. Probably the most difficult one for novices is the first step, learning how to ask structured questions.

The 'PICOT' structure, for a structured set of question about therapy, is outlined below:

- P = patient or group
- I = intervention
- C = comparison
- O = outcome
- T = time.

Questions contain two or more of the above components, for example: for airline passengers (P) do foot and leg exercises (I) prevent the development of deep vein thrombosis (O)? Similar structured questions can be assembled for other types of questions. Structuring questions in this way means that the question is formulated precisely to specifically address the issue in question. Another advantage is that the component terms of such structured questions can be searched separately in databases then combined as necessary to address the questions posed.

Another shift from information to knowledge and wisdom relates to the source of the data retrieved to answer such clinical questions, as information now derives from so many sources. These include the thoughts and opinions of consumers and healthcare professionals, sometimes as individuals and sometimes as members of formal and less formal professional and other groupings such as craft groups, societies and Royal Colleges. To a varying extent the opinions are based upon the scientific evidence available. Media, in its varied and evolving aural and visual formats, provides many additional sources of information, as do scientific publications themselves.

The knowledge to information ratio can be increased in various ways. Reducing bias through considerations of LOE (NHMRC 2000) and of other aspects of the quality of published studies increases the relative proportion of knowledge. Although there is much healthcare information in 'primary' research publications, which can now be obtained easily from huge e-databases like Medline, the knowledge content is also greatly enriched through 'secondary' derivatives of these publications such as systematic reviews (Moynihan 2004). Systematic reviews combine the results of single studies, reduce bias and increase the precision and applicability of the results. They differ from narrative reviews in that the process for developing them is explicit and reproducible. Furthermore, efforts are made to retrieve all of the evidence available and to amalgamate evidence according to agreed principles, increasing the validity of the conclusions. 'Secondary' derivatives of 'primary' research have also evolved. These include critically appraised topics (see the *American College of Physicians (ACP) Journal Club* and *Bandolier*), in which the third step of EBP, critical appraisal, is largely undertaken by others, and clinical pathways (see Map of Medicine), which outline algorithms and steps during diagnostic and therapeutic processes. Clinical practice guidelines, defined as 'systematically developed statements to assist practitioner and patient decisions about appropriate healthcare for specific clinical circumstances' (Field and Lohr 1990) are another example.

The potential of evidence-based practice

Imagine the ideal medical consultation. In non-urgent circumstances, consumers consult clinicians in private, quiet and pleasant surroundings. The leisurely assessment includes an interview and usually a physical examination as well. Healthcare issues, and sometimes other issues of concern to both the consumer and clinician, are raised and discussed. There is always enough time 1) to develop mutual respect and understanding, 2) for the clinician to understand issues from the consumer's perspective, through an appreciation of the consumer's unique personal identity and values, and 3) for further questions and discussions. All consumer and clinician concerns are considered. Aspects possibly unrelated to the consumer's presenting concerns, for example, where the clinician recognized preventive opportunities for the consumer, are always raised and discussed. Medical practitioners would appreciate consumer expectations and, after ascertaining the extent to which the consumers wish to manage their own healthcare issues (NHMRC 2006), they discuss, define and, together with consumers, prioritize healthcare issues.

Following assessment and issue prioritization, consumers and clinicians together develop plans for knowledge-seeking activities, utilizing the three pillars of EBP, discussed above. Clinicians and/or consumers would then formulate questions which reflect the mutually agreed key issues and their priorities. A quest for additional knowledge would usually follow. Computer-derived knowledge and 'decision support systems' might supplement traditional consumer and/or clinician-initiated quests by automatically delivering knowledge to the consumer/clinical 'coal-face'. Consumers acquire not only information, but also the knowledge required to address their concerns, with the ongoing support, care and wisdom offered by clinicians, in parallel with their own evolving healthcare wisdom and self-management skills.

In such ideal circumstances EBP has great potential to improve healthcare outcomes for patients. Furthermore, its application can also embed clinicians' continuing professional development and education within counsultations and the issues which arise from daily practice (Teunissen and Dornan 2008).

Criticisms and limitations of evidence-based practice

In spite of its potential, both the principles and the execution of EBP have been criticized. Using techniques espoused by EBM zealots, the answer to the question, 'Does the practice of EBM, compared to alternative practices lead to better consumer health outcomes?', remains largely unresolved. *The Journal of Evaluation in Clinical Practice* has published ten thematic editions criticizing the evolution and development of EBM. Its editor, in the last of these, vows to continue this approach 'with the aim of leading the international debate towards an intellectual resolution of the many illogicalities and inconsistencies of EBM' (Miles et al. 2007). EBP has even been compared to a religion (Links 2006).

Some key criticisms and limitations of EBP and responses to them are discussed below, in relation to the above definition. Generic criticisms (Sackett et al. 1996) are considered and illustrated with specific examples.

EBM is just 'cookbook' medicine

Increasing consumer autonomy associated with the introduction of EBM threatens medical practitioners' autonomy. Prior to this era the advice of clinicians was seldom challenged. Evidence-based clinical practice 'guidelines', designed to reduce wide variations in clinical advice and practice, for example, were seen as limiting clinicians' choices. In recent years, medical practitioners have largely accepted the concept of such overall 'guidance', as it soon became apparent that there are indeed roles for both clinicians and consumers to specifically adapt the generic guidance available to individual consumers within their own settings.

There's nothing new about EBP, it's just old wine in new bottles

Empirical science has informed clinical practice to varying extents for many years. Although the first RCT was published in 1948 (Medical Research Council 1948), the earliest reference to anything resembling a clinical trial was recorded in biblical times (see *Holy Bible: Old Testament*). Daniel and his colleagues, while captives of the Babylonians, performed better than their Babylonian peers when they consumed their traditional legume/water diet instead of the meat/wine diet of their captors. Since then there have been numerous other examples. Maimonides (1135–1204), philosopher and physician, stated 'He who puts his life in the hands of an empiricist who does not think scientifically is like a mariner who places his trust in good luck'. In 1762, James Lind published clinical trials related to interventions to prevent scurvy. Soon afterwards, the clinical trials of Pierre C.A. Louis (1787–1872) challenged established views and demonstrated that blood-letting was ineffective for patients with pneumonia.

EBP only considers evidence which comes from clinical trials

The reality is that EBP takes all forms of evidence into account, ranging from 'n of 1' trials (Cochrane Collaboration Glossary 2005), where the same patient also serves as the 'control', through systematic reviews and RCTs to case series and anecdotes.

This criticism also refers to the fact that patients included in clinical trials differ from the broader community to which results may subsequently be extrapolated. For example, in cancer trials (Elting et al. 2006) and in a trial of exercise in patients with rheumatoid arthritis (de Jong et al. 2004), participants differ from non-participants in a variety of prognostic factors, thus challenging the broader applicability of results beyond the trial populations.

Another concern is how well the 'efficacy', for example of a therapeutic intervention, which might be unequivocally demonstrable in a clinical trial, may be extrapolated to its 'effectiveness' in the real world, in the setting in which it will be used.

EBM represents a paradigm shift in medicine (Kuhn 1996)

Critics of EBM have very reasonably argued that this statement is a gross overestimation of the status of EBM, in spite of enthusiastic claims (Evidence-based Medicine Working Group 1992) by its proponents. 'For EBM to be meaningfully described as a "paradigm" (let alone the "dominant" paradigm in medicine) it would need to have developed a detailed theoretical structure with explanatory power and substantial empirical corroboration'(Miles et al. 2007).

The clinical research agenda, which informs EBP, bears little relationship to the relative global burden of specific diseases and is determined by industry

A survey of 286 RCTs published in six international peer-reviewed general medical journals showed that only 32 per cent studied one of the top ten contributors to the global burden of diseases; there were no RCTs for almost half of the 35 eligible leading causes (Rochon et al. 2004). In 2000–2001, business funded 25 per cent of Australia's health research and development expenditure, with 13 per cent of the total expenditure being on pharmaceuticals (Australian Society of Medical Research 2003). The Australian pharmaceutical industry currently spends more than $752 million per year on research and development (Medicines Australia 2008). A survey of randomly selected clinical trials published in five influential medical journals reported that 36 per cent reported industry sponsorship, while funding sources were not declared in 28 per cent. Furthermore, the relative sponsorship by industry increased over the 20 years surveyed (Buchowsky and Jewesson 2004). Pleas for a greater proportion of public funding support for large Australian RCTs, which have the potential to both improve consumer outcomes and save community costs, have not yet been heeded (McNeil et al. 2003).

There is insufficient evidence to support most clinical decisions

Although there can never be enough evidence to firmly support all clinical decisions, surveys show a surprisingly high 'evidence-base' across a variety of specialties. For example, in a UK general medical unit in 1995, of 109 consecutive patients with an established diagnosis, 82 per cent reported primary interventions supported by RCT evidence of efficacy (Ellis et al. 1995). Even in surgical units, where ethical considerations mean that the most reliable evidence for some apparently effective interventions cannot always be confirmed by RCTs, 23 per cent of treatments were based on RCTs (Howes et al. 1997). When considering this issue, it is essential to recall that the lack of scientific evidence does not necessarily mean lack of efficacy, but rather that efficacy has not yet been conclusively confirmed or denied.

There are broad variations between and amongst consumers and medical practitioners in the capacity to pose questions about and to access published healthcare knowledge

This valid criticism challenges the ethical justice of differential access, not only to electronic, print and other media and resources, but also to the basic skills required to understand them. The variation in skills between medical practitioners is accounted for in part by the time since graduation, specialty, computer skills, postgraduate professional development, time available to learn new skills and many other factors. Between practitioners and consumers and also amongst consumers the variation is even broader. Fundamental factors like education, health-related literacy (Buchbinder et al. 2006, Safeer and Keenan 2005) and socioeconomic status are especially relevant. Although some countries, including Australia, have made important e-databases like the 'Cochrane Library' universally available at no cost to consumers and practitioners, many consumers and possibly some practitioners are currently excluded from the benefits offered by such resources. Even when the basic skills needed to access healthcare knowledge become available to consumers, many will still lack relevant 'background' information, the more sophisticated skills needed to question this and the additional skills to then pose more specific questions and find the knowledge they seek. Training consumers might serve to rectify some of these problems (Saunders et al. 2008).

There are broad variations between and amongst consumers and medical practitioners in the skills to appraise healthcare knowledge in healthcare decisions

Appraisal of healthcare information requires more than just the capacity to read and comprehend it. Critical appraisal is necessary to determine if the apparent results could reflect 1) the play of chance, 2) bias or confounding, or 3) the way in which results are presented.

Most consumers do not possess appraisal skills at present, although opportunities to acquire them are now becoming available (Cochrane Library, Cochrane Consumer Network, Irwig et al. 2007).

At present, relatively few medical practitioners who graduated more than 15 years ago are fully competent in critical appraisal. Even more recent graduates vary greatly in their appraisal skills, although 'critical appraisal' is now taught as a component of EBM in most undergraduate medical courses. Other determinants of variations amongst clinicians are similar to the issues determining the capacity to pose questions and to access information and knowledge discussed above.

Could reported results reflect the play of chance?

Answers to this question depend on a basic understanding of statistical principles, especially of p values and confidence intervals (Cochrane Collaboration Glossary 2005), which take into account the size of samples, the scatter of the data and the magnitude of the differences between the results in different groups. The answer to this question is always 'yes', and so the practical issue during critical appraisal is to determine the probability that results might reflect chance.

Could reported results reflect confounding or bias?

A confounding factor is associated with both an intervention, or an exposure, and the outcome of interest. For example, if participants given medication in a controlled trial are younger than those in the placebo group, it is difficult to decide if the finding of a smaller risk of death in one group is due to the medication or to the age difference. 'Age' in this context is called a 'confounder', or 'confounding variable' (Cochrane Collaboration Glossary 2005). 'Bias' is defined as 'a systematic error in study design, execution or interpretation) or deviation in results or inferences from the truth' (Cochrane Collaboration Glossary 2005). Bias could reflect, for example, differences in the groups compared (selection bias), exposure to other factors apart from the intervention of interest (performance bias), withdrawals or exclusions of trial participants (attrition bias) or how outcomes are assessed (detection bias) and reported (reporting bias) (Sackett 1979, Yank et al. 2007).

How may results be expressed?

There are many different ways to express the results of clinical studies. Understanding differences in data expression is necessary to comprehend the meaning of results because the manner in which data are 'framed' can affect their interpretation. For example, in a RCT comparing therapeutic interventions with placebo, results may be expressed in absolute or relative terms. If an adverse 'outcome' occurs uncommonly (e.g. 1:100) in the placebo group, even a very effective treatment in relative terms, say with a 'relative risk' (risk in the treated group divided by the risk in the placebo group) of 20 per cent may seem less effective when expressed in 'absolute' terms. The number of people needing treatment to prevent one adverse outcome (NNT) is 125, so although the relative risk is 20 per cent, the chance of one individual benefiting from this treatment is only 1:125. (Consider a group of 1,000 people. With no treatment, 1 per cent (10 people) have an adverse outcome. With this treatment, 20 per cent of 10 (2) have an adverse outcome, so 10–2 (8) benefit when 1,000 are treated. Therefore 1,000/8 (125) people need to be treated for 1 person to benefit.) In order for clinicians and consumers to understand the benefits and risks of interventions, results should be expressed in both relative and absolute terms.

In spite of the fact that appraisal skills are now taught to medical students, trainees and in continuing professional development, subtle appraisal issues remain poorly understood. This means that there are many opportunities to improve the quality of evidence that is incorporated into clinical decisions (Scott and Greenberg 2005, Scott et al. 2006, 2008a).

There are broad variations between and amongst consumers and clinicians in the skills to apply healthcare knowledge in healthcare decisions

Another criticism of EBP is the fact that assumptions of questionable validity may have to be made before data, for example, those derived from clinical trials comparing a drug with a placebo, are extrapolated from the trial to a particular consumer in question. As consumers are not usually included in the trials which might apply to them, the specific applicability of the reported research findings becomes a matter of opinion, especially if the consumer differs in some way from most trial participants, say, for example, in gender, age or race. The consumer's setting might also be quite different from that of the published study. Even when the question of applicability is asked in the negative, for example 'Is there any reason that the published results should *not* apply to this person?', assumptions, some of which may be subsequently shown to be incorrect, are always needed to answer such a question (Dans et al. 1998).

While each consumer is an individual, most clinical studies, for example of prognosis and treatment, address outcomes for the 'average' consumer. Most of us, however, would prefer any estimate, albeit across a defined range of probability, than no estimate at all.

Consider a RCT of the effectiveness and safety of a new medication, which in comparison with another drug, is shown to be both more effective and safer. Statistical tests show that the probability of the study results reflecting the play of chance is <5 per cent. The 'confidence interval', however, is very wide, meaning that the estimation of the size of the benefit is relatively imprecise, the actual effect being somewhere across a broad scatter of possible effects. Under these circumstances, it is especially difficult to be certain about the size of the benefit for an individual considering treatment, as it is not known precisely where individuals' results lie within this scatter. A consumer might only be willing to take medication if their result is towards the higher end of the efficacy spectrum, but this cannot be predicted beforehand. Only the average result and the spread of possible results around this, within the group studied, are known.

When additional data are known about individual consumers, it is sometimes possible to extrapolate from data on groups to data on individuals. Patients with atrial fibrillation (AF), for example, a relatively common disturbance of cardiac rhythm, associated with a randomly irregular pulse, have a higher risk of embolism (transport of clots through the blood stream, which can lodge elsewhere, causing strokes and other problems reflecting sudden reductions of blood flow). RCTs have shown that anticoagulants (AC), 'blood-thinning' drugs, prevent embolism. In addition, the relative benefit of AC, as compared to no AC has been shown to be independent of the risk of stroke, across a range of risks. This means that the absolute benefit, expressed for example as the number of patients needing treatment (NNT) for a defined time to prevent one stroke, is greater for patients at higher risk. As the extent of stroke risk in individual patients with AF can be predicted, so can the size of the benefit. This approach is useful, as the risks of treatment remain relatively constant while the risk of developing a disease varies (Glasziou and Haynes 1995). Structured guides, designed for clinicians, but adaptable for consumers, are available to teach and critically appraise published healthcare information (NHS Public Health Resource Unit, Users' Guides to Evidence-Based Practice). These tools also facilitate the transition from 'information' to 'knowledge'.

Why does the application of evidence result in different findings from different studies apparently addressing the same issue?

There are many examples of this problem. For example, the differences in risk prediction for embolism in patients with AF, discussed above (Fang et al. 2008).Only some can be explained following critical appraisal of the contrasting results of studies, even when the study design is similar. In addition, clinical practice guidelines on the same topic may make different recommendations (Jessup and Brozena 2007).

It is even more difficult, however, to account for large differences when results differ in studies of different design. For example, combining the results of many trials in a systematic review may lead to quite different conclusions from a single large and well-conducted clinical trial (Borzack and Ridker 1995).

What is meant by clinical expertise?

Many factors, including clinical experience, baseline knowledge, the capacity to obtain, evaluate and apply new knowledge, communication, empathy, leadership and clinical judgement contribute to the perception of clinical expertise (Murphy 2008). Different clinicians have different proportions of these qualities and of other components. Defining EBM with clinical expertise as one of its criteria can be regarded as a weakness, as any judgement about clinical expertise is usually a matter of opinion, which is difficult both to measure in absolute terms and to compare between different medical practitioners.

How can judgements be made about the integration of patients' unique values and circumstances into EBP?

Another valid criticism of EBP, as above, is that although it is necessary and even possible to do this (Sadler and Hulgus 1992), there are not yet tools for establishing how well 'patients' values and circumstances' have indeed been integrated into clinical decisions. Should consumer satisfaction be the sole criterion, or should clinical processes and/or outcomes be considered as well? If so, how should the various parameters be included and weighted when such judgements are made?

Heuristics versus knowledge

Clinical decisions and recommendations are seldom based on evidence alone, especially when scientific evidence is unavailable or not known. Even when it is, medical practitioners often use non-scientific principles, axioms and postulates. These ad hoc rules of thumb, or 'heuristics' (McDonald 1996, Scott et al. 2008b) are usually unrecognized and seldom acknowledged, almost never validated and are often applied subconsciously.

One example of such a heuristic is William of Occam's maxim, or 'razor'. The fourteenth-century British monk stated that 'It is vain to do with more what can be done with fewer' (Russell 1961: 462). Although this 'razor' seems valid in many circumstances, medical practitioners are sometimes unaware of its limitations, possibly to the extent of cutting their own throats. Another example in medical diagnosis is 'Sutton's Law', named after Willie Sutton (1901–1980), a US bank robber who is alleged to have told a reporter that he robbed banks 'because that's where the money is'. This very reasonably encourages diagnosticians to consider the prevalence of conditions in diagnosis, and to therefore consider more common conditions.

Knowledge translation

EBP at the consumer/clinician interface is unable to result in better outcomes for individuals or communities on its own. There are many complex processes between integrating ideas and beliefs with scientific evidence and subsequently achieving better results (Glasziou et al. 2005). Consumers and clinicians must firstly become aware of evidence as it evolves (Davis et al. 2003). They must then accept the value of making whatever changes are needed to incorporate the evidence. There must be mechanisms available to deliver the changes required, which must ultimately be deemed acceptable to both individual consumers and to their social groupings. EBP is just one early step along this very tortuous path.

The interaction of individual consumers and their carers and families, medical practitioners and other clinicians occurs within complex social systems. These include consumer groups, professional teaching, training and collegiate institutions, as well as public and for-profit organizations which provide, fund, regulate and insure healthcare. When any of the translational steps between evidence and its uptake are compromised, the probability of better healthcare becomes less. There are always 'gaps' of varying breadth between evidence, on one hand, and better outcomes, on the other. For example, even in countries where healthcare is available and affordable, there are gaps between observed and desirable quality of care (Asch et al. 2006). There are also many unexplained variations in healthcare delivery

(Wennberg 2002). In some countries, including Australia, institutions like the National Institute of Clinical Studies have been established to address such gaps (NICS 2008).

There is now a variety of evidence-dissemination models available. These range from the traditional 'passive diffusion', evidence-packaging and structured approaches, to embrace models which consider those important social and group behaviours which, by influencing innovation-diffusion, cannot be ignored (Scott 2007).

From information to knowledge to wisdom in medical practice

Henri Poincaré (1905) stated that 'Science is facts; just as houses are made of stones, so is science made of facts; but a pile of stones is not a house and a collection of facts is not necessarily science', reminding us of the limitations of information on its own. Some strategies for gleaning knowledge from information have been discussed above. These include the absolute requirement for clinical experience for practitioners wishing to apply information to specific situations, the skill to enrich information using derivatives like critically appraised topics, clinical practice guidelines and critical appraisal tools and the capacity to incorporate consumers' views. Such strategies serve to increase the knowledge:information ratio.

The subsequent distillation of knowledge in medical practice to wisdom, however, is much more difficult, especially as there is even less agreement about the 'gold standards' upon which the success of the process can be measured.

The Canadian author Robertson Davies defines wisdom, in a clinical context, as 'that breadth of the spirit which makes the difference between the first rate healer and the capable technician' (Davies 1984). After an encounter with a medical practitioner whilst a student at Oxford, Robertson reports 'he was a first-rate doctor because he never allowed doctoring to eat him up. He was a humanist first and a physician second'.

To return to ancient Greece, Aristotle in his *Nicomachean Ethics* (~370 BC) (Ross et al. 1998) distinguished two sorts of wisdom, 'sophia' (science), which discerns why the world is the way it is, and 'phronesis', which incorporates the principles of 'sophia' to act in practical situations, based on experience. In medical practice, knowledge (evidence) might be seen as equating with 'sophia', while wisdom equates better with 'phronesis'.

The availability of increasing amounts of information and knowledge in medical practice is a two-edged sword. Medical practitioners and other clinicians need to be constantly aware of what John Keats might have called

'The Hyperion Syndrome'. If not, they risk the consequences of always assuming that 'Knowledge enormous makes a god of me' (Keats 2006).

Acknowledgements

Peter Greenberg acknowledges with much gratitude, the contributions of Associate Professor Caroline Brand, Dr Alan Gijsbers and Dr Yvonne Greenberg, and the secretarial support of Mrs Rita Ward in the preparation of this chapter.

References

American College of Physicians (ACP) Journal Club. Available at: http://www.acpjc.org.

Asch, S., Kerr, E.A., Keesey, J., Adams, J.L., Setodji, C.M., Malik, S. and McGlynn, E.A. 2006. Who is at greatest risk for receiving poor-quality health care? *New England Journal of Medicine*, 354(11), 1147–56.

Australian Society of Medical Research 2003. *Exceptional Returns. The Value of Investing in Health R&D in Australia.* Canberra: Access Economics.

Bacon, F. 1620. Aphorism 95. *The New Organon, or True Directions Concerning the Interpretation of Nature.* Available at: http://www.constitution.org/bacon/nov_org.htm [accessed 29 June 2009].

Bandolier. Available at: http://www.jr2.ox.ac.uk/Bandolier.

Borzak, S. and Ridker, P.M. 1995. Discordance between meta-analyses and large-scale randomized, controlled trials. Examples from the management of acute myocardial infarction. *Annals of Internal Medicine*, 123(11), 873–7.

Buchbinder R., Hall, S. and Youd, J.M. 2006. Functional health literacy of patients with rheumatoid arthritis attending a community-based rheumatology practice. *Journal of Rheumatology*, 33(5), 879–86.

Buchkowsky, S. and Jewesson, P.J. 2004. Industry sponsorship and authorship of clinical trials over 20 years. *The Annals of Pharmacotherapy*, 38(4), 579–85.

Cochrane Collaboration 2005. Glossary of Cochrane Collaboration and research terms. Available at: http://www.cochrane.org/resources/glossary.htm.

Cochrane Consumer Network. Available at: http://www.cochrane.org/consumers/homepage.htm

Cochrane Library. *For Patients.* Available at: http://www3.interscience.wiley.com/cgi-bin/mrwhome/106568753/HOME.

Cowper, W. *The Task.* Project Gutenberg e-text. Available at: http://www.gutenberg.org/etext/3698.

Cullen, W. 1987. An introductory lecture on the practice of physic given at Edinburgh University in the years 1768–89. *Proceedings of the Royal College of Physicians of Edinburgh*, 17, 268–85.

Dans, A., Dans, L.F., Guyatt, G.H. and Richardson, S., for the Evidence-Based Medicine Working Group 1998. Users' guides to the medical literature: XIV. How to decide on the applicability of clinical trial results to your patient. *The Journal of the American Medical Association*, 279(7), 545–9.

Davis, D., Evans, M., Jadad, A., Perrier, L., Rath, D., Ryan, D., Sibbald, G., Straus, S., Rappolt, S., Wowk, M. and Zwarenstein, M. 2003. The case for knowledge translation: shortening the journey from evidence to effect. *British Medical Journal*, 327(7405), 33–5.

Davies, R. 1984. *Can a Doctor be a Humanist?* The David Coit Gillman Lecture, Johns Hopkins Medical School, in Davies, R. 1996. *The Merry Heart*. New York: Viking Press.

Dawes, M., Summerskill, W., Glasziou, P., Cartabellotta, A., Martin, J., Hopayian, K., Porzsolt, F., Burls, A. and Osborne, J. 2005. Sicily statement on evidence-based practice. *BMC Medical Education*, 5,1doi:10.1186/1472-6920-5-1.

de Jong, Z., Munneke, M., Jansen, L.M., Ronday, K., van Schaardenburg, D.J., Brand, R., van den Ende, C.H.M, Vliet Vlieland, T.P.M., Zuijderduin, W.M. and Hazes, J.M.W. 2004. Differences between participants and nonparticipants in an exercise trial for adults with rheumatoid arthritis. *Arthritis and Rheumatism*, 51(4), 593–600.

Eliot, T. 1934. *Choruses from The Rock*. Inside Work e-text. Available at: http://insidework.net/static/downloads/products/choruses_from_the_rock.pdf.

Ellis, J., Mulligan, I., Rowe, J. and Sackett, D.L. 1995. Inpatient general medicine is evidence based. *The Lancet*, 346(8972), 407–10.

Elting, L., Cooksley, C. and Bekele, B.N. 2006. Generalizability of cancer clinical trial results: prognostic differences between participants and nonparticipants. *Cancer*, 106(11), 2452–8.

Evidence-based Medicine Working Group 1992. Evidence-based medicine: a new approach to teaching the practice of medicine. *Journal of the American Medical Association*, 268(17), 2420–25.

Fang, M., Go, A.S., Chang, Y., Borowsky, L., Pomernacki, N.K. and Singer, D.E. 2008. Comparison of risk stratification schemes to predict thromboembolism in people with nonvalvular atrial fibrillation. *Journal of the American College of Cardiology*, 51(8), 810–15.

Field, M.J. and Lohr, K.N. (eds) 1990. *Clinical Practice Guidelines: Directions for a New Program*. Washington: Institute of Medicine. National Academy Press.

Glasziou, P.P. and Haynes, B. 2005. The paths from research to improved health outcomes. *American College of Physicians Journal Club*, 142(2), A8–10.

Glasziou, P.P. and Irwig, L.M. 1995. An evidence based approach to individualising treatment. *British Medical Journal*, 311(7016), 1356–9.

Haynes, B. 2002. 'What kind of evidence is it that evidence-based medicine advocates want health care providers and consumers to pay attention to?, *BMC Health Services Research*, 2, 3doi:10.1186/1472-6963-2-3.

Herodotus 1996. *The Histories*. Harmondsworth: Penguin.

Hill, P. 2008. *Report of a National Review of NHS Health Library Services in England: from Knowledge to Health in the 21st Century*. Available at: http://www.library.nhs.uk/aboutnlh/review.

Old Testament. Book of Daniel, Chapter I, Verse 12.

Howes, N., Chagla, L., Thorpe, M. and McCulloch, P. 1997. Surgical practice is evidence based. *British Journal of Surgery*, 84(9), 1220–23.

Irwig, J., Irwig, L., Sweet, M. and Trevena, L. 2007. *Smart Health Choices*. 2nd Edition. London: Hammersmith Press.

Jessup, M. and Brozena, S.C. 2007. Guidelines for the management of heart failure: differences in guideline perspectives. *Cardiol Clin*, 25(4), 497–506.

Keats, J. 2006. *A Longman Cultural Edition*, edited by S.J. Wolfson. London and New York: Longman Pearson.

Kuhn, T. 1996. *The Structure of Scientific Revolutions*. 3rd Edition. Chicago: University of Chicago Press.

Lind, J. 1762. *An Essay on the Most Effectual Means of Preserving the Health of Seamen, in the Royal Navy*. Available at: http://www.jameslindlibrary.org/trial_records/17th_18th_Century/lind_1762/lind_1762_tp.html.

Links, M. 2006. Analogies between reading of medical and religious texts. *British Medical Journal*, 333(7577), 1068–70.

Map of Medicine. Available at: http://www.mapofmedicine.com.

McDonald, C. 1996. Medical heuristics: the silent adjudicators of clinical practice. *Annals of Internal Medicine*, 124(1), Part 1, 56–62.

McNeil, J.J., Nelson, M.R. and Tonkin A.M. 2003. Public funding of large-scale clinical trials in Australia. *Medical Journal of Australia*, 179(10), 519–20.

Medical Research Council. Streptomycin in Tuberculosis Trials Committee. 1948. Streptomycin treatment for pulmonary tuberculosis. *British Medical Journal*, 2(4582), 769–82.

Medicines Australia 2008. Available at: http://www.medicinesaustralia.com.au/pages/page4.asp.

Miles, A., Loughlin, M. and Polychronis, A. 2007. Medicine and evidence: knowledge and action in clinical practice. *Journal of Evaluation in Clinical Practice*, 13(4), 481–503.

Moynihan, R. 2004. *Evaluating Health Services: A Reporter Covers the Science of Research Synthesis*. Milbank Memorial Fund. Available at: http://www.milbank.org/reports/2004Moynihan/040330Moynihan.html.

Murphy, B. 2008. What has happened to clinical leadership in futile care discussions? *Medical Journal of Australia*, 188(7), 418–9.

Murphy, E. 1976. *The Logic of Medicine*. Baltimore: Johns Hopkins University Press.

National Health and Medical Research Council (NHMRC) Australia 2000. *How to Use the Evidence: Assessment and Application of Scientific Evidence*. Available at: http://www.cebm.net/index.aspx?o=1025.

National Health Service (NHS) 2002. Available at: http://www.nhs.uk.

National Institute of Clinical Studies (NICS) 2008. Available at: http://www.nhmrc.gov.au/nics/asp/index.asp.

Naylor, C. 2002. Putting evidence into practice. *The American Journal of Medicine*, 113(2), 161–3.

NHMRC Australia 2006. *Making Decisions about Tests and Treatments: Principles for Better Communication*. Available at: http://www.nhmrc.gov.au/publications/synopses/hpr25syn.htm.

NHS Public Health Resource Unit. Available at: http://www.phru.nhs.uk/Pages/PHD/resources.htm.

Poincaré, H. 1905. *Science and Hypothesis*, Chapter 9, Hypotheses in physics. London: Walter Scott Publishing. Available at: http://www.brocku.ca/MeadProject/Poincare/Poincare_1905_10.html.

Rochon, P.A., Mashari, A., Cohen, A., Misra, A., Laxer, D., Streiner, D.L., Dergal, J.M., Clark, J.P., Gold, J. and Binns, M.A. 2004. Relationship between randomized controlled trials published in leading general medical journals and the global burden of diseases. *Canadian Medical Association Journal*, 170(11), 1673–7.

Ross, W.D., Ackrill, J.L. and Urmson, J.O. 1998. *Aristotle: The Nicomachean Ethics*. Oxford: Oxford University Press.

Russell, B. 1961. *History of Western Philosophy*. 2nd Edition. London: Routledge.

Sackett, D.L. 1979. Bias in analytic research. *Journal of Chronic Disease*, 32(1–2), 51–63.

Sackett, D.L., Rosenberg, W.M , Gray, J.A. and Haynes, R.B. 1996. Evidence-based medicine: what it is and what it isn't. *British Medical Journal*, 312(7023), 71–2.

Sadler, J.Z. and Hulgus, Y.F. 1992. Clinical problem solving and the biopsychosocial model. *American Journal of Psychiatry*, 149(10), 1315–23.

Safeer, R.S. and Keenan, J. 2005. Health literacy: the gap between physicians and patients. *American Family Physician*, 72(3), 463–8.

Saunders, C., Girgis, A., Butow, P., Crossing, S. and Penman, A. 2008. From inclusion to independence – training consumers to review research. *Health Research Policy and Systems*, 6, 3doi:10.1186/1478-4505-6-3.

Scott, I. 2007. The evolving science of translating research evidence into clinical practice. *American College of Physicians Journal Club*, 146(3), A8–A11.

Scott, I. and Greenberg, P.B. 2005. Cautionary tales in the clinical interpretation of therapeutic trial reports. *Internal Medicine Journal*, 35(10), 611–21.

Scott, I., Greenberg, P.B. and Phillips, P.A. 2008a. Strengthening the scientific approach in the new physician training programme. *Internal Medicine Journal*, 38:6a, 384–7.

Scott I., Greenberg, P.B., and Poole, P.J. 2008b. Cautionary tales in the clinical interpretation of studies of diagnostic tests. *Internal Medicine Journal*, 38(2), 120–9.

Scott I., Greenberg, Poole, P.J. and Campbell, D. 2006. Cautionary tales in the interpretation of systematic reviews of therapy trials. *Internal Medicine Journal*, 36(9), 587–99.

Singer, C. 1962. *A Short History of Medicine*. 2nd Edition. Oxford: Clarendon Press.

Straus, S.E., Richardson, W.S., Glasziou, P. and Haynes, R.B. 2005. *Evidence-Based Medicine. How to Practice and Teach EBM*. 3rd Edition. Sydney: Elsevier Churchill Livingstone.

Teunissen, P.W. and Dornan, T. 2008. Lifelong learning at work. *British Medical Journal*, 336(7645), 667–9.

'Users' Guides to Evidence-Based Practice'. Available at: http://www.cche.net/usersguides/main.asp.

Wennberg, J. 2002. Unwarranted variations in healthcare delivery: implications for academic medical centres. *British Medical Journal*, 325(7370), 961–4.

Yank, V., Rennie, D. and Bero, L.A. 2007. Financial ties and concordance between results and conclusions in meta-analyses: retrospective cohort study. *British Medical Journal*, 335(7631), 1202–5.

3 The practice of the psychiatrist

Alex Holmes

The foundation of psychiatric practice is the diagnosis and treatment of mental illness. That said, the nature of psychiatric practice is hardly visible in the pages of psychiatric texts, or in the reams of new literature published daily. It is built slowly during the course of an arduous clinical apprenticeship where, informed by documented knowledge and fostered by their guild, trainee practitioners develop a deep understanding of how people work and how best to help them. Thereafter the psychiatrist is apportioned complex and disparate roles which require accurate clinical appraisals, considered judgements and the application of treatments attuned to the needs of the patient. Modern in form, the psychiatrist is still guided by the traditions of medicine, the alleviation of suffering, a respect for the autonomy and humanity and *'primum, non nocere'* (Cassell 2004). The psychiatrist has evolved alongside changing understandings of the human mind and the nature of mental illness, and continues to do so in an age of rapid technological advancement. In the end, the practice of psychiatry may be best described as an aspiration to apply the best of knowledge, tradition and experience to help those in psychological pain.

The psychiatrist as doctor

The psychiatrist is a doctor who has undertaken postgraduate specialist training in the field of psychiatry. After graduating from medical school, he or she completes two or more years of residency before applying for entry into a specialist training programme. The psychiatry training programme, in common with other programmes, adopts the *apprenticeship* model of learning. Trainees undertake a series of mandatory and elective clinical placements over five or more years in community or inpatient public mental health services. Concurrently they undertake self-directed learning, attend educational programmes, complete assignments and prepare for written and clinical examinations. The curriculum is wide-ranging, encompassing biological, psychological and social knowledge relevant to understanding the human mind. The trainee is required to become skilled in prescribing medication, psychotherapy and working within complex healthcare systems. When all is completed, the trainee is accepted as a full member of the Royal Australian and New Zealand College of Psychiatrists (or national equivalent) and can call him or herself a psychiatrist. They remain members of the College as long as they engage in ongoing professional development and adhere to standards of practice and professional conduct as stipulated by the College and the boards of medical registration.

The origins of psychiatry in medicine provide the foundation skills for clinical practice and the application of knowledge. Foremost amongst these are diagnostic reasoning and medical decision making. Applying the traditional biomedical method, doctors use history, examination and investigations to diagnose illness. Diagnosis allows for the application of statistical methods to guide decision making and determine effective treatments. Despite this, there is no certainty when making decisions. Treatment decisions are made using published scientific knowledge, previous clinical experience and information carefully collected about the individual patient (Sox et al. 2006). A judgement is made as to the expected outcomes for each course of action (Gigerenzer 2002). Sox et al. (2006) have been so blunt as to suggest that clinical decisions are a choice between two or more gambles. The ability to make clinical decisions in the face of uncertainty and accepting the possibility of serious adverse outcomes is a generic skill in medicine. It defines the practice of all doctors as much as their knowledge base or the authority attributed to their roles. This generic skill is an invaluable basis on which to deal with the complex questions that arise in psychiatry, especially as the focus of activity moves from physical to mental illness.

Mental illness

Disturbances in thinking and behaviour have been observed from the very earliest records. The Ebers and Edwin Smith papyri (1550 BC) describe disorders of concentration and memory, as well as states of sadness and distress (Nasser 1987). Hippocrates (460–370 BC) was the first to describe sustained mental disturbance as an illness, attributing its cause to an imbalance of humours (Lyons and Petrucelli 1979). The designation of 'madness' or 'insanity' in pre-Christian Rome saw the mentally ill as having an impairment of *mens sana in corpore sano* (of healthy mind in a healthy body), a fundamental defect of reason. In early Christian Europe, madness was seen as a deficiency of character or a product of sin, and treated accordingly (Foucault 1988). Seventeenth-century England saw the emergence of mad houses and later asylums to deal with the presence of the mad in increasingly industrialized communities. Consonant with the status attributed to medicine, doctors were allocated positions of leadership within the asylums and with the writing of new laws, such as the Lunacy Act 1845, allocated specific legal authority in reference to those of 'unsound mind' (Shorter 1997).

The notion of disturbances of the mind as constituting an illness is not without controversy. Illness is synonymous with disease. Disease was originally conceptualized as an abnormality in the physical functioning of an organism (Kendell 2001). In medicine, the presence of a disease is suggested by a typical constellation of symptoms and signs, a clinical syndrome. At the origins of modern medicine in the fifteenth century, clinical syndromes were increasingly matched with a pathological process observed post mortem, informed by emerging knowledge of human anatomy and physiology. Thomas Sydenham (1624–1689) (Lyons and Petrucelli 1979), for example, provided detailed descriptions of gout and influenza, the biological causes of which were determined to be disorders of uric acid metabolism and infection by the influenza virus.

Not surprisingly, the same 'medical model' was applied to disturbances of the mind. The first clear descriptions of mental illness occurred during the nineteenth century. Emil Kraepelin (1856–1926), through careful observation of patients, described the features differentiating dementia praecox (now schizophrenia) from manic depression (now bipolar disorder and major depression) (Shorter 1997). Subsequently, a range of other psychiatric disorders, including anxiety, eating and personality disorders were described. In contrast to many disorders in other organ systems, however, the physical causes of these disorders have not been fully elucidated. Their validity continues to rest on the uniformity of the clinical syndrome, alongside associations with anatomical and functional changes revealed through imaging. Proponents of the anti-psychiatry movement have even suggested that mental illness is no more than a social construct, a mechanism of social control (Szasz 1974). The history of modern psychiatry would suggest, however, that, apart from the political and social misuse of the illness model, the 'medical' approach has led to great benefits through the correct treatment of mentally ill patients.

Mental illness can be explained using psychological and sociological paradigms. The term psychological is widely applied, but may be summarized as the exploration of the human mind, manifest in behaviour and language, and described using the abstract concepts of thought and emotion (Carlson and Buskist 1997). Sociology identifies inequalities, acting through stressful life experiences, as fundamental causes of psychological distress (Tausig et al. 1998). What is described psychologically or sociologically is inferred from our observations of others. Typically psychological models of distress or illness are built around how an individual interprets and responds to particular recent and past experiences. There are many eponymous models or theories which typically commence around an individual with a particular insight and gradually build credence through clinical application, research, training and forming associations. Important examples of these are the psychodynamic movement of the early twentieth century and cognitive behavioural theory arising in the 1970s.

Psychiatry and the mind in the modern era

Key ideas about the human mind emerged in the nineteenth century which form the foundation of contemporary psychiatric practice. Previously the mind had been isolated from the body as a consequence of Cartesian dualism (1596–1659) (Descartes 1993) and from the relevance of experience by George Berkeley's (1685–1753) idealism. Immanuel Kant's (1724–1804) refutation of idealism, spurred by British empiricism, determined that although objects in the real world could not be known directly, they could be experienced indirectly through the senses (Kant 2007). As Percy Shelley would contend, we see the world through a 'painted veil'. Kant's work strongly influenced Arthur Schopenhauer (1788–1860), who went on to describe the will as having the force in a man's psyche to be able to affect his behaviour and influence how he perceived the world (Schopenhauer 1995). From this fertile ground emerged the work of Sigmund Freud and colleagues who gave new form and definition to the human psyche.

The work of Freud has been much admired and much maligned. It is an inescapable truth, however, that it has had a great impact on the practice of modern psychiatry. To a large degree this has not been through the use of Freud's therapeutic method, Freudian psychoanalysis, but through the more general application of his theory. Freud shed considerable light on the existence of psychic reality, which, as suggested by Kant, represents an individual's unique internal experience of the external world. Furthermore, according to Freud, our psyches develop from infancy to adulthood by negotiating the conflict between primary narcissism and basic desires (instincts), and the requirements of external reality, most notably the socializing demands of civilization (Freud 1989). Unresolved conflicts or traumas occurring during development were seen to lead to psychological distress or psychosomatic symptoms in later life, requiring treatment with psychotherapy.

Psychodynamic therapy was the first modern psychotherapy. Patients were placed in a relaxed and neutral position and invited to say whatever was on their mind, to 'free associate'. The therapist paid close attention to the content of what was said, the patient's response to the therapist (transference) and his own response to the patient (counter-transference). Observation and interpretations are used by the therapist to bring conflicts into the conscious and work them through, leading to the resolution of symptoms. Despite Freud's repeated reference to the scientific basis of his work and the notion of the therapist as an abstinent 'mirror to the psyche', the therapeutic process is now accepted as an intensely interpersonal process, involving the psyches of both the therapist and the patient.

The emergence of the first effective biological treatments for mental illness and an explosion in neuroscience occurred in the second half of the twentieth century. In 1950 the French chemist Paul Charpentier synthesized the drug chlorpromazine, which was observed to place rats in a state of 'disinterest' or 'detachment'. By 1954 randomized trials had confirmed its effectiveness in treating the symptoms of schizophrenia (Turner 2007). Around the same time, imipramine, a derivative of chlorpromazine, was recognized as the first effective antidepressant. Many agents have followed. The emergence of new medications has occurred alongside rapid expansion in knowledge about the normal and abnormal functioning of the central nervous system. Magnetic resonance imaging has confirmed structural and functional changes in patients diagnosed with psychosis and mood disorders. Neurochemistry has detailed the neurotransmitter systems involved in different mental disorders. Genetic studies have identified gene polymorphisms associated with higher risk of developing major depression.

The volume of new knowledge and treatments requires the use of skills related to knowledge itself. These skills, some of which are documented under the edicts of evidence-based medicine, include the ability to locate and appraise knowledge in reference to making a particular decision, understanding the difference between association and causality, and arguing using logic. These skills are commonly required in order to differentiate marketing and opinion from scientific fact when new treatments are released, and in helping patients explore the strength behind the manifold offerings of help and symptom relief presented to them as part of the information age. Somewhat ironically, we require skills in the use of knowledge as much to determine when it is being misused as to use it directly ourselves in making clinical decisions.

The twentieth century saw the description of a new medical paradigm. In 1977, George Engel (1913–1999) introduced the bio-psychosocial model as a method with which to account for the multifactorial antecedents of disease and to formulate a broad framework of management (Engel 1977). It had long been apparent to physicians that the patient's personal history and social circumstances played a role in the pathogenesis of disease and their interpretation of symptoms (White 2005). Engel was a psychiatrist strongly influenced by psychoanalytic theory who took up work with medically ill patients at the University of Rochester. His model was founded on systems theory, which conceptualized the world as a hierarchy of systems stretching from sub-atomic particles to culture. Relationships between various levels of the system were seen to be dynamic and amenable to change. Impact at one level of the system may affect another. For example, psychological distress may have physical consequences, and social interventions may influence vulnerability to disease. His work not only allowed for non-biological causal factors accommodated into the formulation of an illness, but identified psychological and social strategies which may be used to address the illness. Given that the antecedents of mental health disorders often included psychological and social factors, the bio-psychosocial approach was particularly well suited to the practice of psychiatry. It also allowed for the concurrent use of pharmacological and psychotherapeutic approaches, such as in the management of depression where anti-depressant medication, cognitive behaviour therapy and the provision of social support could be used concurrently.

The bio-psychosocial approach also emphasized the importance of the doctor-patient relationship (White 2005). William Olser (1849–1919), a father of modern medicine, is often quoted as saying 'the good physician treats the disease but the great physician treats the patient who has the disease' (Porter 1996). In previous centuries, when therapeutic efficacy was limited, physicians were well versed in the notion of helping their patients through psychological support (Porter 1996). It has been argued that as medicine developed and interventions became effective, the focus of the doctor moved to treating the illness rather than the patient as a whole. Engel not only placed the person with the illness in their wider context, but placed the treating physician or psychiatrist within the system. Reflecting psychodynamic concepts, the physician was transformed from an objective scientific observer to a participant in an intersubjective relationship. With this relationship came the processes previously identified as occurring in psychotherapy, albeit less overtly. The relationships gave the capacity to identify and work through anxieties, to provide an experience of care and to be subject to transference and counter-transference. Overall, the bio-psychosocial approach placed the doctor in a much more complex, interdependent world in which he was an active participant.

A competent psychiatrist has to be able to apply the biomedical and bio-psychosocial approaches with equal skill. This is not necessarily easily done. One reason for this is that the epistemology inherent in either stance is so fundamental as to be entrenched in the personality of the practitioner. In other words, it is not natural to be both a logical positivist and a relativist. Doctors usually start as logical positivists. The prerequisites for entry into medicine are science and mathematics. Science is reliant on the presumption that observations are separable from the distortions of the observer, from intersubjectivity and the distortions of psychic reality. Science can easily be misconstrued as holding the promise of certainty. As medical students progress, they learn to adapt to uncertainty of clinical practice and the different perspectives held by the doctor and patient. The psychiatry trainee continues this journey, spurred by limitations of the biomedical approach and a need to make sense of intense personal experiences.

The subjective experiences of the trainee psychiatrist form a key component of training. Personal responses, rather than being disavowed or hidden, are embraced as having the potential to aid in understanding the patient, in the same way that transference and counter-transference provide insight when conducting psychotherapy. Inevitably the acknowledgement of these responses requires trainees to explore their own psychic reality, their strengths and vulnerabilities. They aim to acknowledge some of their own internal conflicts, key developmental experiences and the foundations of their self-worth. This encouragement towards self-awareness is supported by the requirement of weekly supervision. A common theme in supervision is the Kantian dilemma – how much of trainee psychiatrists' responses are derived from themselves (their psychic reality) and how much relates to the patient (the patient's psychic reality). Over time a familiarity and fluency in the intersubjective nature of reality develops – 'the truth lies somewhere in between' and the psychiatrist comes to embrace the importance of a life-long commitment to self-appraisal. Having started at the Hippocratic edifice, the psychiatrist now finds him or herself at the oracle at Delphi, adopting the internal ethic, 'know thyself'.

The roles of the psychiatrist

The roles attributed the contemporary psychiatrist are disparate. They include the psychiatrist as individual practitioner, as clinical leader, as holding legal authority under the Mental Health Act, and as holding, transmitting and extending knowledge of the human mind. This may see the psychiatrist as a private practitioner, as a consultant in a public mental health service, providing expert opinion to the courts, as a researcher, a teacher, or undertaking advocacy or even political roles. Of the approximately 2,300 psychiatrists in Australia (Committee MHWA 2001), three-quarters of them are in private practice seeing individual patients (Henderson 2000). About a third of a psychiatrist's time is spent managing patients with psychotic disorders and a third with mood and anxiety disorders (Andrews and Hadzi-Pavlovic 1988). In terms of primary treatment, 30 per cent of patients receive medication and 60 per cent psychotherapy (Andrews and Hadzi-Pavlovic 1988). In 2001, 1.8 per cent of the Australian population consulted a psychiatrist in the last year. Yet among people with a diagnosed mental disorder, only 7.3 per cent consulted a psychiatrist, reminding us that the majority of psychiatric disorders are addressed in primary care or not at all. (Meadows et al. 2002).

Psychiatrists often sub-specialize. Their focus may be on a particular age group (child, adolescent, adult, the elderly), on a subgroup of disorders (psychosis, mood and anxiety disorders, eating disorders), on patients with co-morbidity (physical illness, drug and alcohol), in certain settings (private practice, public mental health services, inpatient units, outpatient care, general hospitals, forensic settings) or applying particular treatments (pharmacotherapy, psychotherapy, electro-convulsive therapy). Commonly a psychiatrist may undertake a number of roles across the working week, although seldom more than two given the requirement to keep up to date with the journal literature and advances in the field.

The psychiatrist in private practice

Psychiatrists receive referrals from general practitioners. When a patient first presents to a general practitioner (GP) with psychological distress, the doctor will attempt to identify the problem and determine if further intervention is required. In many cases, even when a psychiatric disorder is diagnosed, support, reassurance and symptomatic relief are all that are required. Alternatively, the GP may embark on a brief course of physical or psychological treatment. In a minority of cases, the GP will seek the help of a psychiatrist. This usually occurs when there is a lack of clarity about the nature of the presenting problem, or when the seriousness or complexity of the disorder requires greater expertise. This may be the case when the patient is symptomatic to the degree that they cannot function, or when they are severely distressed or psychotic.

To be treated by a psychiatrist is to be involved in a process that is steeped in stigma. In the wider community, when seeing a psychiatrist is suggested, responses like 'I am not mad' or 'I will see a counsellor or psychologist, but not a psychiatrist' are not uncommon. This stigma, arising from contemporary mythology, socialization, stereotyping and atavistic fear, represents one of the greatest impediments to individuals accessing mental health care. There is universal fear of 'madness'. It is commonly assumed that to be mad is to lose control, to lose reason, or even to be dangerous. To have a mental illness is to be marked as deficient, weak or unproductive; to require help for psychological distress is seen as self-indulgent and burdensome on the rest of the hard-working community. The stigma extends to the psychiatrists themselves who become imbued with their own mantle of madness, represented in popular culture by such figures as Hannibal Lecter and the lobotomist in *One Flew Over the Cuckoo's Nest*. Working effectively in practice requires an acceptance of this stigma and the capacity to deal with it. Often the first consultations involve subtly eliciting and casting aside of preconceptions, supported by the appropriate balance of professionalism and emotional availability.

A private psychiatrist receives referrals for patients with a wide range of problems. It may be assumed that the problems are invariably 'psychological or psychiatric', but this is not necessarily the case. The ultimate cause may turn out to be a physical disorder, or alternatively there may be no disorder present at all. The psychiatrist explores the presenting problem by conducting a 'psychiatric interview'. Much of this skill, which incorporates the 'personal' knowledge, intuition and trained insight inherent in good practice, relates to the psychiatrist's capacity to conduct this interview. In the course of the interview the patient is encouraged to tell their own story in their own way. Their telling is facilitated by the use of open-ended questions, clarification and feedback, and strategies used to maintain 'as good as possible' a therapeutic alliance. Throughout the course of the interview, the psychiatrist looks to formulate collaboratively an understanding as to the factors contributing to the patient's problem. A number of provisional hypotheses might be raised which are explored and then presented to the patient in order to test their validity, for example: 'It seems that you feel powerless at home and at work'. At the same time the psychiatrist looks to collect information confirming or excluding particular diagnoses: 'Can you describe your mood'; 'how are you sleeping?'. By the end of the interview the psychiatrist should have consolidated a bio-psychosocial formulation and may have reached a diagnosis. The diagnosis is the presence of one or more mental disorders. The formulation of the diagnosis constitutes a brief explanatory hypothesis as to why the patient is presenting this way at this time, based on salient biological, psychological and social elements from recent and past history.

As part of the psychiatric interview the psychiatrist attempts to assess the patient's reality testing. The psychiatrist tries to identify the individual's particular enduring traits, their 'slant' on the world, or the transference they typically attach to certain types of people. These qualities are aspects of self and personality, and are important determinants as to how someone responds to a particular stress or challenge. For example, an individual may reveal a tendency to see all males in positions of authority as controlling and uncaring, a characteristic that causes them to react strongly to people who share some of these features, especially in the workplace. Alternatively, the psychiatrist may identify temporary alterations in reality testing, which are a consequence of stress or mental disorder. This may be subtle, as in the case of major depression where the patient demonstrates a general pessimism about the world. In psychosis the impairment of reality testing is marked.

The mafia are heard to be crawling through the ceiling of a suburban house, the phone is bugged and no evidence to the contrary will persuade the patient otherwise. In psychosis, the lack of *mens rea*, leads to what Jaspers called a 'non-understandability' and the psychiatrist learns that a plausible understanding is unlikely to be fruitful.

Having made a diagnosis and formulation, the private psychiatrist must decide on a course of action. For some patients the treatment is no more than reassurance. This reassurance is delivered with a judgement that the distress is understandable and likely to be transient. For other patients a simple strategy is suggested. For the overworked manager, who feels tired, unhappy and alienated from his family, the psychiatrist may recommend regular family outings. The apparent simplicity of the solution should not be confused, however, with the process behind it. Suggesting family outings may appear like common sense, but is recommended having excluded other more serious possibilities, including major depression, and determining that the most likely avenue to help involves improved communication within the patient's primary relationships.

Medication may be indicated when a mental illness is present and commonly leads to substantial improvement in function and well-being. Psychotherapeutic medications are single chemicals which exert biochemical effects on the brain. The main categories are anti-psychotics, anti-depressants, mood stabilizers and anti-anxiety agents. Their main mechanism of action is by attaching to specific brain receptors to which neurotransmitters otherwise attach in the process of brain cells communicating with each other. Blocking receptors may have unwarranted effects, experienced as side-effects such as a change in appetite, sleep or sexual function. Sometimes patients state that they simply feel different on medication as opposed to being off it, having both positive (not depressed) and negative (less emotional) aspects. The choice of medication is made according to specific symptom profiles, expected side-effects and previous efficacy. Treatment is guided by evidence-based guidelines derived from a synthesis of clinical trials, but prescribing seldom involves simply following an algorithm. Skilled practice and non-formulated knowledge is applied to make a judgement as to the best treatment for a given individual.

Many patients understandably dislike taking psychotropic medication and seek to cease treatment. They feel stigmatized by treatment, worry about long-term effects and feel resentful of the need to take tablets to maintain their emotional well-being. Fear of dependence and addiction are commonly expressed, despite reassurance that psychotropic medications, with the exception of benzodiazepines, do not lead to physical tolerance. The decision to commence medication is best presented as an informed choice. There is no legal basis for involuntary treatment in the private sector.

The psychiatrist goes over the potential consequences of taking and not taking medication, often a number of times, in order to facilitate this choice.

When medication is used, not all patients improve. The response rate for all medications is less than 100 per cent and often much less. A second or third medication may be trialled. In some individuals, repeated trials of different medications are ineffective. A stage may be reached where all reasonable evidence-based approaches have been applied without adequate benefit. This dilemma is common to all medical specialties and represents one of the most challenging aspects of medical practice. In oncology, for example, this may occur when standard chemotherapy agents are unable to arrest tumour growth. The wish from the patient and doctor alike is for an alleviation of distress, and it is difficult to acknowledge when accepted treatments are ineffective. In these circumstances the teaching, derived form the work of Tom Main (1957), reminds psychiatrists that they are vulnerable to act in one of two ways, both of which are unhelpful to the patient. Firstly, they may undertake a nihilistic withdrawal, becoming blaming and resentful about the patient. Alternatively they may act with therapeutic zeal, leading to the over-use of untested treatments. The middle path is an acceptance as to the limits of treatment and therapeutic capacities, an important and sobering skill.

Psychiatrists practise a range of psychotherapies. Typically, a practitioner will practise one type, be it psychodynamic, cognitive behavioural or supportive. Many psychiatrists choose to limit their psychotherapeutic work to brief supportive work. Some do not practise it at all, either as a personal choice or because it is unsuited to their patient group. The judgement applied in deciding which therapy is recommended is based on the nature of the problem, evidence supporting a particular approach, therapist skills and patient preference. An uncomplicated mood or anxiety disorder may primarily be addressed with cognitive behaviour therapy, requiring once weekly sessions over 12 to 24 weeks. More pervasive difficulties with relationships, self-worth and life direction, may require a psychodynamic approach one or more times a week for some years. An individual dealing with a sudden crisis or loss may be best helped using a time-limited supportive approach.

Psychotherapy is not like surgery or medication. Psychotherapy requires the active participation of both patient and therapist. The notion, often suggested in popular culture, that if a person has a psychological or behavioural problem, they should undergo therapy or counselling makes little theoretical or clinical sense. In practice, people who undertake psychotherapy need not only to have the motivation to do so, but the ability to do the psychological work, the capacity to contribute to the maintenance of the therapeutic relationship and the resilience to deal with the inevitable challenges of disclosure, self-exploration and perceived stigma. Not all patients, even those presenting with significant distress or impulses towards self-harm, possess these qualities. A central skill in conducting therapy, therefore, is the ability to decide when it is better not to begin. As with many medical treatments, psychotherapy can be of benefit, but can also do harm. The judgement regarding whether to undertake a therapy or not is built slowly through experience. Invariably this experience includes having undertaken a number of therapies which have not progressed well or concluded with precipitous termination. To recommend against psychotherapy may be experienced as a further rejection and leave the psychiatrist open to feelings of being withholding or self-serving. Yet the ethic of *prime non nocere* applies as well to psychological interventions as to physical ones. Commencing a therapeutic relationship with little chance of success may simply repeat and replay earlier dissatisfying relationships, adding to a patient's mistrust and nihilism.

Conducting psychotherapy requires significant skill, training and experience. Although psychotherapy may appear similar to 'being kind and supportive', in practice it requires rigour and discipline. In conducting therapy, skilled psychiatrists will tailor their approach to best suit the needs of the patient. Underpinning this is the capacity to maintain a positive therapeutic alliance (Frank and Frank 1961). It is important to have clarity around the goals of therapy, to adhere to method and to maintain limits around availability and responsiveness (boundaries). Once the therapy has begun, the exploration of difficult experiences commonly leads to intense emotions and thoughts. Patients may become fragmented, suicidal or 'act out' their distress outside of therapy. The therapist has to be able to 'sit with' this whilst also responding appropriately at times of high risk.

In formal psychodynamic psychotherapy, much of the work in therapy relates to the patient's experience of others. Inevitably, the therapist becomes a 'significant other'. The patient experiences strong feelings and ideas about the therapist (transference), and the therapist about the patient (counter-transference). The role of the therapist is to remain attuned to the patient and to understand and interpret this transference relationship. The therapist is unable to avoid some disappointment from the patient, by virtue of not being perfectly attuned, instantly available or soothing of all distress. Nonetheless, he or she attempts to remain 'good enough' in order that the relationship can continue. Within this relationship, with time and effort, it is hoped the patient will grow. This growth is built on improved insight and the experience of a relationship that has been authentic and reliable. At termination it is apparent to therapist and patient alike that the goals of therapy have been reached and that it is time for separation to occur. This is negotiated with grief and gratitude on both sides, the natural response to the end of an important and meaningful relationship.

The psychiatrist in public practice

Public mental health services provide for the needs of patients with the most serious and disabling of mental health disorders. Most commonly public patients have schizophrenia, bipolar disorder and severe personality disorders. Their disability is compounded by substance abuse and poor supports. Services are divided into geographical regions and built with a combination of inpatient, outpatient and outreach teams. Within the services the psychiatrist works with nurses, social workers, occupational therapists and psychologists as part of the multidisciplinary team. The psychiatrist also is designated unique authority and responsibilities under the Mental Health Act in regard to the involuntary retention and treatment of patients.

The role of the psychiatrist within the multidisciplinary team is complex and not well articulated. This calls for the use of tacit knowledge often passed between colleagues on an informal basis. The multidisciplinary team evolved in the second half of the twentieth century as one of many manifestations of the shift towards interdisciplinary care. Previous to this, in most health services, the senior doctor was considered the authority, overseeing and guiding the activities of junior doctors and making management decisions to be implemented by nursing and allied health staff. The multidisciplinary approach first emerged in areas of healthcare where the skills of non-medical health staff were most suited to improving function, typically rehabilitation and aged care. The benefits of the multidisciplinary team lie in the capacity to apply a range of discipline-specific strategies, the sum total of which cannot be delivered by a single practitioner. The team works well when united by the common goal of helping the patient, when there is a shared understanding of profession-specific skills, efficient communication, effective decision making and clear lines of clinical responsibility. In practice, however, teams are groups of individuals and prone to processes that can impair the functioning of any group. These processes often relate to tensions around autonomy, authority, responsibility and perceived value within the team. Teams and groups require leadership in order to work through these tensions, a role sometimes, although not invariably, undertaken by the psychiatrist.

Clinical leadership is also required in consolidating the contribution of team members into a single coherent management plan. In this role, familiarity with the bio-psychosocial approach and confidence with decision making come to the fore. Inherent in this process is the dilemma of clinical responsibility in the team setting. The responsibility most difficult to accept when engaged in a professional caring relationship is that relating to the possibility of a major adverse outcome. In mental health the most feared adverse outcomes are suicide and homicide. A common, if not single, aim of mental health care is to reduce the risk of harm to self or others by current patients. This is certainly a commonly articulated community expectation, especially in the aftermath of such an event: 'This should not have happened', 'It should have been prevented', 'The fact that it occurred means that someone did not do their job properly'. As with all healthcare, the wish for perfect foresight must be tempered by the reality that clinical decisions are probabilistic choices influenced, but not determined, by evidence, requiring skill and intuition not present in protocols. Balancing the impulse to intervene in the face of risk is the community's commitment to autonomy. The deprivation of liberty with the aim of reducing risk is a course of action undertaken only in the most severe and imminent of cases. Most psychiatrists have had the experience of a patient under their care committing suicide and have had to negotiate the guilt, rigorous reappraisal of choices made, and self-doubt that follow. In managing the anxiety associated with adverse outcomes, the psychiatrist is most helpful in supporting team members carry their clinical autonomy. This is done through case presentations, conjoint assessment and the oversight of clinical decisions made within the team.

The public psychiatrist holds a unique position within the public mental health service in relationship to mental health legislation and the provision of involuntary care. Mental health legislation has evolved such that involuntary hospitalization and treatment can only occur under specific circumstances. Reflecting the wishes of the community, the Mental Health Act requires that for involuntary treatment to occur, a patient must have a mental illness, that he or she needs treatment and cannot be managed in a less restrictive environment and, in the absence of treatment, that he or she is put at risk of harm or is at risk of harming others. Patients can be brought to hospital without their consent by police or other mental health workers; the decision to retain them in hospital or administer treatment without their consent can only be done under the authority of an authorized psychiatrist. This designation may be understood as reflecting the principle that practitioners with the highest level of training and expertise are best suited to make the difficult judgement as to when it is appropriate to suspend autonomy. Some have argued that it also reflects a hangover from the medically dominated history of mental health care. Either way, judgements around involuntary status are always made with a deep awareness of how it may be experienced by the patient and the tension that between doing good and doing no harm.

This authority held by the psychiatrist to enforce involuntary admission and treatment has been the focus of much debate and criticism. The primary aim of early mental health legislation was to 'remove the mad form the community'. Following the reforms promoted by William Tuke (1732–1822) at the York Retreat in England, the aim of psychiatric care became the treatment or rehabilitation of the mentally ill. In circumstances of mental illness where *mens rea* is impaired, the individual often does not believe that they have an illness or need treatment. Without enforced intervention the patient remains untreated and uncontained. It is sometimes assumed that people with serious mental illness are not distressed, they may even be 'happily mad', like King Lear's fool. Clinical experience shows time and again that this is not the case. The psychotic world, the depressed world and even the manic world are profoundly dysphoric places. Involuntary treatment will likely reduce this suffering, albeit at the cost of the experience of loss of autonomy. Some communities, in particular in Italy, believe that this cost is too high. Others, like jurisdictions in the United States, allow for containment only in the most extreme circumstances, and only for a limited period of time, feeding the dark conclusion to the lives of many homeless men with untreated psychosis who 'die with their rights on'. In Australia the balance formalized in the legislation is to intervene when it is necessary and there is no other option. This is a balance dictated by the community and enacted by the psychiatrist attuned to the prevailing expectations of the community.

This association of psychiatry with the power to remove liberty has greatly coloured the common perception of what psychiatrists do. The association of the psychiatrist with mental health legislation, psychiatric hospitals and the exclusion of madness is manifest in an 'archetypal psychiatrist'. He (rather than she) is austere, authoritative, lacking in compassion and care, bent on control for his own ends. Were he otherwise, he would not do what he does. This stereotype resonates with and is probably driven by basic human fears of being controlled, abused or consumed. These fears cannot but be exacerbated by a psychotic patient's personal experience of involuntary care. Patients can easily feel disempowered and dehumanized, even when the best attempts are made to do otherwise. Psychiatrists, along with other mental health staff, must be able to tolerate and understand this perception while maintaining confidence in their judgement and ensuring the perception does not become a reality.

Conclusion

What a psychiatrist actually does cannot be easily determined through the literature. This truth is common to many, if not all professions, where daily practice looks to provide care tailored to the individual circumstances and needs of the patient. The psychiatrist exercises this task 'to the best of their ability', guided by ever-changing knowledge, accumulated skill and the traditions and ethics of their profession. The practice of psychiatry bridges the body and the mind, instilling a capacity to cross from the biomedical sphere to the bio-psychosocial, and from the objective perspective to the intersubjective. It requires the capacity to make decisions in the face of uncertainty and a belief in of the power of the therapeutic relationship. These skills of the psychiatrist cannot be learned quickly or without struggle, and may never be fully mastered. In the end, as with many professions, commitment to the guild is a commitment to life-long learning.

References

Andrews, G. and Hadzi-Pavlovic, D. 1988. The work of Australian psychiatrists, circa 1986. *Australian and New Zealand Journal of Psychiatry*, 22, 153–65.

Carlson, N. and Buskist, W. 1997. *Psychology. The Science of Behaviour*. Boston: Allyn and Bacon.

Cassell E.J. 2004. *The Nature of Suffering*. Oxford: Oxford University Press.

Committee MHWA 2001. *Mental Health Workforce: Supply of Psychiatrists*. Canberra: Department of Health and Ageing.

Descartes, R. 1993. *Meditations on First Philosophy: In Which the Existence of God and the Distinction of the Soul from the Body are Demonstrated*. Indianapolis: Hackett.

Engel, G.L. 1977. The need for a new medical model: a challenge for biomedicine. *Science*, 196, 129–36.

Foucault, M. 1988. *Madness and Civilization: A History of Insanity in the Age of Reason*. Toronto: Random House.

Frank, J. and Frank, J. 1961. *Persuasion and Healing*. Baltimore: Johns Hopkins University Press.

Freud, S. 1989. *Civilization and Its Discontents*. New York: W.W. Norton and Company.

Gigerenzer, G. 2002. *Reckoning with Risk*. Harmondsworth: Penguin.

Harris, T. 1989. *The Silence of the Lambs*. London: St Martin's Paperbacks.

Henderson, S. 2000. Focus on psychiatry in Australia. *British Journal of Psychiatry*, 176, 97–101.

Kant, E. 2007. *Critique of Pure Reason*. London: Penguin.

Kendell, R.E. 2001. The distinction between mental and physical illness. *British Journal of Psychiatry*, 178, 490–93.

Kesey, K. 1962. *One Flew Over the Cuckoo's Nest*. New York: Viking Press and Signet Books.

Lyons, A. and Petrucelli, J. 1979. *Medicine: An Illustrated History*. London: Macmillan.

Main, T.F. 1957. The ailment. *British Journal of Medical Psychology*, 30, 129–45.

Meadows, G., Singh, B., Burgess, P. and Bobevski, I. 2002. Psychiatry and the need for mental health care in Australia: findings from the National Survey of Mental Health and Wellbeing. *Australian and New Zealand Journal of Psychiatry*, 36, 210–16.

Nasser, M. 1987. Psychiatry in Ancient Egypt. *Bulletin of the Royal College of Psychiatrists*, 11(12), 420-22.

Porter, R. 1996. *Cambridge Illustrated History of Medicine*. Cambridge: Cambridge University Press.

Schopenhauer, A. 1995. *World as Will and Idea*. London: Everyman.

Shorter, E. 1997. *A History of Psychiatry: From the Era of the Asylum to the Age of Prozac*. New York: John Wiley and Sons.

Sox, H., Blatt, M.A., Higgins, M.C. and Marton, K.I. 2006. *Medical Decision Making*. Philadelphia: American College of Physicians.

Szasz, T.S. 1974. *The Myth of Mental Illness*. New York: Harper.

Tausig, M., Michello J. and Subedi, S. 1998. *A Sociology of Mental Illness*. New Jersey: Prentice Hall.

Turner, T. 2007. Chlorpromazine: unlocking psychosis. *British Medical Journal*, 334, Suppl 1, s7.

White, P. 2005. *Biopsychosocial Medicine: An Integrated Approach to Understanding Illness*. Oxford: Oxford University Press.

4 Social work knowledge-in-practice

Heather D'Cruz

Knowledge-in-practice is an important topic for professions such as social work because knowledge is not generated or disseminated for its own sake but to provide services to people who seek professional help for personal and private problems. Thus professional knowledge is *for* practice (Adams et al. 2002: xviii–xx). However, many professions, including social work, are critically engaging with the meanings of 'knowledge', 'practice' and the relationships between these two concepts (Healy 2000: 1–3, Healy 2005: i–xiv) that may be conceptualized as knowledge-*in*-practice, theorized in various ways.

This chapter aims to contribute to an understanding of knowledge-in-practice as a reflexive process, as knowing-in-action (Schön 1983) from my perspective as a social work academic, where 'the academy' is reframed as a 'field of social work practice' and 'academic practices' equate *as social work practices* . This reframing is perhaps contentious because 'social work practice' is generally taken for granted as direct work with individuals, families, groups and communities, although professional associations such as the International Association of Schools of Social Work define social work practice more broadly to include administration, policy, planning and research (IASSW). Furthermore, 'social work academics' are usually qualified social workers (Powell et al. 2004: 2) and hence expected to abide by professional codes of ethics, values and aims. It is just the ways in which social work academics practise social work, through professional education, research and writing for publication, that differ from more traditionally defined social work practice. On this basis, it is possible to argue that as a social work academic, I am a social work practitioner, able to explore what knowledge-in-practice may mean by drawing on an example of my research practice that has been published.

To reflect on knowledge-*in*-practice as a process, a selected example of a research interview is deconstructed according to whether it is representative of the concept of, and the conditions under which general claims can be made about knowledge-in-practice. The process of deconstruction means that critical analysis is applied to how and why I have engaged with an interview participant, including the vocabulary and syntax used and the framing of questions, as well as the consequences for how the participant responded. There are no firm conclusions that can be drawn due to the considerable limitations of the methodology. However, the deconstructive process offers insights and opportunities for dialogue with others in 'communities of practice' (Wenger 2008), whether they are social workers or from other 'caring' professions.

Before I engage with the deconstruction of the selected research interview, the sections below discuss social work knowledge-*for*-practice and social work knowledge-*in*-practice. The former concept recognizes that the knowledge of social workers, as professionals, must enable them to perform their professional roles appropriately and effectively. The latter concept recognizes that there is a continuing preoccupation for all professions as to how abstract and general knowledge is made meaningful in the lives of actual people who seek help.

Social work knowledge-for-practice

All professions recognize that there must be knowledge-*for*-practice, because the purpose of knowledge taught to practitioners as theories, values and ethics, methods of intervention and skills (Healy 2005: 4–8, Adams et al. 2002, Banks 2001) must be translated appropriately and meaningfully in some way in the actual lives of clients so that problems are resolved, prevented or ameliorated. An important symbol of professional identity is the claim of professional autonomy, discretion and judgement (Beauchamp and Childress, cited in Banks 2001: 46, Western et al. 2006) whereby professionals 'know how' to use abstract and general knowledge in particular situations with people who seek their help, as an expression of 'knowledge-*in*-practice'.

For social work, while debates continue about whether there is a unique body of theory, values or skills, knowledge or methods (James 2004: 46, 47), it is nonetheless clear that knowledge-for-practice is both disciplinary and professional (Camilleri 1999; Powell et al. 2004: 1). The definitions of 'theory' and 'practice' articulated by the IASSW and the International Federation of Social Workers (IFSW) explicitly address the need for *disciplinary* knowledge generated through 'research and practice evaluation' as *professional* knowledge, that is, to meet professional aims of 'individual, organizational, social and cultural change' International Federation of Social Workers (IFSW), as opposed to knowledge for its own sake. Social work knowledge relies on disciplinary knowledge that includes psychology, sociology and social policy (James 2004: 47), which is integrated in various ways as social work knowledge-for-practice.

Lyons and Taylor (2004: 78–9) on the other hand distinguish between 'the aims and methods of social work' as an 'academic subject area' that are distinctive as a discipline and the 'body of social work knowledge and the extent to which this is distinctive and created by the discipline itself' (Lyons and Taylor 2004: 78). They go on to say:

> It is apparent that social work has drawn, and continues to draw, on 'knowledge' from a wide variety of other disciplines and professional subject areas (Lyons, 1999) but this is also true of other fields involving professional education, such as medicine, where it does not seem to detract from the discipline's status … The distinctiveness of social work knowledge may lie in the way such knowledge – or understanding – is integrated and applied in professional practice … (Lyons and Taylor 2004: 79).

'The academy', associated with scholars, researchers and educators, is primarily distinguished for knowledge-work related to 'knowledge-creation' and 'knowledge-transmission' (Lyons and Taylor 2004: 72, 76–7, 80–83), with an emphasis on disciplinary knowledge that must be made meaningful 'in practice' (Healy 2000: 1–3). While social work education is primarily associated with 'the academy', there is recognition that 'field education is a core component of the social work education process, [that] has the status of a full academic subject [with procedures] to ensure the promotion of rigorous academic and practice standards' (AASW 2000: section 6.3). 'It is a key activity for the student, providing opportunities to integrate content from classroom learning with practical experience, whilst at the same time developing competence in a range of social work skills. It demands collaborative effort between school and agency staff and students …' (AASW 2000: section 6.3).

Some scholars have contested the above conceptualization of the dichotomy of 'academy' and 'field' by recognizing the knowledge-creation activities of 'practitioners', for example, as 'practitioner-researchers' (Healy 2000: 145–7) or through 'experiential learning' (Gould 2004) to generate 'practice-wisdom' and 'practice-theories' (Fook 1996, 1999, Camilleri 1996, 1999). However, there is still the distinction made between formal and often deductive knowledge-for-practice associated with 'the academy' and the informal and generally emergent knowledge-for-practice associated with 'the field' (Fook 1996, 1999, Camilleri 1996, 1999, Pease and Fook 1999, Miehls and Moffatt 2000, Sheppard 2000, Sheppard et al. 2000, Taylor and White 2000, Webb 2001, Healy 2005). More recently, the values of participatory and emancipatory practice have influenced the validation of service users' knowledge to build theory, and to plan and evaluate services (Beresford 2000, Braye et al. 2008, Millar et al. 2008).

These distinctions, related to the identities and locations of knowers and different knowledges, take into account the relationships between theory, practice and research (Adams et al. 2005), as a dynamic relationship in which each informs and influences the developments of the others (Usher and Bryant, in Powell et al. 2004: 3).

Research, theory and practice are not necessarily separate concepts and practices. Instead, they may be embedded in each other or have other forms of expression, for example, 'practice research' or 'practice theory' (Fook 1996, 1999), where 'knowledge' is emergent, inductively and experientially from 'practitioners in the field' (Healy 2000: 145–7). It is recognized that,

> these three interrelated elements, which may be said together to constitute social work, and ... confirm social work's claim to be both an academic discipline appropriately established in higher education and ... a profession directly affecting the lives of individuals and families. (Powell et al. 2004: 3)

Additionally, social work knowledge-for-practice may be a synthesis of different ways of knowing or generating social work knowledge, described as a 'trinity of sources' – qualitative findings, quantitative findings, and practice-based (or experiential) knowledge (Gould 2004: 132), a proposal that implicitly links formal research approaches with practice-generated knowledge, although it is unclear whether there is also an implicit distinction being made between 'the academy' (and formal research methods) and 'the field' (and practice-based knowledge).

This synthesis 'contributes to 'best attainable knowledge', 'a network of propositions' (Reid, cited by Gould 2004: 141) 'with origins in practice, experience and research' (Gould 2004: 141). This combination of knowledge derived from different epistemological bases and methods 'acknowledges that social work as a form of practice is a complicated and unpredictable activity, involving the reflective synthesis of both inductive and deductive reasoning' (Gould 2004: 141).

Contemporary social work knowledge is framed within debates about the meaning of 'evidence-based practice' (Sheldon 2000, Webb 2001, Sheldon 2001, Dominelli 2005: 223–36), with concerns expressed that a narrow emphasis on 'what works' (Dominelli 2005: 233, Lyons and Taylor 2004: 88) as a utilitarian form of outcome evaluations may disregard more critical questions about knowledge, values and practices. This is especially of concern where social workers are expected to manage risk and uncertainty by standardization and proceduralization of practice (Jordan and Parton 2004: 30), for example, child protection (Parton et al. 1997, D'Cruz 2004), a process described as the 'McDonaldization of social work' (James 2004). The fundamental aim of risk management is to seek certainty and predictability in increasingly complex, diverse and dynamic societies. In such contexts, social work as a discipline and a profession has the continuing problem of the 'question of justification' (Butler and Pugh 2004: 65), that is,

> how to justify choosing between different accounts, goals, methods, explanations, that lie at the heart of the practice of social work, the doing of social work research, and the development of theories of knowledge. (Butler and Pugh 2004: 65)

The next section addresses social work knowledge-in-practice, that is, how social work practice may be 'accomplished' (Dingwall et al. 1983, Margolin 1990, 1992, Pithouse 1987, Scott 1989, Parton et al. 1997, Taylor and White 2000, D'Cruz 2004) through the translation, interpretation, negotiation, social construction or application of abstract and general knowledge in the particular circumstances of individuals, groups or communities.

Social work knowledge-in-practice

Wenger (2008) conceptualizes knowledge-in-practice as 'improvizational engagement' across a 'landscape' whereby the 'practitioner' negotiates multiple sources that include professionalism, theory, research, prescriptions and regulations, local practice and personal experience. These are assertions that do not give insight into *how* practitioners actually engage in these 'improvizational engagements'.

Polanyi (1967) has conceptualized professional knowledge-in-practice as a process: 'tacit knowing'. 'Tacit knowing' involves informed guesses, hunches, emotions and intuitions embedded in the practice and essentially 'hidden from scrutiny' (D'Cruz et al. 2007: 86). The processes of professional knowledge-in-practice include 'a range of rationalities upon which social workers depend in making their judgements', for example, 'practical-moral dimensions' and 'emotion and normative judgement' (Taylor and White 2001: abstract), sensory and conceptual information, and personal experience applied in a particular case.

Schön (1983) and Argyris and Schön (cited by Fook 2002) refer to 'knowing-in-action' as a reflective activity that occurs simultaneously with practice as it unfolds. Schön's (1983) concept of 'knowing-in-action' may be similar to reflexivity, as described in sociological literature (Beck 1992; Fuchs 1992; Elliott 2001: 36–45), and as an ethically sound approach to knowledge-in-practice, for example by Taylor and White (2000: 198, Sheppard 1998, Sheppard et al. 2000, Miehls and Moffatt 2000). Reflexivity (and knowing-in-action) operates 'in the moment' (Sheppard et al. 2000). Knowledge may therefore be situated 'in the moment' (as contextually relevant) *and* transferable to other contexts, while acknowledging that transferability may be conditional upon the extent of 'fit' between contexts.

Thus practice-generated knowledge is simultaneously stable and unstable – it is appropriate to the context in which it emerges, yet the next context may offer both familiar features and new ones which the practitioner must negotiate to construct new knowledge-in-practice (D'Cruz 2004: 241–2).

This definition of knowing-in-action (or reflexivity) also involves a critical approach to professional practice and an awareness of the positioning of the practitioner in the process of knowledge-in-practice as both political and ethical (Sheppard 1998, Sheppard et al. 2000, Taylor and White 2000, Butler and Pugh 2004). Reflexivity is a process of looking '"outward, to the social and cultural artifacts [sic] and forms of thought which saturate our practices" (White 2001: 102) and inward to challenge the processes by which we make sense of the world (White 2001)' (D'Cruz et al. 2007: 78).

D'Cruz et al. (2007: 77–80) differentiate between the above definition of reflexivity, where practitioners are encouraged to engage with the political and ethical dimensions of knowledge in their work with clients, and a 'variation [that] regards reflexivity as an individual's considered response to an immediate context and making choices for further direction'. This variation is represented as an opportunity for adaptation to circumstances, an individualistic process whereby the 'self' may exercise autonomy and choices in the pursuit of self-development and self-definition (D'Cruz et al. 2007: 75–7).

However, it is posited here that it may be possible to distinguish between a *process* of reflexivity as the adaptation by individuals to circumstances and the *aims* of such a process. That is, while a variation of reflexivity may involve adaptation to achieve individualistic life choices or self-development, it does not necessarily follow that the process cannot also be engaged in achieving other outcomes, for example, as part of professional knowledge-in-practice, which practitioners may engage in as they negotiate the particularities of circumstances in their work with clients. This process may nonetheless require them to also engage with the variation of reflexivity/knowing-in-action as mindfulness and critical awareness of the ethics and politics of knowledge (e.g. Taylor and White 2000, Butler and Pugh 2004).

Furthermore, the version of reflexivity (or knowing-in-action) that encourages and prescribes awareness of the relations of knowledge/power as ethical practice is associated with particular paradigms such as social constructionism or post-modernism (Healy 2000; Taylor and White 2000), which are not necessarily shared by all social work professionals, let alone social work practitioners in the field. For example, as mentioned earlier, there are continuing debates about the meaning of evidence-based practice *within* the social work community, with some arguing for fixed, generalizable, objective knowledge and procedures for effective practice (e.g. Sheldon 2000, 2001), and others arguing that there are different ways of knowing and engaging with 'reality', seen as situated, as knowledge-*for*-practice, and *in*-practice (Webb 2001, Taylor and White 2000, 2001, Butler and Pugh 2004). The former perspective proposes that social work practice is a technical activity whereby certainty can be achieved if appropriate procedures for practice are followed, while the latter proposes that social work practice is an 'accomplishment' within uncertainty due to the complexity and unpredictability of human lives and circumstances.

Research studies that have sought to understand how (child welfare/ protection) practice is 'accomplished' as a process of negotiation between practitioners and clients (Dingwall et al. 1983, Margolin 1990, 1992, Parton et al. 1997, Pithouse 1987, Hall et al. 2003, D'Cruz 2004) have offered insights into the assumptions and processes of practice that influence outcomes for children and families. However, none of these studies is able to account for the unfolding of these practices *in the moment of the practice*, as knowledge-*in*-practice. They can only offer retrospective accounts of 'what happened', why and how. Even practitioners' accounts of their practices in these studies, generated through interviews or documentary analysis are retrospective.

While reflection and reflexivity related to knowing-in-action are encouraged to promote ethical and effective practice, some may argue that such expectations are inconsistent with the notion of 'tacit knowing' (Polanyi 1967), which involves that which is ungraspable and unsayable. However, it could be argued that a claim of tacit knowing does not acknowledge self-awareness and the cognitive, ethical and emotional processes involved in any human activity, let alone professional practice. Instead, while it is possible to acknowledge that tacit knowing is a feature of professional practice, it is also possible that as professionals we should able to engage with what is within our awareness so that we can reflect both in and on practice.

To engage with the meaning of knowledge-in-practice, it would perhaps be more illuminating to look at what this might mean actually *in* practice. Ideally, it would be enlightening to ask a social work practitioner to reflect on his or her practice as he or she is actually working with a client. However, this is likely to pose considerable ethical, legal and practical problems. Hence, there is a tendency to rely on retrospective reflection-on-action through critical incidents, even when claims of reflexive practice are made (Fook 1996, Sheppard 1998, Sheppard et al. 2000).

Therefore, because the aim of this chapter is to examine what a process of knowledge-in-practice (as reflection-in-action, and reflexivity) may be from the perspective of someone who is engaged in these processes, it is with some trepidation that I have reframed the taken-for-granted identity of 'social work practitioner' to include my 'present' identity as a 'social work academic–educator–researcher', so that I can engage with this task of writing about 'social work knowledge-*in*-practice'.[1] Some might question this reframing as appropriation (Humphries 1994: 190–91), with potential for colonization, invasion and usurpation of 'practice-space' and more legitimate voices who can, and should, speak about 'social work knowledge-in-practice'. Am I making too much of these distinctions? I believe not, as the literature that represents an institutional meaning of social work as both a discipline and profession also entrenches these definitions of the meaning of social work knowledge and the identities within the 'community of knowers' (Lyons and Taylor 2004: 76). Furthermore, one needs to consider whether my reflections on such 'practices' associated with 'the academy', namely, 'education', 'research' (and 'writing'), have any legitimacy for broader understandings of and for 'social work practice' and 'practitioners' 'out there in the field', or more broadly, for those in 'caring' professions other than social work.

Within these ethical considerations, I make a claim for 'present' identity as 'social work practitioner', located in a particular 'field of practice', namely 'the academy', and engaged in a variety of 'practices' that include 'education' and 'research'. In my view, I have been practising as a 'social worker' over the nearly thirty years since I qualified in 1978. It is just that my occupational identities and locations have changed.

Like many other 'social work academics', I believe that I could claim some legitimacy by re-connecting to my 'past' identity as a 'social work practitioner from the field':

> These differences in self-identity reflect the biographies of many social work educators, and their often strong and continuing commitment to social work practice, alongside the sometimes competing demands of the academy in relation to disciplinary development and knowledge creation *per se*. (Powell et al. 2004: 2, original emphasis)

Methodology and positioning

In deconstructing my own knowledge-in-practice in the section below, I examine an extract taken from a research interview that has been discussed in several publications, for different reasons and with slightly different

---

1   My other option, briefly considered, was to examine the process of writing this chapter which is 'doing' knowledge-in-practice. However, it did not seem viable as it could prove quite irritating to readers due to the messiness of actual knowledge-in-practice, when 'academic writing' is (required to be) so linear and tidy. There is also a particular narrative structure required with a distinct beginning, middle and end, which the almost endless circularity of introspection associated with 'writing about writing this chapter' would significantly disrupt.

emphases in each publication. Together these differences in representation of what is 'the same interview' may offer insights into (social work)[2] knowledge-in-practice as both reflection-in-action and reflexivity. I also consider whether my representation of this example of 'knowledge-in-practice' is necessarily seen as such by others. Thus this example is offered as a way of beginning dialogue about a rather elusive, partial and invisible process for professionals in practice, rather than as definitive of what knowledge-in-practice '*is*'.

This re-presentation of an interview extract as an example of '(social work) knowledge-in-practice' has several methodological and ethical limitations. The first methodological limitation is that the interview extract and all the related publications are about research that has already been completed, so they do not have the advantage of being 'in process' and perhaps more immediate. Secondly, I will be engaging in a retrospective process of critique and analysis, relying on piecing together my reflections about the interview extract from other publications to construct a close approximation of (social work) knowledge-in-practice as if it is 'in the moment'. Thirdly, the reflections from past publications may be tangentially relevant to the 'main point' of the original publication, but for this chapter they become central.

From an ethical perspective commensurate with the expressed concerns above about appropriation of identity and legitimate knowledge about knowledge-in-practice, there is a danger of considerable introspection and the placement of 'the self' at the centre of the process, which may become self-indulgent (Gill 1995; White 2001). The question is how to transform such a process into one that is meaningful to a community of knowers, whether to social workers only or more widely amongst other professions. This is especially problematic when the chapter focuses on (social work) knowledge-in-practice which may seem exclusive of other professions. Furthermore, the introspective style and focus on 'small things' may also deter readers who prefer other ways of knowing. It is hoped that this chapter will offer opportunities for dialogue rather than dismissal of such differences as valueless.

The next section explores the selected interview extract as an example of (social work) knowledge-in-practice. I reflect on whether the selected extract offers insights into a version of (social work) knowledge-in-practice (as knowing-in-action and reflexive practice).

---

2   I have bracketed the words 'social work' to indicate that while I am primarily wanting to explore the practical meaning of knowledge-in-practice, I am using social work as an example from which I hope to theorize more broadly about professional knowledge-in-practice.

(Social work) knowledge-in-practice in social work research

In this section, I re-present and critically examine an extract of an interview from a research project, which has been previously analyzed in two publications (D'Cruz 2002, 2004). The analysis will consider whether the extract may be considered an example of (social work) knowledge-in-practice and its relevance for other social workers and other professionals in the 'caring professions'. The idea of 'relevance' would need to include readers' recognition of similar experiences, as well as discomfort or dissonance with the example, content and processes. Similarities and differences could offer opportunities for further dialogue and theory development about knowledge-in-practice, and perhaps encourage others to write their own versions of what this concept may mean.

The publications are 1) a peer-reviewed article in an electronic journal, 'Constructing the Identities of "Responsible Mothers, Invisible Men" in Child Protection Practice' (D'Cruz 2002), and 2) a book on original research, 'Constructing Meanings and Identities in Child Protection Practice' (D'Cruz 2004). The extract of the interview is part of a larger study undertaken for my PhD (1993–1999) (D'Cruz 1999, 2004).

The aims of the PhD were to explore how official meanings and identities are constructed in child protection practice rather than being outcomes representing an objective 'truth' that can be ascertained by the rigorous application of risk assessment criteria (D'Cruz 1999, 2004). Social work knowledge-in-practice was understood as 'accomplished' through a process of negotiation between all participants involved in situated interactions (Dingwall et al. 1983, Margolin 1990, 1992). It is assumed that a child protection practitioner must consider different, yet often equally plausible meanings of reported events involving the care of a child and those people identified as 'responsible' for the events that led to the report. Thus the practitioner must consider and decide between different explanations given by parents, children and other professionals, to achieve an outcome that may or may not be officially categorized as 'maltreatment' and with a 'person believed responsible' (D'Cruz 2004: 241–50).

The methods involved semi-structured interviews with 15 child protection practitioners, most of whom were social workers, about 20 cases for which they were responsible. The interviews were audio-taped with consent and then transcribed verbatim, with line numbering added. Additionally, a documentary analysis of case files and policy documents was conducted, as well as an ethnographic study of the cultures of the two offices where the practitioners were located (D'Cruz 2004: 27–8, 106–30). Through critical discourse analysis, I explored the deployment of language as a rhetorical device of knowledge and power. That is, how workers and clients use language, consisting of vocabulary and syntax, as resources of persuasion and contestation to construct meanings and identities of normality and abnormality and thereby legitimize or marginalize particular versions of 'knowledge' (Potter 1996). Within such professional processes there is no simple, neutral description of 'what happened' or 'who was responsible' because language is a resource to advance a particular, preferred version of meaning and to dismiss the less preferred version.

Each practitioner interviewed about his or her case was invited to 'talk about the case' (D'Cruz 2000: paragraph 8.12). This process involved first asking participants 'some prepared questions to begin the discussion about the case, enhanced by additional questions *related to issues emerging from the reading of the case files prior to the interviews*' (D'Cruz 2004: 36, emphasis added).

The interview extract

I want to start this analysis with the interview extract, as this is what would be normally seen or heard by the practitioner, the client and any observers of the interaction (such as supervisors or peers). It is unusual for a social work practitioner to declare explicitly what his or her 'knowledge' is so that it is manifested 'in-practice' (for example, as an interview question or in the whole interview process). The analysis follows immediately after the extract and moves 'outwards' to reflections about theoretical assumptions, ethics and values that provide a version of knowledge-in-action and reflexivity as knowledge-in-practice in the extract.

While the identities of participants in the extract are myself as the researcher (HD), and worker (as research participant/informant), it is possible to imagine a similar interaction between a practitioner and a client. Thus, the researcher (HD) could be equated with 'practitioner' and worker (research participant) could be equated with 'client'.

> HD: the girl ... identified three separate incidents where she was hit by both her parents [A] ... So is it the most recent incident that you would investigate in terms of person responsible? [B] [*Note that the worker's response to this question took 305 lines (2146–51) which I have interpreted as her extreme discomfort with a question that dealt with an aspect of her practice that was taken for granted. I have only included the 'relevant' lines, not the 'digressions'.*]

> Worker: ... in terms of dad, I don't remember [1] what I did with dad. I suppose I focused primarily on ... the incidents with mum [...] When I phoned, mum was home [2a] ... Mum answered the phone [2b] and she agreed to come in ... I suppose ... I could have got side tracked in that the focus of [girl's] concerns [3a]

were mum. This stuff [4a] to do with dad was not the primary thing she talked about … and there was an incident … that day [5a] … mum had been cross [3b] with her … the stuff [4b] to do with dad got lost in the conflict [3c] with mum […] … the conflict between the two children, the pressure that puts on mum and how she responds [6] … The issue [4c] with dad was not a current concern [5b] … and it got lost.

HD: … maybe mum was the person … primarily responsible for the daily care of the children? [C]

Worker: certainly […] I suppose my assessment was that the [family] conflict [was] … parent teen stuff … the primary issue … that was the thrust of the intervention with mother and child [7] (emphasis added). (D'Cruz, 2002: paragraph 3.25, 2004: 172–3).

Analysis of the interview extract

The interview extract will be analyzed according to three dimensions:

- Structure and purpose of the extract – similarities and differences compared with (social work) knowledge-in-practice by practitioners with clients
- Content and process of a social work research interview and how this may or may not represent (social work) knowledge-in-practice
- Concluding comments related to the analysis of the extract and how these may represent another form of (social work) knowledge-in-practice.

Structure and purpose of the interview extract

There are five features related to the structure and purpose of the extract that must be considered for their relevance as (social work) knowledge-in-practice. The first is that the extract is an interview, a 'structured, purposeful conversation' (Chandler 1990: 129). It has a conventional, familiar question-and-answer format in a particular context, where a designated person asks the questions and the other answers them (Wooffitt 2005: 56–7, 171–2). This is unlike an informal conversation where both participants take turns to speak and listen, there may be statements or questions used by participants more or less equally, without 'the rigidity of order of participation, [and] the kinds of turns expected of participants' (Wooffitt 2005: 57).

Secondly, although the interview is taken verbatim from the transcribed audio-taping, it is not reproduced in its entirety, as indicated by the 'Note' in italics in the above extract. This process may be similar to how the outcomes of formal interviews may be recorded on case files (Smith 1974), where I as the researcher (or practitioner) consider what is 'relevant' for the purpose of the interaction (research in this case), with 'digressions' excluded.

Thirdly, as a practitioner, I may only include the client's response and not my actual questions, which therefore hides how knowledge-in-practice may be embedded in an interview question and its influence in eliciting a particular response (Wooffitt 2005: 171–2, Wood and Kroger 2000: 72–3). The inclusion of my questions in the interview extract offers an opportunity for further exploration of (social work) knowledge-in-practice as the worker's responses are seen as meaningful in relation to the question being asked, rather than as a neutral, objective set of 'facts'. The interview is seen as an 'active' process (Holstein and Gubrium 1995) whereby participants generate meaning together and where the outcome of the interview may differ with different participants who may pose their questions differently or pose different questions. 'Answers that are produced in the interaction are not simply "there" waiting to be elicited; they may never have been produced before that moment' (Wood and Kroger 2000: 72).

Fourthly, the numbers in square brackets are taken from the original research analysis. These artefacts from the original research process have been included here to show how my knowledge-in-practice was subsequently expressed after the interview as an analysis of the interview transcript and publication (D'Cruz 2002: paragraph 3.26, 2004: 172–3).

Finally, the letters in upper case and in square brackets [A, B, C] have been added for the purposes of this chapter as features of interest in regard to knowledge-in-practice as they allow a reading of the extract that goes beyond what is taken for granted by practitioners (due to its familiarity) and makes the familiar a topic for scrutiny and understanding of professional practices and processes. This analysis will be set out in the section immediately below.

In summary, while the extract is taken from an interview between me as researcher and a social work practitioner as research participant/informant, I am using it in this chapter as an example of (social work) knowledge-in-practice, where the purpose is not dissimilar from professional interviewing where knowledge-in-practice is regularly expressed.

Content and process: the social work research interview as knowledge-in-practice?

In this section, I deconstruct the interview extract, with a particular focus on my questions as the researcher (as 'practitioner') and how these questions as (social work) knowledge-in-practice influenced the worker/ research participant's responses (comparable to a 'client's' responses to a practitioner). The focus taken here differs from that of the original research analyses (D'Cruz 2002: paragraph 3.20–3.27, 2004: 171–4) that focused primarily on the informant's responses and backgrounded my questions. For this chapter, the interview text is the starting point. It offers opportunities for being read in different ways, as there is no explanation given explicitly for why the questions are asked and how they are asked, unless and until the practitioner is called upon to explain (usually retrospectively) why she asked a particular question, for example, in a supervisory relationship (Pithouse 1987). The potential for understanding how 'knowledge' *is* 'in-practice' in the interview will be explicated below in a way that begins from the interview and moves 'outwards' to reconstructed explanations.

> *Interview extract: Statements A and B:* HD: the girl … identified three separate incidents where she was hit by both her parents [A] … So is it the most recent incident that you would investigate in terms of person responsible? [B]

My question as an expression of 'knowledge-in-practice' that begins this segment of the interview with the worker does not explicate the normative assumptions about children and parenting and 'knowledge' expressed 'in-[my]-'practice'. The question consists of two parts [A, B], a structure common to most formal interviews (Wooffitt 2005: 57). Part one (Statement A) refers to 'three [1] separate [2] incidents where she was hit by both her parents [3]', which is based on the known information about the case, recorded in the file by the worker being interviewed.[3] The structure of Statement A is a 'preface', a 'statement of fact (or what is offered as fact) …' (Wooffitt 2005: 57), followed by part two, a question. The question [Statement B] asks 'So is it the most recent incident that you would investigate in terms of person responsible?' As a surface reading of this question, an observer may wonder why the question was asked and why it has this structure (vocabulary and syntax). How does the question express knowledge-in-practice in the interview?

Put together, Statement A contextualizes the second part of my question, as on its own Statement B is less meaningful. Statement B may be read with Statement A as being asked by someone who is puzzled as to why the worker has intervened in a way that has only accounted for a part of the recorded information (that is, investigation of one incident, the most recent of three,

---

3   Mr and Mrs Gilman's teenage daughter Laurel reported to Suburbia 'that she is being hit at home: (1) [date] she was hit with the wooden handle of the broom across the arm, back and behind her right ear … by mum (2) [previous night] hit by mum across her face as mum thought she had hit her sister across her face [in keeping with] the [family] rule […] (3) a week after the last school holidays ended, dad hit her with a strap across her face …' (D'Cruz 2004: 171).

and only involving one parent, the mother). Statement B may also be read as someone offering to the worker a possible explanation of this apparent anomaly by normalizing the worker's intervention in terms of 'the most recent incident', as the two other reported incidents were perhaps 'not recent enough' to provide relevant information or the urgency to intervene (Potter 1996). The phrasing of the question in this way is perhaps less critical than a more direct question might be, for example, a supervisor may ask: 'Why did you not interview both the parents?' or 'Did you investigate the three incidents involving both the parents that were reported?'

My question that puts two seemingly unrelated Statements [A and B] together expresses the practice anomaly indirectly. This approach perhaps allows some leeway for the practitioner to respond however she wishes, while knowing she has to provide an explanation that I would find plausible, given my 'shared identity as a former practitioner' (D'Cruz 2004: 34–5, D'Cruz 2000: paragraph 8.3) and the perceived relatively higher status as a researcher in the context. This explanation of the ethics and values for my knowledge-in-practice in this research context has been expressed, 'as knowledge/power in practice' (D'Cruz 2000) and in particular, through 'the active interviews' (Holstein and Gubrium 1995) with child protection practitioners where 'I aimed to equalise relationships … where respondents were not objects to be judged by a "superior and detached researcher" (Stanley and Wise, 1993)'. (D'Cruz 2000: paragraph 8.4).

I have noted in other publications (D'Cruz 2000, 2004) that when workers were asked to 'talk about the case', this

> increased informants' anxieties. I represented a pseudo-supervisor, asking for details of practice which normally would be given to supervisors within a carefully preserved identity of competence (Pithouse 1987). I also asked awkward questions which the worker(s) had either not thought about previously or preferred not to discuss: *for example, how it came about that, although both biological parents were reported for 'physical abuse', only the mother was interviewed?* … I had to disguise the tone and intent of the questions, including posing as ignorant and naïve, to avoid offence or judgement (not always possible), while pursuing clearly important issues for the thesis. (D'Cruz, 2000: paragraph 8.12, D'Cruz, 2004: 36–7, emphasis added).

I have also commented in D'Cruz (2000) that

> Whilst occupying an identity as pseudo-supervisor I was trying to hold together both the 'realist' and 'relativist' ethical and epistemological positions, rather than polarise them … I acknowledged as 'real', children's reported experiences of oppressive practices, and the social, legal and ethical necessity for child protection intervention … However, I also wanted to explore the 'relative' meanings given to these reports called 'child maltreatment' and how and when practitioners categorised them as such … *inquiring into particular assumptions and*

practices ... seemed intrusive and made me uneasy about seemingly taking the high moral ground about complex and contentious work. (D'Cruz 2000: paragraph 8.13, emphasis added)

In addition to these insights into how a practitioner's espoused ethics and values may influence how she expresses 'knowledge-in-practice', there is a possible further insight into my theoretical perspective, expressed in my introductory statements immediately *preceding* the interview extract in two publications (D'Cruz 2002, 2004), and set out in Table 4.1 below.

Table 4.1   Positioning within the literature, curiosity about the practice: the interview question

Column 1	Column 2
Having noted that at the conclusion of this case [1] only the mother was categorized as 'person believed responsible for physical abuse' [2], although both parents had been reported [3], *I was curious about the practical construction of 'responsible mothers, invisible men' (Stark and Flitcraft, 1988; Korbin, 1989; Milner, 1993)* [4]: [interview extract follows]. (D'Cruz 2004: 172) (emphasis added).	'Responsible mothers, invisible men' in practice 3.25 I was *curious to understand why* only the mother was the focus of the investigation [5]. *Positioned as I was within the literature* [6], *this seemed to be a practical construction of 'responsible mothers, invisible men.'* [7] [interview extract follows]. (D'Cruz 2002: paragraph 3.25) (emphasis added).

The extracts in Table 4.1 above perhaps offer some support for how particular theories and concepts influenced my interest in asking about the apparent practice anomaly that I noticed when I read the case file (Table 4.1, column 1: 1), although these explanations of my theoretical interest are expressed retrospectively. However, the process of generating the question I asked in the interview segment began with the reading of the case file. I had noticed this 'practice anomaly' which someone else may not have because I was 'positioned within the literature' and 'curious about the practical construction' of an abstract concept in the particular case (Table 4.1, column 1: 4, column 2: 6–7).

The process of 'writing' about research may encourage greater expression of knowledge-in-practice, although in usual case practice neither the interview questions nor the positioning of the interviewer is made explicit in the actual interview or on a file record, therefore rendering knowledge-in-practice relatively invisible.

Further support for my claim that the theoretical perspective 'responsible mothers, invisible men' (Milner 1993) was 'behind' my initial question is that the worker's response seemed to be meaningful to me. If she had 'not answered the question' I would have continued to ask further questions until I could conclude the interview segment to my satisfaction (Wooffitt 2005: 32–3, 56–7). However, the length of time the worker took to answer the question (suggested by the lines of transcript which I refer to in 'Note' above as 'digressions') was perhaps indicative of some discomfort (my interpretation), yet she responded in a way that was plausible to me (D'Cruz 2004: 172, 2002: n18, 2000: paragraph 8.12). Even though I did not make explicit my ethical or theoretical positioning, she seemed to have heard the question as critical of her practice *and* as a comment on the gendered nature of her intervention. Hence despite my expressed wish to attend to the ethics and politics of the research process, I could not completely avoid contributing to a colleague's discomfort and sense of inequality towards me (D'Cruz 2000: paragraphs 8.1, 8.3, 8.4, 8.12), although I achieved the aim of my 'knowledge-in-practice' in that first question. After the worker had responded to my initial question [A and B], I then asked another question [C].

Interview extract: Statement C: HD: … maybe mum was the person … primarily responsible for the daily care of the children? [C]

This question is more of a statement in structure although it is somewhat ambiguous as it is punctuated by a question mark. It is possible that this section of the interview was heard as a question on the audio-tape and transcribed in that way. However the ambiguous structure including the 'maybe' is another attempt by me to soften the discomfort experienced by the worker by my initial question, in keeping with the espoused ethics and values discussed above. Furthermore, the structure of my question picks up on the worker's response where she explains why and how she focused exclusively on the mother, paraphrasing a central theme of the worker's explanation: that the mother was primarily responsible for the care of the children. Finally, my reflexive comments contained in an endnote (D'Cruz 2002: n16 and n17), which were unexpressed in the interview, link the practices I read and heard in this case to theoretical views expressed by Donzelot (1980) and Hirst (1981: 69) about the primacy of women's roles and responsibilities in the family, which has 'repressive implications' for them.

The worker's concluding response to my ambiguously phrased remark seems to have been heard as a reinforcement of her competence as she replies 'certainly,' and then goes on to add a justification of 'the thrust of the intervention with mother and child'. This response concluded that particular segment of the interview (and extract above), and also appeared to achieve the aim of my initial question within an ethical awareness of the process of the interview.

In summary, this section of the analysis that has focused on the content and process of the social work research interview as a possible example of (social work) knowledge-in-practice as it unfolded has offered some insights, however limited. First, what is expressed explicitly, whether verbally (such as in an interview) or in writing (such as in a case file), may not directly reflect what is kept silenced yet is influential in how a practitioner may practise his or her knowledge. That is, there are invariably multiple surface readings of what is said/heard, written/read, and the practitioner may have various explanations and assumptions unknown to observers of the meaning of what is said or written. There has been some support offered for these processes of how formal knowledge as theories and concepts may be influential in framing questions. Secondly, knowledge-in-practice, at least for social work, may also include ethics and values that are integrated with formal theories and concepts to engage potentially more vulnerable participants. Thus while the practitioner's ethics and values may remain invisible, particular ways of expressing questions may integrate purpose with values and ethics, thus also requiring particular verbal and writing skills of the practitioner. In the case extract discussed here, even though the initial question posed seemed somewhat oblique, it nonetheless achieved its purpose in as ethical a way as was possible in the context.

The next section briefly considers how social work knowledge-in-practice through an interview may also be expressed in the conclusions to the interview: as the outcomes of a research analysis or of a social work intervention.

'Conclusions': outcomes of research analyses or social work interventions

The concluding comments I made as part of the research analysis of the interview extract are considered here from the perspective of how it may be similar to social work knowledge-in-practice with clients. Due to space limitations, I have only included my first sentence immediately after the extract of the interview is concluded. (The remainder of the conclusion, not reproduced here, is a summary of the analysis linked to the numbered sections [1–6] in the worker's response in the interview extract above.)

> This extract clearly demonstrates [1] how assumptions of 'patriarchal mothering' (Stark and Flitcraft 1988) [2] intersect with the discursive formation, that 'someone did something to the child' [3], constructing 'responsible mothers, invisible men' (Stark and Flitcraft 1988; Milner 1993) [4]. (D'Cruz 2004: 173, also 2002: paragraph 3.26)

Most case files would record a similar conclusion as if there is a 'clear' linear connection between a theoretical perspective and a practice outcome in regard to 'what was happening in a case'. This practice is not dissimilar to what I as a social work researcher have done in the extract above, where I claim that the interview with the worker has 'clearly demonstrated' a particular theoretical and conceptual approach that I have read, accepted and practised in the interview. Statements numbered 1–4 above make these connections explicit in a somewhat circular fashion. I have reflected on this problem in D'Cruz (2002: paragraph 4.2):

> From the social constructionist position in which I have problematised my own constructionist practices, is there any validity in my conclusions or is the whole argument merely a consequence of my positioned subjectivity? Have I only seen what I want to see because of 'bias' or is there any possibility of a version of an 'objective truth' that also accounts for positioned subjectivity?

These reflections are essential to those espousing a social constructionist perspective as an ethically and methodologically sound practice (Taylor and White 2000). Nonetheless, this theoretical and practice problem for social work research that seems to be associated solely with social constructionism is also valid for social work knowledge-in-practice more generally – regardless of which theoretical approach is preferred by a practitioner – because *all* theoretical approaches position practitioners in particular ways vis-à-vis clients, their experiences, problems and circumstances (Riessman 1994).

In summary, this section, in which I have considered the implications of 'conclusions' drawn from 'interviews' for (social work) knowledge-in-practice, raises the importance of awareness of the ethical and theoretical positioning of practitioners and the apparently 'clear' conclusions that can be drawn about an issue or problem. Reflection-on- and -in-practice by practitioners is important to minimize rigidity and arrogance about what is known and practised.

(Social work) knowledge-in-practice: reflections-on-practice

This chapter has considered the meaning of knowledge-in-practice by focusing on social work as a discipline and profession. In addition to a general theoretical overview of social work knowledge-for-practice, and social work knowledge-in-practice as two dimensions representing, respectively, the disciplinary and professional nature of social work, I have deconstructed a single example from my knowledge-in-practice as a researcher by drawing on relevant publications to construct a rough approximation of what knowledge-in-practice may be. This small example is not intended to be definitive or conclusive. It is instead offered as a means of beginning a dialogue between social workers, and perhaps between social workers and professionals from other 'caring' professions, as to the representativeness of the example for others.

To begin this dialogue, it is important to summarize and reflect upon the interview extract – its content, structure, purpose and participants in respect of the similarities and differences between a social work research interview and a social work interview as part of an interview with a client. The similarities are in the recognisable structure of a professional interview, with the participants positioned strictly as 'interviewer' (researcher or practitioner) and 'respondent' (research participant or client). Furthermore, in this extract, the research interview is semi-structured, thus allowing for the expression of discretion and autonomy by the 'interviewer' in how she shapes the question and what she is allowed to ask. This level of discretion is dissimilar to contexts where practitioners are obliged to follow procedures and interview schedules designed as organizational requirements, for example, in child protection risk assessment. The content of the extract reflects its purpose – that of a research interview with a particular set of aims, which differs from a professional interview with a client. The former process requires a researcher to engage in a process of disinterested inquiry to generate knowledge for practice. The latter process requires a practitioner to attend to resolution of a problem that is experienced by a client or by a significant other. However, despite these differences between a social work research interview and a social work practitioner's interview with a client, the extract has offered some insights into how a professional may express knowledge-in-practice as a practical skill, with the influences of values and ethics, as well as theories and concepts, on the content and structure of questions. The question is how recognizable as knowledge-in-practice is this relatively introspective process into the minutiae of a social work research interview for other social workers and for others in 'caring' professions? What can be offered by others as a basis for expanding our understanding of professional knowledge-in-practice in the 'caring' professions?

References

Adams, R., Dominelli, L. and Payne, M. (eds) 2002. *Social Work: Themes, Issues and Critical Debates*. 2nd Edition. Basingstoke: Palgrave/The Open University.

Adams, R., Dominelli, L. and Payne, M. (eds) 2005. *Social Work Futures: Crossing Boundaries, Transforming Practice*. Basingstoke: Palgrave Macmillan.

Australian Association of Social Workers (AASW) 2000. *Policy and Procedures for Establishing Eligibility for Membership of the AASW*. Available at: http://www.aasw.asn.au/becomeamember/becomingasw/POLICYand PROCEDURES%201-IV_Dec2006%20.pdf [accessed 1 April 2008].

Banks, S. 2001. *Ethics and Values in Social Work*. 2nd Edition. Basingstoke: Palgrave Macmillan.

Beck, U. 1992. *Risk Society: Towards a New Modernity*. London: Sage.

Beresford, P. 2000. Service users' knowledge and social work theory: conflict or collaboration? *British Journal of Social Work*, 30(4), 489–503.

Braye, S., Preston-Shoot, M. and Thorpe, A. 2008. *Beyond the Classroom: Integrating Legal Knowledge, Practice Learning and User Experience to Prepare Students for Ethical Practice in the Human Services*, 8th International PEPE Conference, Practical Learning: Achieving Excellence in the Human Services, Edinburgh, Scotland, 23–25 January 2008.

Butler, I. and Pugh, R. 2004. The politics of social work research, in *Reflecting on Social Work – Discipline and Profession*, edited by R. Lovelock, K. Lyons, and J. Powell. Aldershot: Ashgate, 55–71.

Camilleri, P. 1996. *(Re)constructing Social Work: Exploring Social Work Through Text and Talk*. Aldershot: Avebury.

Camilleri, P. 1999. Social work and its search for meaning: theories, narratives and practices, in *Transforming Social Work Practice: Post-modern Critical Perspectives*, edited by B. Pease and J. Fook. St Leonards: Allen and Unwin, 25–39.

Chandler, J. 1990. Researching and the relevance of gender, in *Studies in Qualitative Methodology: Reflections of Field Experience*, edited by R. Burgess. Greenwich, Connecticut: JAI Press, 119–40.

D'Cruz, H. 1999. Constructing Meanings and Identities in Practice: Child Protection in Western Australia, unpublished PhD thesis, Lancaster University, Lancaster, UK.

D'Cruz, H. 2000. Social work research as knowledge/power in practice. *Sociological Research Online*, 5(1). Available at: http://www.socresonline. org.uk/5/1/dcruz.html.

D'Cruz, H. 2002. Constructing the identities of 'responsible mothers, invisible men' in Child Protection Practice. Sociological Research Online, 7(1). Available at: http://www.socresonline.org.uk/7/1/d'cruz.html.

D'Cruz, H. 2004. *Constructing Meanings and Identities in Child Protection Practice*. Croydon: Tertiary Press.

D'Cruz, H., Gillingham, P. and Melendez, S. 2007. Reflexivity, its meanings and relevance for social work: a critical review of the literature. *British Journal of Social Work*, 37, 73–90.

Dingwall, R., Eekelaar, J. and Murray, T. 1983. *The Protection of Children: State Intervention in Family Life*. Oxford: Basil Blackwell.

Dominelli, L. 2005. Social work research: contested knowledge for practice, in *Social Work Futures: Crossing Boundaries, Transforming Practice*, edited by R. Adams, L. Dominelli. L. and M. Payne. Basingstoke: Palgrave Macmillan, 223–36.

Donzelot, J. 1980. *The Policing of Families: Welfare versus the State*. London: Hutchinson.

Elliott, A. 2001. *Concepts of the Self*. Cambridge: Polity Press, 36–45.

Fook, J. (ed.) 1996. *The Reflective Researcher*. St Leonards: Allen and Unwin.

Fook, J. 1999. Critical reflectivity in education and practice, in *Transforming Social Work Practice: Postmodern Critical Perspectives*, edited by B. Pease and J. Fook. St Leonards: Allen and Unwin, 195–208.

Fook, J. 2002. *Social Work: Critical Theory and Practice*. London: Sage.

Fuchs, S. 1992. Relativism and reflexivity in the sociology of scientific knowledge, in *Metatheorizing*, edited by L. Ritzer. Newbury Park: Sage.

Gill, R. 1995. Relativism, reflexivity and politics: interrogating discourse analysis from a feminist perspective, in *Feminism and Discourse: Psychological Perspectives*, edited by S. Wilkinson and C. Kitzinger. London: Sage.

Gould, N. 2004. Qualitative research and social work: the methodological repertoire in a practice-oriented discipline, in *Reflecting on Social Work – Discipline and Profession*, edited by R. Lovelock, K. Lyons and J. Powell. Aldershot: Ashgate, 130–44.

Hall, C., Juhila, K., Parton, N. and Pösö, T. (eds) 2003. *Constructing Clienthood in Social Work and the Human Services: Interaction, Identities and Practices*. London: Jessica Kingsley Publishers.

Healy, K. 2000. *Social Work Practices: Contemporary Perspectives on Change*. London: Sage.

Healy, K. 2005. *Social Work Theories in Context: Creating Frameworks for Practice*. Basingstoke: Palgrave Macmillan.

Hirst, P. 1981. The Genesis of the Social. *Politics and Power*, 3, 67–82.

Holstein, J.A. and Gubrium, J.F. 1995. *The Active Interview*. Qualitative Research Methods Series, volume 37. Thousand Oaks: Sage.

Humphries, B. 1994. Empowerment and social research: elements for an analytic framework, in *Re-thinking Social Research*, edited by B. Humphries and C. Truman. Aldershot: Avebury, 185–204.

International Association of the Schools of Social Work (IASSW). Available at: http://www.iassw-aiets.org/ [accessed 15 January 2008].

James, A. 2004. The McDonaldization of social work – or 'come back Florence Hollis, all is (or should be) forgiven', in *Reflecting on Social Work – Discipline and Profession*, edited by R. Lovelock, K. Lyons and J. Powell. Aldershot: Ashgate, 37–54.

Jordan, B. and Parton, N. 2004. Social work, the public sphere and civil society, in *Reflecting on Social Work – Discipline and Profession*, edited by R. Lovelock, K. Lyons and J. Powell. Aldershot: Ashgate, pp. 20–36.

Lyons, K. and Taylor, I. 2004. Gender and knowledge in social work, in *Reflecting on Social Work – Discipline and Profession*, edited by R. Lovelock, K. Lyons and J. Powell. Aldershot: Ashgate, 72–94.

Margolin, L. 1990. When vocabularies of motive fail: the example of fatal child abuse. *Qualitative Sociology*, 13(4), 373–85.

Margolin, L. 1992. Deviance on record: techniques for labeling child abusers in official documents. *Social Problems*, 39(1), 58–70.

Miehls, D. and Moffatt, K. 2000. Constructing social work identity based on the reflexive self. *British Journal of Social Work*, 30(3), 339–48.

Millar, J., Thomson, J., Rae, W. and Horne, A. 2008. *'We're Here Tae Make a Difference'*, 8th International PEPE Conference, Practical Learning: Achieving Excellence in the Human Services, Edinburgh, Scotland, 23–25 January 2008.

Milner, J. 1993. A disappearing act: the differing career paths of fathers and mothers in child protection investigations. *Critical Social Policy*, 38, 48–68.

Parton, N., Thorpe, D. and Wattam, C. 1997. *Child Protection: Risk and the Moral Order*. Basingstoke: Macmillan.

Pease, B. and Fook, J. (eds) 1999. *Transforming Social Work Practice: Postmodern Critical Perspectives*. St Leonards: Allen and Unwin, 70–83.

Pithouse, A. 1987. *Social Work: The Social Organisation of an Invisible Trade*. Aldershot: Avebury.

Polanyi, M. 1967. *The Tacit Dimension*. New York: Anchor Books.

Potter, J. 1996. *Representing Reality: Discourse, Rhetoric and Social Construction*. London: Sage.

Powell, J., Lovelock, R. and Lyons, K. 2004. Introduction, in *Reflecting on Social Work – Discipline and Profession*, edited by R. Lovelock, K. Lyons and J. Powell. Aldershot: Ashgate, 1–19.

Riessman, C.K. 1994. Subjectivity matters: the positioned investigator, in *Qualitative Studies in Social Work Research*, edited by C.K. Riessman. Newbury Park: Sage, 133–8.

Schön, D.A. 1983. *The Reflective Practitioner: How Professionals Think in Action*. New York: Basic Books

Scott, D. 1989. Meaning construction and social work practice. *Social Service Review*, 63(1), 39–51.

Sheldon, B. 2000. *Evidence-based Practice*, Lyme Regis: Russell House Publishing.

Sheldon, B. 2001. The validity of evidence-based practice in social work: a reply to Stephen Webb. *British Journal of Social Work*, 31(5), 801–9.

Sheppard, J. 2000. Learning from personal experience: reflexions on social work practice with mothers in child and family care. *Journal of Social Work Practice*, 14(1), 37–50.

Sheppard, M. 1998. Practice validity, reflexivity and knowledge for social work. *British Journal of Social Work*, 28, 763–81.

Sheppard, M., Newstead, S., Caccavo, A. and Ryan, K. 2000. Reflexivity and the development of process knowledge in social work: a classification and empirical study. *British Journal of Social Work*, 30, 465–88.

Smith, D. 1974. The social construction of documentary reality. *Sociological Inquiry*, 44, 257–68.

Taylor, C. and White, S. 2000 *Practising Reflexivity in Health and Welfare: Making Knowledge*. Buckingham: Open University Press.

Taylor, C. and White, S. 2001. Knowledge, truth and reflexivity: the problem of judgement in social work. *Journal of Social Work*, 1(1), 37–59.

Webb, S.A. 2001. Some considerations on the validity of evidence-based practice in social work. *British Journal of Social Work*, 31, 57–79.

Wenger, E. 2008. *Communities of Practice: A Social Discipline of Learning*, Keynote Speech 1, 8th International PEPE Conference, Practical Learning: Achieving Excellence in the Human Services, Edinburgh, Scotland, 23–25 January 2008.

Western, J., Haynes, M., Durrington, D. and Dwan, K. 2006. Characteristics and benefits of professional work: assessment of their importance over a 30-year career. *Journal of Sociology*, 42(2), 165–88.

White, S. 2001. Auto-ethnography as reflexive enquiry: the research act as self-surveillance, in *Qualitative Research in Social Work*, edited by I. Shaw and N. Gould. London: Sage,100–15.

Wood, L. and Kroger, R.O. 2000. *Doing Discourse Analysis: Methods for Studying Action in Talk and Text*. Thousand Oaks and London: Sage.

Wooffitt, R. 2005. *Conversation Analysis and Discourse Analysis: A Comparative and Critical Introduction*. London: Sage.

5 Disability: a personal approach

Lisa Chaffey

Health professions are largely seen as 'helping professions', traditionally helping people with disabilities. Approximately 20 per cent of the Australian population live with an impairment which affects their everyday life, potentially leading to disability. Disability is not a single entity, with each person presenting with their own beliefs, values, assumptions and abilities. The Ecological Model of Professional Reasoning, from the occupational therapy literature, suggests that each therapist brings a personal lens to therapy, influenced by their own beliefs, values and assumptions, impacting on knowledge use in practice. In addition to therapists' personal views, the framework in which they situate their practice may be shaped by either the biomedical or social models of disability, which also influences knowledge use. Increasing diversity in the health professional workforce and becoming a reflective practitioner are two strategies to broaden a profession's collective beliefs. In recognition of the many influences on practice, there has been a call to increase diversity in the profile of clinicians. Reflecting on practice enables therapists to become aware of their own beliefs and values and how these impact on their knowledge use in therapeutic encounters.

This chapter is concerned with health professionals' knowledge use in therapeutic encounters with people with disabilities. It is entitled 'Disability: A Personal Approach' for two reasons. The first is that rather than discussing the types of knowledge used by health professionals, or the origin of that knowledge, the focus is on the factors that shape individual health workers' knowledge use in practice. That is, factors that influence how health professionals think and, therefore, how they act with a client with a disability will be explored. For each worker, this is a unique and personal approach.

How health professionals think in action, also known as clinical reasoning, will be considered whilst raising issues that may influence this thinking and knowledge use. The frameworks in which a health professional works undoubtedly influence their professional practice. Two common disability models will be examined: the biomedical and social models of disability, with a view to understanding how these models shape action.

Some common examples of conflicting beliefs and values will be highlighted. Two strategies are then suggested as ways to minimize the negative impact of different beliefs on therapeutic encounters. Increasing diversity in the healthcare workforce and reflecting on individual practice could decrease potential conflicts in belief between health professionals and their clients.

The second reason for the title of this chapter, 'Disability: A Personal Approach', is that I am a health professional – an occupational therapist – with a physical disability. I will share my personal experience of incidents in which I have had both clashing and congruent beliefs with colleagues and clients.

At the end of this chapter, it is hoped that readers will have an understanding of the factors and beliefs that shape their knowledge use in therapeutic encounters with a person with a disability. It is also hoped that readers will have identified the impact of clashing beliefs, as well as strategies that could minimize such conflicts between health professionals and clients.

Who lives with a disability?

Approximately 20 per cent of the Australian population live with a disability. In determining this statistic, disability is defined as a limitation, restriction or impairment which impacts on everyday activities (Australian Bureau of Statistics 2004). Physical conditions are the most common of these impairments (84 per cent), with the remaining 16 per cent being behavioural or mental disorders.

Some people live with their families, some with their partners, some live alone, some in formal care settings and others with friends. Some work, some are not employed, some do volunteer work and others are job-seeking. Many are spouses, parents, carers, workers, students, community members and, occasionally, clients of health professionals. People with disabilities are present in every role in society, experiencing unique and meaningful lives. So it can be said that disability is not one single entity.

In the literature written by people with disabilities, words such as 'frustration, anger, loss, isolation, guilt, helplessness, personal worthlessness, depression and pain' are often used. However, the words 'joy, excitement, pride, accomplishment, power, intelligence, fulfilment, and triumph' are also used (Beer 2003). There is no one single experience of disability, just as there is no one single experience of humanity.

Each person seeking assistance from a health professional arrives with their own unique beliefs, values, assumptions and abilities. In addition, professionals also bring their own beliefs and values about disability into the therapeutic encounter. A health worker's values and beliefs about the world directly influence the way they practise and use their knowledge (Stewart and Law 2003). This leads, now, to an exploration of health professionals' thinking in action and highlights how a clash of beliefs, values and assumptions between a client and therapist could be problematic.

Personal knowledge – thinking in action

Within the health professions, there is increased interest in understanding how professionals think in action. Thinking in action within a health profession is also known as clinical, or professional, reasoning (Mattingly and Fleming 1994, Boyt Schell and Schell 2008, Unsworth 2004). Reasoning contains, but is not limited to knowledge manipulation. It is focused action, providing clinicians with a framework for interaction, assessment and intervention (Higgs and Jones 2000). There are a number of different models of clinical reasoning. Here, the Clinical Reasoning Study (Mattingly and Fleming 1994), and the Ecological Model of Professional Reasoning (Boyt Schell and Schell 2008) are briefly discussed to illustrate the role of beliefs and values in shaping reasoning and knowledge use. Both of these ideas are from the occupational therapy literature, but similar concepts have been developed in other health professions.

In 1986, Cheryl Mattingly and Maureen Fleming began the first study of occupational therapists' thinking in practice, the Clinical Reasoning Study (Mattingly and Fleming 1994). This project was a four year study that combined ethnographic and action research methodologies. Data was collected from 14 therapists by participant observation, in-depth interviewing and videotaping of treatment sessions. Story-telling and narrative analysis was used to analyze data, with an emphasis on therapists reflecting on their own practice. This study was an attempt to create a language for therapists to describe their thinking in practice. Mattingly and Fleming concluded that therapists think in three styles, which they called tracks, during the course of interventions with clients. They often thought in two or more tracks simultaneously. These tracks are procedural reasoning, interactive reasoning and conditional reasoning.

Procedural reasoning occurs when a therapist is defining problems and selecting treatments (Fleming 1991). In determining how a therapist's beliefs and values may influence this reasoning track, consider the task of problem identification. What the therapist may view as the main issue may be minor for the client. For example, not being able to care for their children may be more pressing for the client than pain management. *Interactive reasoning* occurs when a therapist is attempting to understand the client as an individual and build a collaborative relationship with them (Fleming 1991). The more a therapist tries to understand their client, and avoid making assumptions about their life, the more use they will have from interactive reasoning. Finally, *conditional reasoning* is considering a client's whole condition within broader social and temporal contexts (Fleming 1991). A therapist's underlying views and beliefs about the role and contribution of people with disabilities in society will colour this track of reasoning.

Since the publication of Mattingly and Fleming's study in 1991, a number of clinical and professional reasoning models have been developed in the health professions. It is generally accepted that professionals' values and beliefs about the world directly influence the way they practice and use their knowledge (Stewart and Law 2003), with most contemporary models containing an element relating to health professionals' values and beliefs. One such model is the Ecological Model of Professional Reasoning (Boyt Schell and Schell 2008).

This model (Boyt Schell and Schell 2008) illustrates that each health worker thinks through a professional 'lens', comprising practice theories, knowledge, experience and therapy skills. In addition to this professional lens, each health worker also brings a personal lens to therapy, consisting of their own beliefs, values and assumptions. This personal lens impacts on the professional lens, influencing knowledge use and action. What makes this model of professional reasoning interesting is the inclusion of the client. Within this model, clients bring to therapy a personal lens, which is a history of life experience, in addition to their own beliefs, values, intelligence and embodied sense and abilities. They collaborate with a health worker whose personal lens may be congruent or clashing. Later, there will be a discussion of the potential difficulties when a health worker's personal lens is incongruent with a client's personal lens.

So, how does a personal lens develop? What influences our beliefs about people with disabilities? Each health professional's own personal history and experiences will influence their values and beliefs. In addition, the values and beliefs of the professions to which we belong also influence our personal lens. Of course, individual professions are influenced by the society around them, so societal viewpoints about disability are relevant here.

Societal knowledge – viewpoints on disability

Individuals' beliefs and values arise from their experiences. During a health professional's training, they are influenced by the frameworks of their profession. There appear to be two views on disability which guide the health professions in Western society; the biomedical and the social model of practice. For the greater part of the twentieth century, views of disability centred on the biomedical model. The biomedical model places emphasis on the disease, trauma or health condition, and views disability as a feature of the person. A more contemporary view of disability is represented in the social model. The social model of disability emphasizes the role of the environment in creating disability. In describing these models, and the underlying beliefs, we can see how each influences the actions and practice of health professionals.

The biomedical model of disability

The idea of sickness and disability within the biomedical model is that of deviation from the norm. In 1951, Parsons, spoke of individuals who were experiencing illnesses as people who have deviated from their roles in society. He called this situation *sickness*, and noted that this was socially acceptable. However, these individuals were not free of roles. They needed to assume the sick role, which meant that their role was to participate in activities and tasks that would alleviate their illness. For example, part of the sick role was to seek and follow a health practitioner's advice.

Evidence of the influence of the biomedical model can easily be seen in our healthcare system today. Many health services, apart from emergency services, are only available during business hours, with the assumption that a patient will be free of other responsibilities (or at least be able to take time away from them) to attend to the business of regaining their health.

The sick role, as described by Parsons (1951), is a temporary one. The condition is a deviation from an individual's everyday life. Once the illness is alleviated, the individual is expected to resume his or her roles. However, many health professionals are involved with people who will not regain previous function in their physical, emotional or psychological systems. Disability then ensues.

Disability, within the biomedical model, is a feature of an individual. It is the impairment of a physical, psychological or emotional system (Stewart and Law 2003). The health professional places the emphasis of disability on the impairment, and rarely on the person themselves. Sometimes, the health professional's emphasis is entirely on the affected part, and not on the person at all. In healthcare settings where the biomedical model dominates, it is not uncommon to hear of the 'stroke in bed 7', or 'the wheelchair arriving by taxi'. In these examples, the disability *is* the individual.

Health professionals guided by the biomedical model work to 'fix' the anomaly and correct the problem. The overall aim of a therapeutic encounter within this model is to 'get back to normal'. Knowledge use is focused on assessing function in a part of the body and using remedial or compensatory techniques to return that injured part to normal. These are admirable tasks within therapy, but there is no mention of the client and how they wish to live their life. So, being influenced by the biomedical model, a therapist's values and beliefs may be influenced in such a way as to see disability as an individual's difference or anomaly, rather than just one part of a client's life.

The social model of disability

Arising as a result of criticisms of the biomedical model, the social model of disability is a contemporary view of disability. Proponents of this model assert that many external physical and behavioural factors intersect with an individual's own capacities, skills and function, resulting in disability (Stewart and Law 2003). Some of these factors include tangible factors such as the built environment, housing and public transport. Other factors are more intangible, such as social exclusion, stigma and prejudice. All of these factors combine to determine an individual level of disability that is specific to an individual's cultural and social setting.

A therapist influenced by the social model of disability considers the individual client within the context of their physical and social environment. The therapist here considers 'fixing the problem' to be more than just addressing the client's impairments. Interventions could centre on similar techniques to the biomedical model but extend further to include public health measures and larger scale adjustments to the physical and social environment.

The World Health Organization developed the International Classification of Functioning (ICF) as a way to conceptualize the impact of impairment on an individual's life (World Health Organization 2001). The ICF was developed within the guides of the social model of disability and provides a framework for therapists to situate the impact of impairment on a client's participation in their cultural and social world.

Both models of disability have their place in our healthcare system. A skilled health professional may use both accordingly. However, what happens when a professional sees through one model, whilst a client sees through another?

Conflicting beliefs

As previously discussed, a person with a disability brings their own personal lens, based on their lived experience of disability, to the therapeutic encounter. Simultaneously, a health professional also brings a personal lens, influenced by their experiences, but also by the model guiding their professional practice. It is conceivable that the professional's and the client's personal lenses may clash.

Does it matter if the client and professional have differing views, beliefs and ideas about knowledge use and the direction of therapy? I will now explore some areas where clashing personal lenses may impact on a therapeutic encounter. I will consider problems that may arise when a health professional values their ideas and time more than those of their clients, and highlight how these clashes may manifest.

Health professions are largely seen as 'helping professions', traditionally helping people with disabilities. The professional has been seen as the 'healer', while the person with a disability is seen as a submissive recipient of care (Mattingly and Lawlor 2003). How often have you heard a professional talk about 'doing an assessment *on* a client', not *with*? This simple use of language speaks volumes about a professional's views. Completing an assessment *on* a client implies little or no collaboration, valuing the professional's knowledge, values and beliefs over those of the client. Completing an assessment *with* the client implies a partnership.

Another way that over-valuing the therapist's ideas and minimizing collaboration and client's values and beliefs could manifest is in non-compliance. Non-compliance is demonstrated by a client when they do not follow health professionals' recommendations. In occupational therapy, this is usually in the form of clients not using prescribed equipment, or not completing exercises outside of therapy times. The underlying meaning of describing a client as 'non-compliant' is almost similar to 'disobedient'. This client description implies that the health professional's goals should supersede those of the client. It is assumed that the health professional knows best and that the client must follow their advice. In this context, non-compliance could be a manifestation of a clash between a therapist's and a client's personal lenses.

Additionally, a lack of collaboration with clients and placing more emphasis on the health professional's beliefs rather than those of the client, could lead to irrelevant therapeutic action. For example, occupational therapists occasionally prescribe equipment that they feel is important for the client but the client does not feel is required and will never use as intended. The therapist's beliefs about 'improving function' do not fit with the client's values of 'quality of life' or 'dignity'. The under-use of equipment is quite a common phenomenon in occupational therapy, and one I have encountered many times. On one occasion, in a service in which I worked, we had a client who, the occupational therapist felt, would benefit from a wheeled walking frame. She was given one, but she never used it when she came in for therapy. On a regulation home visit, the occupational therapist spotted the walking frame … in the garden, being used as a mobile pot-plant.

Not only do these clashes in values and beliefs lead to frustrations, considerable cost and time can also be wasted, for both the client and therapist. It is important that health professionals are aware of strategies to improve therapeutic encounters.

Strategies to encourage an understanding of values and beliefs

Now that possible manifestations of a clash of values and beliefs, or personal lens, have been identified, it is time to think about strategies to minimize these issues. Namely, increasing diversity in the health profession workforce and reflecting on our own practice may be used to overt therapist's values and beliefs and encourage congruence with those of our clients.

Increasing diversity within the healthcare workforce

In the biomedical model, which is still a dominant model in health professions, the emphasis of disability is on an individual's difference or anomaly, so it is easy to see how people with disabilities could be seen as 'other'. Abreu and Peloquin (2004), in describing cultural diversity in the occupational therapy profession, speak of *otherism*. Otherism emerges from our natural tendency to categorize the things around us in order to make sense of the world. However, in categorizing people with disabilities as others, health professions are clearly creating a separation.

Furthering this belief, the social environment in which we work may also shape the construction of otherness (Abreu and Peloquin 2004). The social environments in which we work, play and live our daily lives, influence our values and beliefs. If a health worker is in a professional environment in which there is little diversity, they may not appreciate the differing values and beliefs of others. If the only time this worker sees people with disabilities is when they are 'helping' them, can the health professional make that leap into believing 'they' should, or could, be one of 'us'? Toward the end of this chapter, I will recount my experiences of going from a 'them' to an 'us', from a 'helpee' to a 'helper', a 'client' to a 'therapist'.

In recognition of the many influences on practice, there has been a call to increase diversity amongst clinicians. Increasing diversity refers to the idea of widening participation in the profession. It involves encouraging people from non-traditional backgrounds into the health professions (Taylor 2007).

Increasing diversity within health professions will present different ways of thinking (Taylor 2007). Values will be challenged, and health professionals may find a new way of seeing situations. This change may enhance health professionals' ability to understand and appreciate the values of their clients which in turn could increase the responsiveness of therapeutic alliances.

The call to increase diversity in health professions is supported by research conducted with healthcare consumers. From a qualitative study of the experience of consumers who name themselves as members of a minority group in terms of religion and sexuality, an identified need was for the health professions to understand a diverse range of viewpoints to provide appropriate recognition of clients' cultural values and beliefs (Kirsh et al. 2006).

Reflecting on practice

All health professionals have a significant body of knowledge from which they draw. However, it is not enough just to have knowledge. Reflection allows us to use that knowledge judiciously and conscientiously. Reflection, in a simple definition, is when you 'arrest a particular moment in time, ponder over it, go back through it, and only then … gain new insight into different aspects of the situation' (Alsop and Ryan 1996: 170).

Essentially, reflection is thinking about what we do, why we do it, and wondering if there is another way. A respected author on the use of reflection was Schön. He asserted that reflecting on experiences increases specialist knowledge and improves clinical reasoning (1983). A reflective therapist develops into a skilled therapist as they learn from each experience.

According to Van Manen (cited in Alsop and Ryan 1996), there are three levels of reflection. The first two levels will be discussed here, as they are the most relevant to our individual practice. Firstly, the initial stage of reflection is thinking about whether a professional's actions helped to reach their stated outcome. For health professionals, this stage of reflection concerns interventions chosen, actions taken and goals that have been developed. In some health sectors this level of reflection is required when providing a written treatment report or plan.

The second stage of reflection, according to Van Manen (in Alsop and Ryan 1996) is of particular interest when considering health professionals' knowledge use. The second stage involves reflecting on assumptions and how they impact on actions.

As discussed earlier, a health professional's beliefs, values and assumptions will influence their actions (Stewart and Law 2003). Reflection can facilitate an exploration of a professional's attitudes to minimize clashing with those of their client. To understand others, we need to understand ourselves. Reflecting on our own beliefs, values, norms and practices allows us to understand the diversity in others (Taylor 2007).

Reflection requires adequate time and a safe space to explore values, beliefs and attitudes. Diaries, supervision or peer discussions are good methods to use to understand what factors influence actions, reasoning and knowledge use.

The following questions may be helpful to facilitate reflection:

- What do I know about my client as a person?
- What am I trying to achieve with this client?
- What does the client want to achieve?
- What did I do as an intervention/therapy?
- Why did I choose to do that?
- Was there any other alternative to my chosen activity?
- If I had to do it differently, what else could I have done?

A Personal Story: What Happens when the Helpee becomes the Helper?

Our job as health professionals is to support people to gain or regain the life they want. It is not our job to decide what would make a life meaningful. Do we place our expectations on others' lives, reflecting our values and beliefs, not theirs? Do we sometimes lead a client rather than walking alongside them? I want you to think about those questions, and I am going to tell you about my life and others' expectations of me.

I was born with a significant and rare spinal abnormality, resulting in lower limb paralysis. I require the use of a wheelchair for mobility. My prognosis wasn't good, but I defied expectations, and pretty soon, I was old enough to go to school. Because I lived in a rural city, in the mid-1970s, the assumption about people with disabilities was that they could not attend a mainstream school, and it was assumed that I would go to a special school. I did, but as I had learnt to read at age three, I spent a few bored years not learning very much at all. My parents moved me to mainstream schooling, and I finished, and then moved to university to study occupational therapy.

It was after university that I first felt expectations from the health professions. My first position, after graduation, was at a psychiatric disability service. My position involved supporting clients as they worked towards their own goals. As part of the job, I was often involved in negotiating and advocating for clients with other services. The clients did not care that I owned a wheelchair, but often, the other services did. They didn't expect someone with a disability to be in the helping professions. On one occasion, I accompanied a client with schizophrenia to his local doctor because he had hurt his wrist. The doctor could not make eye contact with me during the consultation, and asked who would help me to remember all of the details to help my client. Clearly, this doctor's values and beliefs about people with disabilities did not extend to having the ability to help others.

One of the clearest examples of beliefs clashing with another health professional occurred frequently in my role as a consultant. My task was to visit mainstream nursing homes to establish systems to assist nursing staff to manage residents with dementia. The role involved me visiting two different facilities each week. I would spend time with the manager, discussing needs and strategies. Then, as I was pressing the code in to leave the locked facility, almost routinely, a member of staff would try to stop me and suggest that I go back to my bedroom and wait for lunch. On one occasion, despite producing my hospital identity badge, the staff member allowed me to leave through the locked doors only after the facility manager vouched for my identity!

A significant advantage to being a health professional with a disability is that clients usually feel open to discuss issues that they hide from other therapists. Clients would often say that they were too embarrassed to ask about a particular issue, but they thought I would understand because sometimes I would need to ask for help too. Clients reported that they never felt judged, and were able to express fears that they avoided showing in front of others.

Summary

This chapter has been concerned with the way therapists use their knowledge in an encounter with a person with a disability. Knowledge use, in this context, is a personal approach as an individual health professional's beliefs, values and attitudes influence their actions and reasoning.

Approximately 20 per cent of Australians live with an impairment that affects their everyday lives. Each person's experience of disability is unique. Each client presenting to a health professional is also unique, and has unique values, beliefs and attitudes.

Clinical reasoning models provide an understanding of how health professionals think and use knowledge in practice. These models demonstrate that the way professionals think is strongly influenced by their values, beliefs and attitudes.

In addition to personal viewpoints about disability, societal viewpoints also impact on the way health professionals practise. The biomedical model of disability sees an individual's impairment as the sole cause of disability. A health worker's job is to 'fix' this problem. However, the social model of disability situates individuals and their impairment within a cultural and social context. Disability, in the social model, is an intersection of the individual's capacity and skills with the physical and behavioural aspects of their environment.

When a health professional and a client have clashing values, beliefs and attitudes about disability, there may be consequences for the therapeutic encounter. Over-valuing of the health worker's ideas could lead to lack of collaboration and non-compliance in therapy participation. Placing more emphasis on the health worker's beliefs about people with disabilities, rather than the person's beliefs about themselves, could lead to irrelevant therapeutic action.

Increasing diversity in the health profession workforce and reflecting on our own practice may be used to avert conflicts between health professionals' values and beliefs and those of their clients.

Knowledge use is influenced by many factors. Personal beliefs, values and attitudes all impact on behaviour and reasoning. Health professionals need to consider more than just techniques and interventions when in a therapeutic encounter with a person with a disability.

References

Abreu, B. and Peloquin, S. 2004. Embracing diversity in our profession. *American Journal of Occupational Therapy*, 58(3), 353–9.

Alsop, A. and Ryan, S. 1996. *Making the Most of Fieldwork Education: A Practical Approach*. London: Chapman Hall.

Australian Bureau of Statistics. 2004. *Disability, Ageing and Carers, Australia*. Canberra: Australian Bureau of Statistics, 4430.0.

Beer, D. 2003. The illness and disability experience from an individual perspective, in *Willard and Spackman's Occupational Therapy*, edited by E. Blesdell Crepeau, E.S. Cohn and B.A. Boyt Schell. Philadelphia: Lippincott Williams and Wilkins.

Boyt Schell, B.A. and Schell, J.W. 2008. *Clinical and Professional Reasoning in Occupational Therapy*. Baltimore: Lippincott, Williams and Wilkins.

Fleming, M.H. 1991. The therapist with the three-track mind. *American Journal of Occupational Therapy*, 45(11), 1007–14.

Higgs, J. and Jones, M. 2000. *Clinical Reasoning in the Health Professions*. 2nd Edition. Melbourne: Butterworth Heinemann.

Kirsh, B., Trentham, B. and Cole, S. 2006. Diversity in occupational therapy: experiences of consumers who identify themselves as minority group members. *Australian Occupational Therapy Journal*, 53(4), 302–13.

Mattingly, C. and Fleming, M.H. 1994. *Clinical Reasoning: Forms of Inquiry in a Therapeutic Practice*. Philadelphia: F.A. Davis Company.

Mattingly, C. and Lawlor, M.C. 2003. Disability experience from a family perspective, in *Willard and Spackman's Occupational Therapy*, edited by E. Blesdell Crepeau, E.S. Cohn and B.A. Boyt Schell. Philadelphia: Lippincott Williams and Wilkins.

Parsons, T. 1951. *The Social System*. New York: Free Press.

Schön, D. 1983. *The Reflective Practitioner: How Professionals Think in Action*. New York: Basic Books.

Stewart, D. and Law, M. 2003. The environment: paradigms and practice in health, occupational therapy and inquiry, in *Using Environment to Enable Occupational Performance*, edited by L. Letts and Debra Stewart. Thorofare: Slack, 3–16.

Taylor, M.C. 2007. The Casson Memorial Lecture 2007: diversity amongst occupational therapists – rhetoric or reality? *British Journal of Occupational Therapy*, 70(7), 276–83.

Unsworth, C.A. 2004. Clinical reasoning: how do worldview, pragmatic reasoning and client-centredness fit? *British Journal of Occupational Therapy*, 67(1), 10–19.

World Health Organization. 2001. *International Classification of Functioning, Disability and Health (ICF)*. Geneva: World Health Organization.

6 Knowledge in the making: an analytical psychology perspective

Joy Norton

Introduction

As a psychotherapist, not knowing is unbearable. Subjectively it robs me of any professional edifice and strips me bare, subject to the wails and wiles of the other in pain. I am cast into misery, aloneness, uncertainty and despair. I am incompetent. It is as if the thirty-something years of practising as a psychologist do not exist and there is no thought possible about anything. The raw human condition is starkly present, unavoidable and unpalatable. I can only be present in the rawness of my humanity.

In writing this chapter, the agony of not knowing has been with me, surfacing each time I attempted to communicate to the reader knowledge as it is conventionally understood. With 33 years of experience working as a psychologist, it is a rude shock to be confronted, yet again, by the undermining agony of not knowing anything at all. And yet this is a necessary starting point for this chapter, as it has been in work with my client. The client, too, could not let herself know anything, so together we struggled, slouching towards an emergent knowing.

Writing this chapter was a replay of the struggle with this client who, more than any other, confronted me with a major dialectic embedded in Carl Gustav Jung's way of explaining the work of an analytical psychologist; the tension between not knowing and being informed by existing knowledge. The encounter with this client starkly represents the dilemma in the clinical setting and this chapter is an effort to track this tension.

Knowledge and clinical practice are always mediated and informed by the experience of the client. Moreover, the significance of the relationship between the client and the analyst is a vehicle of potential influence in the psychological work. In order to present the challenges embedded in my dilemma and to ground this chapter I will introduce the reader to

Anya,[1] describing how she presented herself. The shape of my subjective response as it flowed then follows, as well as some dawning attempts to link my experience and observations with the knowledge base of analytical psychology. A more explicit link to the body of knowledge will then be developed.

A client, not knowing anything

Initially Anya had consulted another psychologist about sleep difficulties, and deeply disturbing nightmares were found to be at its core. Exploring the nightmares was recommended as potentially useful to Anya, so she was referred to the author. Our first contact was via the telephone, where a weak voice communicated an urgent desperation to meet, although with no articulated intention. I found myself assisting Anya in getting transport to the appointments as she was too weak to drive and her family members were not initially free to help. This was unusual behaviour for me. I had been mobilized to be helpful, even before we met.

Anya was 23 years old on referral, though for much of the time she looked physically like a child of eight, and a very thin and emaciated one at that. She was dressed in a girl-like way. There seemed to be a desperate air in her attempt to be in charge, to be an adult, and this contrasted with her extremely weak physicality and mode of engagement. Anya was exhausted, like a reed with no strength, yet determined not to collapse emotionally. Her face was grey. When she arrived in the room she seemed ghostly. She would go to the couch, remove her shoes and curl up is the shape of a foetus.

I was immediately sympathetic to her bodily weakness and frailty. I felt protective, with a desire to be enfolding, even though there was minimal eye contact. The image of a baby bird, eyes not yet open, was with me. She rarely cried and when she did was contemptuous of her weakness. I felt extremely wary of approaching any feeling state, felt controlled, and in particular I sensed that I was expected to know things about her experience without asking or being told. Further, I sensed that I was expected to comprehend her being and get it right away. I should be all knowing – and I had better not say the wrong thing. I felt silenced and pressured by these seeming, unspoken commands.

Anya seemed impenetrable. There was a closing down of her experience, as if the world were a dangerous place. I intuited her to be objectified by the world. What really struck me was her inability to take anything in, psychologically or physically. The tight rigidity in her frail, curled-up

---

1   Permission to use this clinical material has been given. The personal details have been disguised to protect identity.

body seemed a reflection of the rigidity in her thinking. She was unable to reflect, but was active in revealing her antagonism to the medical and helping professions, about which she was deeply ambivalent and distrusting. Anya insisted her body reflected nothing emotional to her. For Anya her problems were all physical yet her medical consultants diagnosed psychological underpinnings of some serious concern: chronic fatigue, fibro myalgia, anorexia, borderline personality disorder, depression. Each of these opinions she rejected. I felt manipulated into a collusion of negation of all understanding of the expressions of her body. This young woman was seriously ill. I learned she was also at times suicidal.

Initially Anya said almost nothing. She seemed too tired, as if words exhausted her. She seemed ambivalent about whether or, perhaps how I would diagnose her. I sensed I must not say the wrong thing. I must not interpret. I must agree about the physical nature of her demise, even agree with her denial of the severity of her condition. She was distrustful of words. She wrote down a flood of dreams and emailed them to me. This she could manage.

She was usually in physical pain in the sessions and would drink from her water bottle. Many of the early sessions were silent, because she slept. She would gradually drop off, slip away, and initially I registered some anger and helplessness as I searched for a way of contact. I felt locked out by her sleeping, but I did not then feel sleepy. On other occasions I felt quietly present, curious about her dreams and how we might join around them. As time went on when she slept I would sit quietly or read her dreams silently. It seemed at times she did not breathe. She would not read her dreams after writing them, nor did she read the dreams aloud in the sessions. She faced away from direct engagement always sitting or lying at 45 degrees, facing away from me.

Paradoxically, she spoke as if the dreams were something I could tell her about. I felt this was a trap, inviting premature knowing from me. It was like an invitation to be inauthentic as I would need to be all-knowing without any understanding of her experience of these dreams; it was an invitation to objectify her. To Anya the dreams meant nothing other than that they were things that disturbed her at night, but the disturbance continued in the day as an aftermath, and she was frightened by them. She had no thoughts about their meaning, she could not identify any as more or less of concern, but was prepared to keep a record of them and email them to me each week. They did scare her, though she could not elaborate how. It seemed I was meant to digest and regurgitate them, but if I attempted to do so, they were not received by her thinking self at all. It was like a seduction to be known, but a rejection always followed.

As time went by, I was very aware of the pain in her body, especially her stomach and arms. When she arrived I frequently began to experience the sensations of aching in my arms and of tightness in my stomach, like I had been gripping something. Stabbing pain in these areas then developed in me. For the first 16 weeks we continued in this way, she attended and would lie on my couch sometimes sleeping, sometimes telling me a little about the week's medical events. I felt trapped by the expectation that I should be doing something, know something – and by her desire to be in charge.

Generally, in working psychologically with someone, I am able to engage empathically, be person-centred, find a focus, and locate the conflicting internal states. Under such circumstances a dialogue would begin. However, my responses were not receivable by Anya. Increasingly I found myself pushed towards a state of waiting, and I began to wonder if she was able to register any interest in herself.

The reader may sense from this description of our early meetings that there is a tension of expectations both in the analyst and in the client. The client is hostile to professional knowledge and contemptuous of it, distrustful and refusing to be objectified by the knowledge of diagnostic categories or any predictable terms of engagement. She barely speaks, does not keep eye contact, refutes any approach and yet is deeply affective in her unspoken presence. She does not want this knowledge. Yet she continues to attend sessions twice each week. The analyst is unable to mobilize words to engage meaningfully, is stripped of knowing anything useful, expected to present her knowledge of dreams and resorts to a soliloquy, sitting in the paradox of waiting with another who continues to come with apparently no engagement yet a sense of connection. The analyst finds herself into a not-knowing position.

Besides the immersion in the subjectivity of the encounter with the client, the analyst is also tracking other sources of understanding this experience. The raw data of the encounter begins to gather into islands of potential knowledge based on practical clinical experience, self-knowledge and theories of the discipline.

The next section examines Jung's position on theory and knowledge. The key elements are then applied to the raw data to take the reader through this thinking process.

Theories as instruments of knowledge or therapy

Theories are to be avoided, except as mere auxiliaries. As soon as a dogma is made of them, it is evident that an inner doubt is being stifled ... Theories are not articles of faith, they are either instruments of knowledge and of therapy or they are no good at all. (Jung 1985c: 88)

Jung's ideas about the nature of knowledge

Carl Gustav Jung was a psychiatrist who wrote many volumes of his version of psychology now known by the name of its author, or as analytical psychology. Jung considered himself to be an empiricist. To Jung, knowledge is empirical and is based on clinical observation of the experiences with the client. As with others like Husserl, phenomena are psychological facts. For Jung, 'All knowledge is the result of imposing some kind of order upon the reactions of the psychic system as they flow into our consciousness' (Jung 1973: 81).

By using this definition of knowledge, the reactions of the psychic systems experienced and observed in the client and in the analyst assist knowledge to develop. The emphasis, therefore, is on the emergent phenomenal experience – within the client and between the client and the analyst.

Jung also regarded knowledge as based on a dialectical process, and thus the analytic process is also dialectical:

> Psychotherapy has … become a kind of dialectical process, a dialogue or discussion between two persons. Dialectic was originally the art of conversation among the ancient philosophers but very early became the term for creating new syntheses. A person is a psychic system which, when it affects another person, enters into a reciprocal reaction with another psychic system. This formulation of a therapeutic relation between physician and patient is clearly very far removed from the original view that psychotherapy was a method which anybody could apply in stereotyped fashion to reach the desired result. (Jung 1985a: 3)

Further, the analyst is deeply involved in the dialectic process, and it is mutual.

> If I wish to treat another individual psychologically at all I must, for better or worse, give up all pretension to superior knowledge, all authority and desire to influence. I must perforce adopt a dialectical procedure consisting in a comparison of our mutual findings. But this only becomes possible if I give the other person a chance to play his hand to the full, unhampered by my assumptions. (Jung 1985a: 5)

The dialectical procedure and the reciprocal reaction between Anya and myself, was one of not knowing, waiting and being radically disinterested in objectified interpretations. I needed to be in the psychic experience with her, to be affected by her for some mutual psychological experience to arise and for psychological movement to occur. Jung (1985d: 176) writes of this as a need for the *doctor to be infected* by the patient. This was a significant orienting thought. Jung cautioned about theory and never wanted clinical work to be formulaic.

Jung argued that the analyst has to be him- or herself, open to the influence of the client's process, and willing to create a theory anew each time with the client from the experiences arising in the engagement, empirically gathered. The challenge is to be open to each encounter in each session. Knowledge comes from this emergent process over time and, with these experiences, client and analyst come to know something together. Knowledge is phenomenologically empirical. The art of practice is to bear not knowing, to allow the unfolding to occur and to stay open to what is creating itself in the client. Jung also acknowledged that the therapist is a participant observer in the process and needs to be skilled in understanding the dynamic interactive influences that operate within and between the client and the therapist, both known and unknown. The therapist needs to be attuned to the timely communication of such understandings that maximize the agency of the client.

In order to be facilitative in this way, the analyst needs to be very self-aware, and also open to the possibilities of being unaware for periods of time. The analyst, through self-knowledge, needs to be able to process such disassemblies, to find ways to engage and be with such transactions interpersonally and intra psychically whilst remaining open to the possibility of some emergent understanding or meaning. The tension is very much between knowing and not knowing. A long analysis and ongoing supervision are necessary to develop this art as a clinician to enable him or her to remain alive in the therapeutic encounter. Trainings in the Analytical Psychology field orient strongly to this aspect of skill in practice and the development of a kind of intra psychic *radar* and *language* for use as a readout in the affective and somatic register. Comprehending the processes involved in the development of meaning and consciousness need to be intricately understood intellectually and experientially. Preverbal processes, defensive organization in the body, images and disengagements are all vital as communications. They are embedded in the training experiences, personal analysis and the intensive supervision required when developing as a practitioner. Process is privileged over theory and the fullness of the personality of the analyst is emphasized.

What follows is an attempt to report on such an emergent process as it occurred between the writer and her client.

Emergent meaning

The raw data of this engagement with Anya began to shape themselves in the thinking of the analyst. What was flowing into consciousness was gathered in the theorizing track of the analyst's experience. It is important to note that this theorizing held no weight in the mind of the client at this point.

It was refuted when placed in the interaction. I place it in this discussion to clarify that the analyst continues where she is able to think, holding the emergent thoughts as tentative representations of potential issues within the client, not yet formulated in or outside of the client's consciousness. They remain tentative until experienced as meaningful by the client and, if not, discarded.

The interaction with this particular person, Anya, did influence the analyst. Fragments of thought surfaced, and were held in mind. These empirical data coalesced around the maternal matrix, as many different aspects of Anya's experience pointed towards a disturbance in maternal attunement. In her dreams, babies and baby animals were described as abandoned. The client's instinctual responses to her body were in disarray. Feeding, sleeping, pain management and other bodily functions like the menses were not regulated. Eye contact was avoided, she presented in a foetal position often and she sucked on her water bottle. It seemed she brought her baby self into the sessions. She was unable to work in her vocational field of childcare. Anya seemed unable to be comforted. She was fiercely defensive about mothers, both personal and collective, defending them as all-giving, and knowing best for babies. She could not comprehend why she was dreaming such destructive scenarios.

The analyst's response to Anya's frailty seemed to represent a maternal response, un-worded. Words did not appear to reach into Anya's experience in any meaningful way. My eyes searched her for connection through eye contact, which was rarely reciprocated. It felt as if my eyes surrounded her body, communicating a holding presence. Her physical presence repelled holding or acknowledgement of any need. I theorized about a baby in need who cannot trust expression of her need. To need anything puts one in a vulnerable place and others then have control, therefore, maybe, it is better to not need anything and cut off that experience and be the one in charge.

Affective expressions in such a state were closed down and not allowed to come into experience. Perhaps her pain was to do with affective states locked in her body? Were we preoccupied with her bodily states in an attempt to unlock or open up affective expression? She regarded tears with contempt. This baby state was guarded from view and any approach towards it, any support, would collapse her self-system. I was identified with her baby state, feeling the pain in her body as well as warned off by the omnipotent aspects of her that were in control and denying access. Non-worded attempts to connect with her made me ponder maternal attunement to a baby not yet up to speech but needing to receive care. Something was deeply worrying, but we seemed not able to focus on it because of fear, thus keeping aspects of her potential from expression.

Developmental theories were also in my thinking, together with structural ways of conceiving the psyche. I began to ponder defences of the self, psychological mechanisms keeping parts of the personality apart. When feeling states, particularly anger or fear, were approached in the sessions, she would dissociate and retreat into pain or sleep. Had she jumped from a baby state to being a girl who needed to be grown up? If so, what had shaped this leap? Her baby self seemed abandoned by her. Her creative self closed down. She was not self-reflexive. It was as if no one was at home.

I also thought about the functional significance of the bodily symptoms and the freeze on developing reflexivity. It kept our focus on the body in an urgent way. Affective states that have not been modulated by the adult caring for a baby can present in such ways. Sidoli (2000) posited that when the carer is not able to provide words to make sense of affect-loaded somatizations, they remain mute and locked in the body as symptoms or as pain. Generally, a mother digests and translates these somatizations for the infant, and then they are regulated and transformed through the reverie of the mother. This allows play and thinking to develop. Meeting the silence and aggression in this client made it difficult for us to think and reflect together. We certainly could not be playful. Maybe a reverie was being created for such a purpose? I looked for the teleology in the symptoms, meaningful signs of forward development.

In the implicit communication in the sessions, I found it difficult to hold onto thoughts. They would fragment if they were in my mind, fade off, be forgotten. I began to conceptualize this difficulty in being unable to hold onto thought processes as a manifestation of the dissociability in the client at that time. Where islands of thought coalesced in my client, they seemed to be put to sleep or slip out of mind. Parts of her personality were not able to come together or interact. Her energy for life was fixed, stuck.

The other implicit communication was experienced in my body as pain, quite like what Anya described. It was as if her experience was in me. This experience reflects the psychic infection about which Jung writes. This is conceptualized as part of the data being gathered through the transference and counter-transference, which Jung (1985b: 71) described as 'a highly important organ of information' for the analysis.

> In any effective psychological treatment the doctor is bound to influence the patient; but this influence can only take place if the patient has a reciprocal influence on the doctor. You can exert no influence if you are not susceptible to influence. It is futile for the doctor to shield himself from the influence of the patient. By doing so he only denies himself the use of a highly important organ of information … one of the best known symptoms of this kind is the countertransference evoked by the transference. (Jung 1985b: 71)

My sleepiness, reverie and maternal focus are other examples of gathering information, using my counter-transference as a register.

The other emergent arena of thought focused on archetypal understanding given that the body and imagery were strong aspects on her presentation. Jung defined the Archetypes as mental representations of instinctual drives, and/or the innate predisposition to experience life according to certain patterns. He also saw them as a powerful way of representing affects. They were conceived as organizers of experience which operate within the self in the service of the ego, and determine the structure and relationship between the internal and external worlds. In Jung's view the affects were the life-blood of the psyche and the bridge between the body and psyche. The archetypal pattern, in this case, involved the maternal matrix and creation.

These islands of thinking contributed to the emergent understanding. In this interaction with the client, they were part of the stream of coming to know. Such knowledge is partial, emergent and tentative. It is part of the process of making knowledge. It is incomplete and not yet overtly beneficial to the client.

Experiences, such as those just described, are common for analysts and they reflect ways in which understanding emerges through a type of dialectical resonance that takes place between client and analyst. It is also expected that the processes, as described, illustrate how theoretical knowledge needs to emerge in the practice of analysis and not be predetermined by existing, formalized thinking. They are two very different processes yet they remain in a dialectical relationship with one another. This issue is explored next.

Theory as an auxiliary to knowledge

The process of respecting the emergent meaning for a client is in tension with generalized ways of comprehending psychological phenomena. Theory might usefully be conceived as ways writers make overt, knowledge derived from how we think about experiences in the clinic and invite a wider professional scrutiny and engagement. Theorizing is also a way we chart the evolution of knowledge in a professional field and how we identify themes in practice that come to be valued as therapeutic. Theory is also used to differentiate orientations to practice (Samuels 1994: 15). Critical, contested areas are identified and this process allows for areas of difference to be considered and argued, and for the edges of the knowledge to be enlivening for practice, but none of this explains what should happen between an analyst and a client.

It is important to comprehend that with Anya all of this professional knowledge was of no use between us at this time. She was fiercely protective of her mother and family; it created anxiety in her to move towards reflections about her upbringing, and such explorations failed in that she became very defensive. Attempts to engage her in the narratives and themes of the dreams failed. All attempts to engage around her body symptoms led to nothing. The pervasive experience was of knowing nothing, being unable to act, staying in the frozenness of now, and allowing ourselves to not know anything yet. It was like we were waiting for something to emerge and be born, and this had to be referenced in Anya or credibly exchanged between us. So structural ways of understanding how the psyche works were helpful to me as an orienting way, but experientially the process was extremely painful and levelling. Taking up these areas of knowledge after the event is much easier than knowing at the time.

The elements of Jungian theory that best relate to understanding of this woman even presented as hypotheses failed to help because they involved interpreting the client to herself and this, she was determined, would not happen. We both needed to know nothing until she became interested in something she had created, something which arose in her that was of interest to her. An attitude of disinterest seemed required and Analytical Psychology knowledge did serve as an anchor for me as we began to engage in a radical form of disinterest in the processes that were emerging in the client. It could be speculated that my relationship to not knowing finally enabled her to relinquish control.

A dialectical theory of practice in Jungian analysis

> Since individuality is absolutely unique, unpredictable, and uninterpretable ... the therapist must abandon all his preconceptions and techniques and confine himself to a purely dialectical procedure, adopting the attitude that shuns all methods. (Jung 1985a: 7)

Theory and knowledge are in a dialectical tension within the analyst's experience in this work. Whilst methods and techniques do abound in the work of Analytical Psychology – sand play, dream work, active imagination, to name a few – they do not address the way the synthesis in this dialectic between theory and knowledge occurs. Such methods could be thought of as the craft of what to do, or what happens. They do not tell us how we *know* what we know. There are also structural theoretical ways that a psychological synthesis would be understood by analytical psychologists, for example in terms of the transcendent function.[2] For the practitioner, he or she does not carry out the transcendent function, it is a conceptual way of understanding a transformation after it has occurred. I am interested in

---

2   The transcendent function is defined in Samuels et al. (2000: 150) as 'the function that ... facilitates a transition from one psychological state or condition to another'.

what brings the thesis and antithesis into a synthesis. My view is that it is the relational process that brings these two aspects together. I propose that the relational process is the *techne*, as a process art that brings together the theory and the emergent knowledge. It is this synthesis that emerged within my work with Anya.

Techne, as a process art, embodies skills, particularly process skills in relating. In particular the skill of tracking self-awareness, thoughts, feelings, behaviours, body sensations and the minute, partly formed experiences as they wash through consciousness. The capacity to articulate unfolding meanings tentatively, to remain open to not knowing, to be respectful of the client's experiences, to be genuine and real in the engagement, to be prepared to self-disclose where helpful, to be prepared to be affected by the other in ways that are unknown, to trust that the process with the client will unfold through this connection, are all aspects of this relational matrix which provides what is often called a *transforming vessel* for the other. Embodiment of the client's experiences, immediacy of expression, modelling self-reflexivity and the willingness to be affected by the client are embedded in this relational process.

Papadopoulos (2006) points out that in Greek philosophy there is a long debate about the meaning of the word *episteme*, mainly between Aristotle and Socrates, about its opposition to *techne*, which is often translated as art, craft or practice (Papadopoulos 2006: 9). He reports that the general trend has been to attribute *episteme* to theoretical knowledge and *techne* to applied technology. I am proposing that the synthesis of this apparent opposition might be thought of in psychological work as the mediating relationship. A kind of higher order of process of understanding arises from both theory and knowledge in the analyst, which is then taken up through a synthesis arising in the client from theory she makes about herself and her psychic contents. A synthesis is experienced as a clear shift in felt sense (Gendlin 1973).

The emergence of knowing in the client

Anya continued to go to sleep in sessions and I found myself quietly reading the dreams aloud to her. She began to remain awake, listening and I became aware that this behaviour felt like telling a child a bedtime story, creating a particular space before sleep. As I was reading aloud, I noted that within the dream material, the protagonists often fell asleep or became unconscious, so I began to realize that we were enacting something of the same dynamic in the sessions. I commented on this as a possibility and wondered with Anya what this going to sleep, or becoming unconscious, might mean. She was taken by the immediacy of the dynamic between us. This was real in her experience and she was astounded at the parallel. Out of this effect, she took up an inquiry into her dreams and noted in them that the protagonists were fearful before this loss of consciousness occurred in the dreaming. She carried out an analysis of this content from her then current dream material and became interested and curious in the narrative. The working metaphor she developed seemed to ask: What was asleep in her? Anya told me that this was now her question. She had become awake to her own process.

Some time later she noticed a strange word in a dream (Pinja) and wanted to know what it meant. Anya had now taken on the role of asking and exploring what words, images and symbols meant for her. This process had been modelled by the analyst throughout. She initiated exploration and Googled this word on the internet. She found that it was an Aboriginal word for *painting stick*. She wondered about this, a word she had never heard[3] and why she had dreamed it. She wondered how could she know something like this, where had it come from, what part of her generated this word, for what purpose, and so she became aware of knowledge in the making.

Anya had the thought she might need to draw her dreams, and so she took up drawing some dream series and their associations. This process occurred over many months. The images in these drawings came in three different groupings over time. The first series had about 12 images. Thematically the pictures represented many eyes surrounding and looking out from imprisoned walls. There were images of eyes all over the pages, searching. The eyes were black. Other images included babies wrapped in teardrops falling like rain, split caverns with mountain-like breasts, with many crying eyes on their peaked surface. There were images of feeding bottles with measures on them and breasts marked on the bottle like eyes, weeping blood. There was a confusing merging of eyes and breasts in this first series. There were babies reflected in the bloodshot eyes of another, there were eyes in the black torsos where breasts would be, bleeding red tears. These images recurred and she became aware of the distressed baby part of herself. She did not link these images to her personal mother as this was not important to her. What mattered was she felt she was in communication with a part of herself that was engaging. She felt she was in dialogue with something unknown to her, that she could explore it in my company and not be controlled or directed by me. She was in charge of her own exploration, and she was developing a capacity to reflect and gather her experience into pockets of understanding. She was also able to trust a conversation about things not yet known. She was making a different relationship with herself.

---

3   Anya had not consciously ever heard or read this word.

The second group of images represented dark figures, either looming or torsos of faceless heads with arms outstretched. There were crosses, weeping blood. This grouping she associated with grief and loss.

The third grouping represented figures with knives in them surrounded by bleeding skin. This grouping she linked to feelings of pain and anger. The images became more figurative and whole over time.

At the end of this series of drawings, Anya dreamed about a mother needing counselling and took this as a cue for herself to dialogue in an imaginary conversation with the mother and baby parts of herself. Feeling experiences dominated these emergent, intra psychic conversations, which she shared with me, with anger and fear being the dominant affects. She had become agential in her own inquiry. The analyst became a person with whom a dialogue could now occur, a person who could be both witness and companion in these explorations. As she worked through these experiences, returning again to those requiring further work, her pain levels began to reduce, her energy improved, she gained weight and enlivened. These relationships with herself opened up many areas of her life to be explored, past trauma and loss, her primary relationship, her desire for a baby, and her emotional and creative expression.

Conclusion

The relationship between theory and knowledge within the work of an Analytical Psychologist is characterized by a number of significant factors. Theory is proposed as a form of cultural conservation (Moreno 1960: 12), in the sense that it is a corpus of formal explanations associated with practice that stand as a professional discourse. The proposal in this chapter is that such a corpus, while of considerable significance, should not be mistaken by practitioners as being a road map for client work. What is needed, instead, is a form of sensitive engagement with clients that may have generalized character but needs to emerge *de novo* within each, unique analytic encounter. This has been described in this chapter as knowledge in the making, derived from the phenomenological and empirical data arising in the client. There is a tension between theory and knowledge which is mediated and synthesized into a high order of understanding, with the relational matrix being defined as the key *techne*, a process art at the heart of the analytic work.

References

Gendlin, E. 1973. Experiential psychotherapy, in *Current Psychotherapies*, edited by R. Corsini. Itasca: Peacock, 317–52.

Jung, C. 1985a [1935]. The principles of practical psychotherapy, in *The Collected Works of C.G. Jung*, volume 16, Princeton: Princeton University Press.

Jung, C. 1985b [1931]. Problems of modern psychotherapy, in *The Collected Works of C.G. Jung*, volume 16, Princeton: Princeton University Press.

Jung, C. 1985c. [1945] Medicine and psychotherapy in *The Collected Works of C. G. Jung*, volume 16, Princeton: Princeton University Press.

Jung, C. 1985d [1945]. The psychology of the transference, in *The Collected Works of C.G. Jung*, volume 16. Princeton: Princeton University Press.

Jung, C. 1973 [1954]. On the nature of the psyche, in *The Collected Works of C.G. Jung*, volume 8. London: Routledge and Kegan Paul.

Moreno, J. 1960. *The Sociometry Reader*. New York: Free Press.

Papadopoulos, R.K. 2006. *The Handbook of Jungian Psychology*. London: Routledge.

Samuels, A. 1994. *Jung and the Post Jungians*. London: Routledge.

Samuels, A., Shorter, B. and Plaut, F. (eds) 2000. *A Critical Dictionary of Jungian Analysis*. London: Routledge.

Sidoli, M. 2000. *When the Body Speaks*. London: Routledge.

7 Knowledge to action in the practice of nursing

Alison Hutchinson and Tracey Bucknall

Introduction

The development of knowledge in nursing has grown at an exponential rate since 1952 when Virginia Henderson collected all published nursing research papers in only two slim volumes (McKenna 2004). Although there is much debate on the definition of nursing knowledge and what counts as knowledge, contemporary nursing has challenged the view that propositional knowledge (knowing that) accounts for all knowledge. Moreover, there is a growing acceptance that nursing incorporates other forms of knowledge, such as practical knowledge (knowing how). Nursing not only uses traditional forms, but also non-traditional methods for accessing or constructing knowledge relevant to nursing. This is hardly surprising given nursing is an applied discipline, whereby knowledge and practice are inextricably linked. As a result, when knowledge changes so too should practice, and as practice changes so too should knowledge.

The purpose of this chapter is to explore nursing knowledge and its development and contribution to nursing practice. We will begin with an overview of the development of knowledge in nursing and the current challenges being faced by nurses in a changing healthcare context. We will examine the types of knowledge that provide a basis for nursing decisions in practice, including traditional and non-traditional sources. This section will be followed with an analysis of the significance and use of knowledge in practice and an outline of models used to describe the process of knowledge use. We will then turn to a discussion about what constitutes evidence for nurses, from where this knowledge is derived, and the barriers and enablers to using empirical evidence in practice. Finally, we will examine how research evidence is integrated and blended with other forms of knowledge (expertise, patient preference and knowledge of available resources) to inform clinical decision making.

History of knowledge development in nursing

This section will provide a brief overview of knowledge development in nursing, providing an historical context for the current challenges.

Historically, nursing knowledge was based on intuition, experience and knowledge borrowed from other disciplines. In the last 30 years, however, there has been greater examination of practice to distinguish knowledge that is unique to nursing. The literature has comprised discussions of knowledge development (Fawcett 2000, Gortner 1990, Meleis 1997), the diversity of knowledge (Carper 1978), processes associated with knowledge (Chinn and Kramer 2008), the distinctiveness of nursing knowledge (Benner 1984, Carper 1978), its relationship with research and theory (Fawcett et al. 2001) and, importantly, the relationship between research and nursing practice (Rolfe 2006, Rolfe and Gardner 2005) to mention a few examples.

The profession has been keen to identify and clarify nursing knowledge, differentiating it from the knowledge of other disciplines. Yet arguably, like many disciplines, nursing knowledge has been borrowed, then adapted and applied in a nursing context. Concerns about the uniqueness of knowledge appear to be related to a pursuit for professional recognition in a sector dominated by the biomedical and scientific paradigms. Nurses have endeavoured to distinguish the nursing contribution to a person's health and illness experience to validate evolving roles and changes in professional boundaries in the health sector.

The classic work of Carper (1978) identified four patterns of knowing in nursing: empirics, ethics, personal and aesthetics. She recognized the limitations of knowledge based on averages in populations and the importance of knowledge based both on theory and practice. Similar to Carper, Gadamer (1996) identified the limitations of empirical knowledge in clinical practice. Decision making in practice relies on health professionals to apply diverse forms of knowledge to a specific context and to discover the best course of action for each individual. For this reason, making diagnostic, treatment and prognostic decisions with any certainty presents significant difficulty in practice. Indeed outcome prediction in advance of a patient encounter is often impossible.

In contrast to empirics, Carper's (1978) other patterns of knowing are less conventional, particularly given the relatively recent focus on evidence-based practice. Ethical obligations, individual perceptions and interpersonal processes and relationships have been downgraded or deleted from the hierarchies of evidence dominant in evidence-based practice, thus in some way contributing to the theory-practice gap, widely reported in healthcare, in which research findings are not necessarily used in practice by nurses.

Rolfe (2006: 39) argues that the theory–practice gap may in fact be related to 'inappropriate findings resulting from inappropriate research methodologies'. He suggests that researchers have frequently attempted to generalize findings to the wider population, even when selective sampling has been used in the process. This approach fails to recognize the fact that nursing practice involves interactions with unique individuals who have had unique experiences. Rolfe strongly believes that a better approach for nursing would be to adopt Schön's (1983) reflection-in-action, generating informal theories about unique clinical situations, and developing theory and practice simultaneously. Not surprisingly, methods such as this are being examined and tested in nursing practice (Bucknall et al. 2008a).

It would appear that the traditional view of what constitutes knowledge is being challenged to incorporate other types of knowledge and that non-traditional methods for developing knowledge are being more widely explored. The next section will examine in greater detail the different types of knowledge accessed and used in nursing.

Knowledge in nursing

This section provides an overview of the forms of knowledge from which nurses draw when delivering care. As previously discussed, Carper (1978) outlined four patterns of knowing considered fundamental to nursing practice. Carper refers to these knowledge domains as *empirics* or scientific knowledge, *aesthetics* or the art of nursing practice, *personal* knowledge, and *ethics* or moral knowledge. Since publication of Carper's patterns of knowing there has been an assumption within the nursing literature that non-scientific as well as scientific patterns of knowing exist (Paley et al. 2007). Empirical knowing is described as observed, factual, descriptive, replicable and generalizable, and is generated through research and scholarship. This form of knowing is akin to propositional (Kuhn 1970, Polanyi 1958) or codified knowledge (Eraut 1985, 2000). Scientific knowledge has received dominant status in healthcare decision making because of the strength of its validity and reliability when compared with the more subjective forms of knowing: aesthetics, personal and ethical knowing (Higgs and Titchen 1995). Aesthetic knowing encompasses craft and tacit knowledge, including technical skills required for care delivery and awareness of characteristics of the individual patient. Such knowledge is acquired and mastered through practice experience. This is similar to the situational knowledge described by Bucknall and Thomas (1996) that arises from a nurse's repeated exposure to particular clinical situations and settings. A nurse's decision making is influenced through constant data comparison with earlier encounters with individual patients, families, staff, equipment, policies and procedures. Personal knowing refers to knowledge of how to conduct oneself to promote a therapeutic nurse–patient relationship and learning through reflection on the nurse–patient encounter. Ethical knowing draws on an understanding of the values, norms and belief systems of individuals and groups with whom the nurse interacts. Aesthetic, personal and ethical forms of knowing equate with non-propositional (Kuhn 1970, Polanyi 1958) or personal forms of knowledge (Eraut 1985, 2000). Chinn and Kramer (2008: 2) have developed Carper's (1978) patterns of knowing to describe knowledge development and use within each pattern and the interrelationship between the patterns to produce knowing as a whole. They define *knowing* as 'ways of perceiving and understanding the self and the world'. According to Fawcett et al. (2001) the patterns of knowing described by Carper encompass most, and possibly all, knowledge required for nursing practice and provide the foundation for multiple forms of evidence.

However, White (1995) criticized Carper's definition of empirical knowledge as being too narrowly focused on realist approaches to knowing that result in knowledge which can be generalized. White calls at minimum for acknowledgement of the limitations of this definition and, preferably, for modification of the definition to include relativist approaches to knowledge generation, thereby encompassing knowledge developed from contextualized descriptions that are intended to deepen understanding of certain phenomena. White, amongst others (Fiandt et al. 2003, Hagedorn 1995), also recommends the addition of *sociopolitical knowing* to Carper's typology, to encompass knowledge related to the sociopolitical context in which nursing care delivery takes place. Chinn and Kramer (2008) term this the fifth form of knowing, emancipatory knowing, defined as 'the human capacity to critically examine the social, cultural, and political status quo' (Chinn and Kramer 2008: 4).

Having discussed conceptualizations of the different forms of knowledge from which nurses draw in their practice, we will turn to an examination of the meaning of knowledge utilization and the forms and sources of knowledge on which nurses rely.

Using knowledge in nursing

Knowledge has been defined as '*knowing* that is expressed in a form that can be shared or communicated with others' (Chinn and Kramer 2008: 2). A range of terms, including knowledge utilization, knowledge translation, knowledge transfer, innovation diffusion, research utilization and evidence-based practice are used interchangeably to describe *knowledge utilization*. Strictly speaking, these terms have different meanings.

Larsen (1980: 424) described knowledge utilization as 'a complex process involving political, organizational, socioeconomic, and attitudinal components in addition to specific information or knowledge'. Knowledge utilization has been conceptualized in terms of *instrumental* or *conceptual* utilization (Rich 1975, 1977, Weiss 1979). Instrumental utilization refers to the application of specific knowledge to practice. This may include, for example, the use of aseptic technique when undertaking a wound dressing based on knowledge of the importance of asepsis to minimization of infection. Conceptual utilization, on the other hand, refers to a change in thinking in response to research findings. Conceptual knowledge use occurs in the absence of actual application of knowledge in practice. For example, based on new knowledge the practitioner may change the way they think about the causes of eating disorders. *Symbolic* utilization has subsequently been added to the classification of knowledge utilization (Beyer and Trice 1982), and refers to the use of certain knowledge to persuade others regarding a predetermined position.

Some scholars (Loomis 1985, Shaperman and Backer 1995) maintain that research utilization is encompassed within the domain of knowledge utilization. It has been argued that research constitutes a specific type of knowledge (Estabrooks 1999, Loomis 1985). Like knowledge utilization, research utilization has been conceptualized to comprise instrumental, conceptual and symbolic forms of use (Berggren 1996, Stetler 1994a, 1994b). It has been argued that conceptual use of research is likely to be the most frequent form of research utilization employed by nurses (Estabrooks 2004). However, given the invisible nature of conceptual research use, measurement of this phenomenon presents an enormous challenge to researchers (Estabrooks 2004).

Estabrooks et al. (2005), in examining data from two ethnographic case studies, identified four groups of practice knowledge sources: social interactions, experiential knowledge, documents and *a priori* knowledge. Social interactions, involving formal and informal means of communication and information sharing amongst and between health professionals and patients, were identified as the dominant source of knowledge. Estabrooks et al. likened the social interaction and clinical experience knowledge source to Carper's (1978) aesthetic way of knowing and the professional craft knowledge described by Higgs and Titchen (1995). Experiential knowledge was the next most important source of knowledge and comprised knowledge acquired mostly from the individual's, but also from their colleagues', observations during practice. This knowledge encompassed nurses' experiences of practices that had worked or failed and their intuition. Documentary sources of knowledge included written or printed unit-based documents, such as policies, procedures, patient charts, the Internet and communication books, as well as books and journals. Finally, *a priori* knowledge was an individual's internalized knowledge and included knowledge acquired during undergraduate or postgraduate education, common sense and life experiences. In contrast with the tenets of the evidence-based practice movement, according to which empirical knowledge should take precedence, the findings of this study highlighted the tendency for nurses to privilege social interaction and experiential sources of knowledge. Reliance on these sources of knowledge in preference to what has been perceived as a more legitimate form of knowledge, empirical knowledge, has been demonstrated in other work (Gerrish and Clayton 2004, Hutchinson and Johnston 2008). In the following section we will examine the types of evidence used by nurses in their practice.

Evidence in nursing practice

A substantial global investment has been made to ensure patients receive care based on the best available evidence, despite the lack of consensus on what constitutes best evidence and the hierarchy of evidence. The concept of evidence in healthcare is based on the notion of proof and rationality. Yet, Freshwater and Rolfe (2004: 38) argue that 'the evidence for a particular practice is actually a lack of evidence against it'.

A common assumption is that evidence comprises only research evidence. In the current climate of fiscal constraint, risk management and professional accountability, greater value has been placed on quantitative research evidence to the neglect of other types of evidence. Indeed, Tonelli (2007) argued that evidence-based practice (EBP) is based on the 'fundamental primacy of empirical evidence'. He claims that hierarchies diminish the personal experience of the clinician and consider anything other than rigorously conducted, peer-reviewed published clinical research to be inferior. Similarly, Murray and colleagues (2007: 484) argue the focus of EBP movement has been 'outrageously exclusionary and dangerously normative with regards to scientific knowledge'.

In contrast, nursing has been receptive to different types of evidence. Nursing has argued in support of the contribution of different methodological approaches to generate empirical/scientific evidence, as well as promoting the value of other forms of evidence, such as clinical experience, patient experience and information from the local context (Rycroft-Malone et al. 2004). Rycroft-Malone and colleagues have advocated four sources of evidence from two theoretical paradigms: the external scientific and the internal intuitive. These paradigms are usually presented as separate and distinct. However Hamm (1988) considered both to be part of a cognitive continuum, with the rational and scientific/empirical evidence at one end and intuitive/humanistic evidence at the other. Nevertheless, Dawes and Godwin (2000) suggest that regardless of the type of evidence, it needs to be independently observed and verified.

Research evidence

Research evidence can be obtained from multiple methodological approaches even when studying the same phenomenon. Thus research evidence is frequently uncertain, rarely definitive and mostly evolutionary (Upshur 2001). Rycroft-Malone and colleagues (2004) claim research evidence is socially and historically constructed. As it is processed for local use, it becomes dynamic and eclectic in nature. Many believe that even scientific/empirical research at the 'gold standard' level requires a degree of interpretation and thus is not certain or value free as frequently portrayed (Bucknall et al. 2008a, Downie and Macnaughton 2000, Rycroft-Malone et al. 2004).

Not surprisingly, the levels of evidence and quality of the research are central to the debate on evidence. In recognition of interdisciplinary differences, the Scottish Intercollegiate Guidelines Network (SIGN) developed a standardized system to assist clinicians to appraise and grade research that was internationally adopted by the Guidelines International Network (GIN). However, the National Health and Medical Research Council (1999) in Australia departed from the conventional appraisal system and developed an approach to enable a more comprehensive assessment of research evidence. It includes the volume of evidence, consistency of results, clinical impact, generalizability and applicability of evidence to other contexts. These characteristics are rated on a scale of excellent to poor within a matrix to assist clinicians in deciding the quality and usefulness of the research.

In recognition of the value of qualitative research, other tools have been developed to assess qualitative research evidence. Qualitative researchers tend to use the term validity in a different way to quantitative researchers. Qualitative research validity is appraised in terms of rigour, credibility, trustworthiness and believability. Similar to the variability found in quantitative methods, qualitative research also needs to be conducted appropriately for each different convention.

Evidence from clinical practice/experience

Clinical practice and life experience provide a substantive contribution to a nurse's decision making. As previously discussed, knowledge derived from practical experience becomes increasingly prevalent as more experiences are obtained. Such knowledge may even present as intuitive and without rational thought. Arguably such knowledge is idiosyncratic and subject to bias and thus may lack credibility in practice when discussing the evidence for treatment decisions (Bucknall et al. 2008a). However, Stetler and colleagues (1998) assert that if clinical experience can be reflected upon, critiqued externally and then verified, it can provide evidence suitable for practice. Ferlie and colleagues (1999) suggest that research is more powerful when it combines well with clinical experiences. Conversely, if clinical experience differs from research it may not be used in practice by a clinician. Rycroft-Malone and colleagues (2004) reason that this highlights the social construction of evidence, which is only beginning to be explored.

Patient, client and carer evidence

Farrell and Gilbert (1996) present two types of patient, client and carer evidence: 1) past experience, and 2) knowledge of themselves and their condition. This type of evidence is becoming increasingly important in EBP, particularly as patients are more informed about their conditions through greater access to credible information sources. Integrating the patient perspective as a form of evidence is complex and has been the subject of little research despite considerable support for patient-centred care in nursing and calls for nurses to elicit patient preferences and opinions on treatments and care planning. It is possible that nurses who do not incorporate patient preferences with treatment plans may find lower compliance and no improvement in outcomes despite using the research evidence to inform and design care.

Contextual evidence

This type of evidence is derived from the local environment. It may include micro or macro factors related to the physical resources, staffing, type and timing of feedback systems and the culture of an organization. Although locally obtained, this type of evidence can still be systematically gathered and appraised to evaluate local outcomes. Integration of international research evidence into practice has been shown to lead to variable outcomes. It has been shown to be more dependent upon the local context, the nursing model of care and nurses' decision making responsibility than it is on the characteristics of the research evidence itself (Bucknall et al. 2008b). Rycroft-Malone et al. (2004) correctly advocate furthering our understanding of the role of local data in integration with other kinds of evidence and its influence on nurses' decision making.

   In summary, the interaction between research evidence, clinical experience, patient experience and the local context remains largely unexplored. Although the EBP movement and its supporters have led a paradigm shift away from non-scientific evidence, clearly a broader evidence base that demonstrates rigour and trustworthiness is required

(Rycroft-Malone et al. 2004). Nutley and colleagues (2002) have argued for methodological pluralism to ensure that specific practice questions are dealt with by the appropriate research technique. We will now turn to an examination of the development of knowledge utilization in nursing.

Knowing and using evidence to inform practice decisions

The development of EBP and research utilization in nursing

In the face of growing interest in EBP and research utilization, the nursing literature has been flooded with information about the limited use of research in practice and perceived barriers to research utilization. The research–practice gap has been discussed in this literature for over thirty years and many examples of apparent lack of research use by nurses have been highlighted (Gould 1986, Hunt 1981, Walsh and Ford 1989). This gap has been described as 'one of the profession's most pressing dilemmas' (Crane 1995: 567). While there is a strong theme in the nursing literature in support of research utilization to further the professional status of nurses, the primary and most morally persuasive motivation for the use of research evidence in practice is nurses' social responsibility and the potential to improve patient health outcomes and promote the health of the community. Hunt (1981) argues that, as professionals, nurses have a responsibility to themselves, their profession and most of all to their patients, to keep abreast of current knowledge and relevant research findings.

The establishment of research utilization in nursing has been traced to the work of Florence Nightingale and her use of systematically collected epidemiological data to influence social policy (McDonald 2001). In 1952, *Nursing Research* commenced publication as the first nursing journal devoted purely to publication of nursing research. However, it was not until the early 1970s that the first efforts were made to address the nursing research–practice gap (Estabrooks et al. 2004, Titler 1993, Titler et al. 2001). In 1970, a study conducted by the Royal College of Nursing (RCN) to evaluate the effectiveness of nursing care in the United Kingdom provided some evidence of the research–practice gap (McFarlane 1970). In 1972, the first study to explore research utilization by nurses was published (Shore 1972).

In the mid- to late 1970s, the first of a number of research utilization models began to emerge. These models were intended to provide a framework to facilitate the translation of research into practice. Early and well-known models included the Conduct and Utilisation of Research in Nursing (CURN) Model (Horsley et al. 1978, Horsley et al. 1983), the Western Institute Commission for Higher Education in Nursing (WICHEN) Model (Krueger et al. 1978, Lindeman and Krueger 1977), the Nursing Child Assessment Satellite Training (NCAST) Model (Barnard and Hoehn 1978), the Stetler-Marram Model (later the Stetler Model) (Stetler 1994b, 2001, Stetler and Marram 1976), the Iowa Model of Research in Practice (Titler et al. 1994, Titler et al. 2001) and the Ottawa Model of Research Use (Logan and Graham 1998). More recently, the Multidimensional Framework of Research Utilisation, developed by the Royal College of Nursing Research Institute, has received considerable attention in the literature (Harvey et al. 2002, A. Kitson et al. 1998, Kitson et al. 2008, McCormack et al. 2002, Rycroft-Malone et al. 2002, Rycroft-Malone et al. 2004).

While nursing research utilization models were being developed, implemented and evaluated, and demonstration projects and programmes promoted research utilization, research designed to explore the extent of and factors influencing research utilization by nurses began to increase. Interest in the field grew and, further influenced by the advent of the EBP movement, there was a surge in research utilization activities in nursing during the 1990s (Estabrooks et al. 2004).

The EBP movement gained momentum in the early 1990s in Canada (Evidence-Based Medicine Working Group 1992), drawing the attention of the international medical community to the importance of incorporating research findings into practice. As such the EBP movement has largely been medically driven and the term 'evidence-based medicine' has been widely adopted. In 1998 the *Evidence-Based Nursing* journal was launched and the term evidence-based nursing was added to the nomenclature by DiCenso and colleagues (1998) who argued that evidence-based decision making in nursing takes into consideration 'clinical expertise, patient preference for alternative forms of care, clinical research evidence, and available resources' (DiCenso et al. 1998: 38). Also in the 1990s, a number of initiatives were implemented to promote the use of research in practice, including the establishment of the Cochrane Collaboration and Cochrane Library; the National Institute for Clinical Effectiveness in the United Kingdom; the Nursing Research Initiative for Scotland; the Joanna Briggs Institute in Australia and New Zealand; the Agency for Healthcare Research and Quality in the United States; and the Canadian Health Services Research Foundation.

The twenty-first century has witnessed an increase in international cooperation and collaborative efforts to examine the effectiveness of interventions to promote the uptake of research evidence (Estabrooks et al. 2004). Funding bodies have recognized the importance of knowledge utilization and funding opportunities that focus on knowledge translation have created further impetus for research in this field (Estabrooks et al.

2004). An increase in interdisciplinary approaches to overcome barriers to research use and formulate strategies to implement evidence-based changes in practice has also been evident (Estabrooks et al. 2004). In 2004, *Worldviews on Evidence-Based Nursing*, a publication of Sigma Theta Tau International, was launched in recognition of the importance of nurses acquiring an evidential base for their practice. In Australia, the Royal College of Nursing (1998) sought to uphold and promote a culture of research use and EBP through its Position Statement on Nursing Research, which states: 'By providing sound evidence for nursing practices, the way is paved for quality outcomes in nursing. A prerequisite for this development is an environment in which research is widely appreciated and positively nurtured for its real contribution to improving the quality of nursing practice' (Royal College of Nursing 1998: 1). At an international level, the International Council of Nurses' (unpublished) 2008 'Nursing research: a tool for action' urges nurses to seek and use new knowledge, including research evidence in their practice, and emphasizes nurses' societal obligation to practice in accordance with current, scientifically defensible evidence.

Models and frameworks to guide the translation of evidence into practice

As previously noted, since the 1970s several scholars have sought to develop nursing models for research utilization. The models have tended to focus upon problem identification, and most have identified the individual practitioner as the key player in the research utilization process (Stetler 1994b, 2001, Stetler and Marram 1976). In addition, some models have sought to address organizational issues related to research utilization (Horsley et al. 1978, Horsley et al. 1983, Titler et al. 1994). All models have, however, identified a committed and supportive environment as being important to the process of research utilization. The models tend to be prescriptive in nature, assume the individual will rationally choose to use research findings and that research utilization is a linear process (Estabrooks 2001, Kitson et al. 1998, Kitson et al. 2008). By contrast, Kitson, Harvey and McCormack (1998) offer a multidimensional framework that represents the interaction between many factors that influence the utilization of research in practice. They argue that the effectiveness of efforts to integrate research into practice is determined by the simultaneous interaction between 'three core elements – the level and nature of the evidence, the context or environment into which the research is to be placed, and the method or way in which the process is facilitated' (Kitson et al. 1998: 149).

Rogers (2003) has written extensively on the subject of diffusion of innovation and his classic and oft-cited work *Diffusion of Innovations* has been extremely influential in promoting the innovation diffusion conceptual paradigm. According to this theory, an innovation such as a new idea, practice or object is communicated, over time, through social systems representing those involved in joint problem solving to achieve a common goal. Nursing has drawn extensively on Rogers' work in exploring issues surrounding research utilization and the research–practice gap (Brett 1987, 1989, Funk et al. 1995, Funk et al. 1991a, 1991b, Horsley et al. 1983, Kirchhoff 1982, Michel and Sneed 1995). In the following section we examine the process of decision making in practice.

Making decisions in the real world

Clinical decision making involves locating, comparing and evaluating information to form an opinion or judgement about future patient treatments or plans for care. The accessibility and availability of evidence to make those decisions is a critical requirement for decision making and is therefore a key attribute for the profession (Bucknall et al. 2008a). The discussion surrounding types of evidence assumes that if evidence is available to support the correct treatment options then that knowledge will be used to treat an individual. In fact the uptake of research may depend on the type of research, the patient population concerned, the characteristics of the individuals using the research and the context in which the research is being applied. Given the interplay between these factors, it is not surprising that research uptake has been historically slow (Melnyk et al. 2004).

Nevertheless, patients and families are reassured when a nurse displays competent clinical judgement and a caring manner in delivering patient-centred care. Patient-centred care occurs when a nurse engages with the patient to establish their preferences for treatment and support. Kitson (2002) highlighted the importance of establishing individualized relationships with patients as critical to the nature of nursing. This would suggest that practice knowledge is socially constructed, derived from a variety of sources and may be weighted differently during different encounters, even with the same patient. Downie and Macnaughton (2000) support Kitson in recognizing that scientific facts (wherever derived) only become evidence when the information is applied to a specific patient. Frequently, clinical decisions are based on a mixture of factual information and value judgements, made with varying amounts of relevant information, from a variety of sources, in a climate of significant uncertainty (Bucknall et al. 2008a). Therefore, in determining treatment, information must be judged to be important enough and relevant to the specific situation (Downie and Macnaughton 2000).

Although a critical component in clinical decision making is a nurse's individual knowledge, values and capabilities, the specific context of a nurse's decision making will often be an influencing factor for an individual's decision (Bucknall et al. 2008a). For example, restricted access to resources may mean that certain information is unavailable or it is not available in a timely manner. Resource availability has been shown to impact on the types, speed and processing of nurses' decisions in critical care (Bucknall and Thomas 1996). Technology may be time-saving and offer clearer, consistent and objective measurements, thereby improving communication, decreasing the risk in patient treatment decisions and ultimately improving patient outcomes. Staffing mix (different levels of education and experience among nurses) has also been shown to influence patient outcomes (Aiken et al. 2003). Thus, the balance between the level of education and experience amongst nurses can mean specific evidence may be available but overlooked or dismissed due to lack of knowledge; consequently treatment decisions may vary between nurses.

Just as contexts and the relationships between patients and nurses influence decisions, so do interprofessional relationships and interactions. Experiential hierarchies, appointment levels, interdisciplinary role boundaries, teamwork and organizational culture exert influences that have rarely been explored in relation to the use of evidence, although Firth-Couzens (2001) has argued that increased communication and collaboration within and across healthcare teams is more likely to increase the use of evidence in actual clinical decisions. Similarly, with greater access to information through technological advancements and increasing calls for shared decision making between clinicians and consumers, input from patients and families may also promote the use of research in practice.

In summary, the type of patient problem confronting the nurse, the available evidence to support nursing care decisions and the context within which the decisions are being made will determine the use of evidence and the importance placed upon it. By ensuring nurses are aware of contextual influences on their decisions in practice, and knowledge of evidence available to support their decisions, better nursing practice and improved patient outcomes should be the end result.

Conclusion

This chapter has focused on the nature and sources of nursing knowledge and the use of knowledge to inform clinical practice. In particular, we have considered its development and contribution to nursing practice in a rapidly changing healthcare context. We have examined sources of knowledge, both traditional and non-traditional approaches that reflect the socially constructed, dynamic and personalized nature of nursing care. For this reason, there is increasing support in the profession for the simultaneous development of theory and practice, that is, the generation of informal theories from contemplating unique patient situations. Whilst this approach could overcome the criticisms regarding the gap between theory and practice, there are also criticisms about the impracticality of such knowledge development in the real world of clinical practice whereby significant time constraints, amongst other barriers, exist.

Nonetheless, these practical challenges also offer opportunities to explore new ways of thinking. New technologies and greater consumer input into decision making regarding treatments and plans for care afford clinicians new possibilities in blending traditional with non-traditional knowledge to create new knowledge for clinical practice.

References

Aiken, L.H., Clarke, S.P. and Cheung, R.B. 2003. Educational levels of hospital nurses and surgical patient mortality. *Journal of the American Medical Association*, 290(12), 1617–23.

Barnard, K.E. and Hoehn, R.E. 1978. *Nursing Child Assessment Satellite Training: Final Report*. Seattle: Washington University Press.

Benner, P. 1984. *From Novice to Expert*. Menlo Park: Addison-Wesley Publishing).

Berggren, A. 1996. Swedish midwives' awareness of, attitudes to and use of selected research findings. *Journal of Advanced Nursing*, 23(3), 462–70.

Beyer, J.M. and Trice, H.M. 1982. The utilization process: a conceptual framework and synthesis of empirical findings. *Administrative Science Quarterly*, 27, 591–622.

Brett, J.L.L. 1987. Use of nursing practice research findings. *Nursing Research*, 36(6), 344–9.

Brett, J.L.L. 1989. Organizational integrative mechanisms and adoption of innovations by nurses. *Nursing Research*, 38(2), 105–10.

Bucknall, T. and Thomas, S. 1996. Critical care nurse satisfaction with levels of involvement in clinical decisions. *Journal of Advanced Nursing*, 23(3), 571–7.

Bucknall, T.K., Kent, B. and Manley, K. 2008a. Evidence use and evidence generation in practice development, in *International Practice Development in Nursing and Healthcare*, edited by K. Manley, B. McCormack, and V. Wilson. Oxford: Blackwell Publishing, 84–104.

Bucknall, T.K., Manias, E.M. and Presneill, J. 2008b. A randomized trial of protocol-directed sedation management for mechanical ventilation in an Australian intensive care unit. *Critical Care Medicine*, 36(5), 1444–50.

Carper, B.A. 1978. Fundamental patterns of knowing in nursing. *Advances in Nursing Science*, 1(1), 13–23.

Chinn, P.L. and Kramer, M.K. 2008. *Integrated Theory and Knowledge Development in Nursing.* 7th Edition. St Louis: Mosby Elsevier.

Crane, J. 1995. The future of research utilization. *Nursing Clinics of North America*, 30(3), 565–77.

Dawes, M. and Godwin, M. 2000. Global medical knowledge database is proposed. *British Medical Journal*, 320, 1340.

DiCenso, A., Cullum, N. and Ciliska, D. 1998. Implementing evidence-based nursing: some misconceptions. *Evidence-Based Nursing*, 1(1), 38–40.

Downie, R.S. and Macnaughton, J. 2000. *Clinical Judgement: Evidence in Practice.* New York: Oxford University Press.

Eraut, M. 1985. Knowledge creation and knowledge use in professional contexts. *Studies in Higher Education*, 10(2), 117–33.

Eraut, M. 2000. Non-formal learning and tacit knowledge in professional work. *British Journal of Educational Psychology*, 70, 113–36.

Estabrooks, C.A. 1999. The conceptual structure of research utilisation. *Research in Nursing and Health*, 22, 203–16.

Estabrooks, C.A. 2001. Research utilization and qualitative research, in *The Nature of Qualitative Evidence*, edited by J.M. Morse, J.M. Swanson and A.J. Kuzel. Thousand Oaks: Sage, 275–98.

Estabrooks, C.A. 2004. Thoughts on evidence-based nursing and its science – a Canadian perspective. *Worldviews on Evidence-Based Nursing*, 1(2), 88–91.

Estabrooks, C.A., Scott-Findlay, S. and Winther, C. 2004. A nursing and allied health sciences perspective on knowledge utilization, in *Using Knowledge and Evidence in Health Care. Multidisciplinary Perspectives*, edited by L. Lemieux-Charles and F. Champagne. Toronto: University of Toronto Press, 242–80.

Estabrooks, C.A., Rutakumwa, W., O'Leary, K.A., Profetto-McGrath, J., Milner, M., Levers, M.J. and Scott-Findlay, S. 2005. Sources of practice knowledge among nurses. *Qualitative Health Research*, 15(4), 460–76.

Evidence-Based Medicine Working Group. 1992. A new approach to teaching the practice of medicine. *Journal of the American Medical Association*, 268, 2420–2425.

Farrell, C. and Gilbert, H. 1996. *Health Care Partnerships: Debates and Strategies for Increasing Patient Involvement in Health Care and Health Services.* Kings Fund.

Fawcett, J. 2000. *Analysis and Evaluation of Contemporary Nursing Knowledge: Nursing Models and Theories.* 1st Edition. Philadelphia: F.A. Davis Company).

Fawcett, J., Watson, J., Neuman, B., Walker, P.H. and Fitzpatrick, J.J. 2001. On nursing theories and evidence. *Journal of Nursing Scholarship*, 33(2), 115–19.

Ferlie, E., Wood, M. and Fitzgerald, L. 1999. Some limits to evidence-based medicine: a case study from elective orthopaedics. *Quality in Health Care*, 8, 99–107.

Fiandt, K., Forman, J., Erickson, M.M., Pakieser, R.A. and Burge, S. 2003. Integral nursing: an emerging framework for engaging the evolution of the profession. *Nursing Outlook*, 51(3), 130–37.

Firth-Couzens, J. 2001. Cultures for improving patient safety through learning: the role of teamwork. *Quality In Health Care*, 10, Supplement II, ii26–ii31.

Freshwater, D. and Rolfe, G. 2004. *Deconstructing Evidence-based Practice*. Abingdon: Routledge.

Funk, S.G., Champagne, M.T., Tornquist, E.M. and Wiese, R. 1995. Administrators' views on barriers to research utilization. *Applied Nursing Research*, 8(1), 44–9.

Funk, S.G., Champagne, M.T., Wiese, R.A. and Tornquist, E.M. 1991a. Barriers to using research findings in practice: the clinician's perspective. *Applied Nursing Research*, 4(2), 90–95.

Funk, S.G., Champagne, M.T., Wiese, R.A. and Tornquist, E.M. 1991b. Barriers: the barriers to research utilization scale. *Applied Nursing Research*, 4(1), 39–45.

Gadamer, H. 1996. *The Enigma of Health: The Art of Healing in a Scientific Age*. Stanford: Stanford University Press.

Gerrish, K. and Clayton, J. 2004. Promoting evidence-based practice: an organizational approach. *Journal of Nursing Management*, 12, 114–23.

Gortner, S.R. 1990. Nursing values and science: toward a science philosophy. *Journal of Nursing Scholarship*, 22(2), 101–5.

Gould, D. 1986. Pressure sore prevention and treatment: an example of nurses' failure to implement research findings. *Journal of Advanced Nursing*, 11(4), 389–94.

Hagedorn, S. 1995. The politics of caring. The role of activism in primary care. *Advances in Nursing Science*, 17(4), 1–11.

Hamm, R.M. 1988. Clinical intuition and clinical analysis: expertise and the cognitive continuum, in *Professional Judgment: A Reader in Clinical Decision Making*, edited by J. Dowie and A. Elstein. Cambridge: Cambridge University Press, 78–106.

Harvey, G., Loftus-Hills, A., Rycroft-Malone, J., Titchen, A., Kitson, A., McCormack, B. and Seers, K. 2002. Getting evidence into practice: the role and function of facilitation. *Journal of Advanced Nursing*, 37(6), 577–88.

Higgs, J. and Titchen, A. 1995. The nature, generation and verification of knowledge. *Physiotherapy*, 81(9), 521–30.

Horsley, J.A., Crane, J. and Bingle, J.D. 1978. Research utilization as an organizational process. *Journal of Nursing Administration*, 8(7), 4–6.

Horsley, J.A., Crane, J., Crabtree, M.K. and Wood, D.J. 1983. *Using Research to Improve Nursing Practice: A Guide*. New York: Grune and Stratton.

Hunt, J. 1981. Indicators for nursing practice: the use of research findings. *Journal of Advanced Nursing*, 6, 189–94.

Hutchinson, A.M. and Johnston, L. 2008. An observational study of health professionals' use of evidence to inform the development of clinical management tools. *Journal of Clinical Nursing*, 17(16), 2203–11.

Kirchhoff, K.T. 1982. A diffusion survey of coronary precautions. *Nursing Research*, 31(4), 196–201.

Kitson, A. 2002. Recognising relationships: reflections on evidence-based practice. *Nursing Inquiry*, 9(3), 179–86.

Kitson, A., Harvey, G. and McCormack, B. 1998. Enabling the implementation of evidence based practice: a conceptual framework. *Quality in Health Care*, 7, 149–158.

Kitson, A.L., Rycroft-Malone, J., Harvey, G., McCormack, B., Seers, K. and Titchen, A. 2008. Evaluating the Successful Implementation of Evidence into Practice Using the PARiHS Framework: Theoretical and Practical Challenges. *Implementation Science* [Online], 3(1). Available at: http://www.implementationscience.com/content/3/1/1/abstract/ [accessed: 7 January 2008].

Krueger, J., Nelson, A. and Wolanin, M. 1978. *Nursing Research: Development, Collaboration, and Utilization*. Germantown: Aspen.

Kuhn, T.S. 1970. *The Structure of Scientific Revolutions*. 2nd Edition. Chicago: University of Chicago Press.

Larsen, J.K. 1980. Knowledge utilization. What is it? *Knowledge: Creation, Diffusion, Utilization*, 1(3), 421–42.

Lindeman, C.A. and Krueger, J. 1977. Increasing the quality, quantity, and use of nursing research. *Nursing Outlook*, 25(7), 450–54.

Logan, J.O. and Graham, I.D. 1998. Toward a comprehensive interdisciplinary model of health care research use. *Science Communication*, 20(2), 227–46.

Loomis, M.E. 1985. Knowledge utilization and research utilization in nursing. *Image: The Journal of Nursing Scholarship*, XVII(2), 35–9.

McCormack, B., Kitson, A., Harvey, G., Rycroft-Malone, J., Titchen, A. and Seers, K. 2002. Getting evidence into practice: the meaning of 'context'. *Journal of Advanced Nursing*, 38(1), 94–104.

McDonald, L. 2001. Florence Nightingale and the early origins of evidence-based nursing. *Evidence-Based Nursing*, 4, 68–9.

McFarlane, J.K. 1970. *The Proper Study of the Nurse*. London: Royal College of Nursing.

McKenna, H. 2004. Foreword, *Knowledge for Contemporary Nursing Practice*, edited by P.C.K. Rawlings-Anderson. Edinburgh: Mosby.

Meleis, A.I. 1997. *Theoretical Nursing: Development and Progress*. 3rd Edition. Philadelphia: J.B. Lippincott.

Melnyk, B.M., Rycroft-Malone, J. and Bucknall, T. 2004. Sparking a change to evidence-based practice in health care organizations. *Worldviews on Evidence-Based Nursing*, 1(2), 83–4.

Michel, Y. and Sneed, N.V. 1995. Dissemination and use of research findings in nursing practice. *Journal of Professional Nursing*, 11(5), 306–11.

Murray, S.J., Holmes, D., Perron, A. and Rail, G. 2007. No exit? Intellectual integrity under the regime of 'evidence' and 'best practice'. *Journal of Evaluation in Clinical Practice*, 13, 512–16.

National Health and Medical Research Council. 1999. *A Guide to the Development, Implementation, and Evaluation of Clinical Practice Guidelines*. Canberra: National Health and Medical Research Council.

Nutley, S., Davies, H. and Walter, I. 2002. Evidence Based Policy and Practice: Cross Sector Lessons from the UK, Research Unit for Research Utilisation. Available at:http://www.st-andrews.ac.uk/%7Eruru/NZ%20conference%20paper%20final%20170602.pdf [accessed: 11 March 2004].

Paley, J., Cheyne, H., Dalgleish, L., Duncan, E.A.S. and Niven, C.A. 2007. Nursing's ways of knowing and dual process theories of cognition. *Journal of Advanced Nursing*, 60(6), 692–701.

Polanyi, M. 1958. *Personal Knowledge: Towards a Post-Critical Philosophy*. London: Routledge and Kegan Paul.

Rich, R.F. 1975. Selective utilization of social science related information by federal policy-makers. *Inquiry*, XII, 239–45.

Rich, R.F. 1977. Uses of social science information by federal bureaucrats: knowledge for action versus knowledge for understanding, in *Uses of Social Research in Public Policy*, edited by C.H. Weiss. Lexington: DC Heath, 199–211.

Rogers, E.M. 2003. *Diffusion of Innovations*. Fifth Edition. New York: Free Press.

Rolfe, G. 2006. Nursing praxis and science of the unique. *Nursing Science Quarterly*, 19(1), 39–43.

Rolfe, G. and Gardner, L. 2005. Towards a geology of evidence-based practice: a discussion paper. *International Journal of Nursing Studies*, 43, 903–13.

Royal College of Nursing. 1998. *Position Statement: Nursing Research*. Australian Capital Territory: Royal College of Nursing.

Rycroft-Malone, J., Kitson, A., Harvey, G., McCormack, B., Seers, K., Titchen, A. and Estabrooks, C. 2002. Ingredients for change: revisiting a conceptual framework. *Quality and Safety in Health Care*, 11(2), 174–80.

Rycroft-Malone, J., Seers, K., Titchen, A., Harvey, G., Kitson, A. and McCormack, B. 2004. What counts as evidence in evidence-based practice? *Journal of Advanced Nursing*, 47(1), 81–90.

Schön, D. 1983. *The Reflective Practitioner. How Professionals Think in Action*. London: Temple Smith.

Shaperman, J. and Backer, T.E. 1995. The role of knowledge utilization in adopting innovations from academic medical centers. *Hospital and Health Services Administration*, 40, 401–13.

Shore, H.L. 1972. Adopters and laggards. *The Canadian Nurse*, 68(7), 36–9.

Stetler, C.B. 1994a. Problems and issues of research utilization, in *Nursing Issues in the 1990s*, edited by O.L. Strickland and D.L. Fishman. New York: Delmar, 459–70.

Stetler, C.B. 1994b. Refinement of the Stetler/Marram model for application of research findings to practice. *Nursing Outlook*, 42, 15–25.

Stetler, C.B. 2001. Updating the Stetler model of research utilization to facilitate evidence-based practice. *Nursing Outlook*, 49(6), 272–9.

Stetler, C.B. and Marram, G. 1976. Evaluating research findings for applicability in practice. *Nursing Outlook*, 24(9), 559–63.

Stetler, C.B., Brunell, M., Giuliano, K.K., Morsi, D., Prince, L. and Newell-Stokes, V. 1998. Evidence-based practice and the role of nursing leadership. *Journal of Nursing Administration*, 28(7/8), 45–53.

Titler, M.G. 1993. Critical analysis of research utilisation (RU): an historical perspective. *American Journal of Critical Care*, 2, 264.

Titler, M.G., Kleiber, C., Steelman, V., Goode, C., Rakel, B., Barry-Walker, J., Small, S. and Buckwalter, K. 1994. Infusing research into practice to promote quality care. *Nursing Research*, 43(5), 307–13.

Titler, M.G., Kleiber, C., Steelman, V.J., Rakel, B.A., Budreau, G., Everett, L.Q., et al. 2001. The Iowa model of evidence-based practice to promote quality care. *Critical Care Nursing Clinics of North America*, 13(4), 497–509.

Tonelli, M.R. 2007. Advancing a causistic model of clinical decision making: a response to commentators. *Journal of Evaluation in Clinical Practice*, 13, 504–7.

Upshur, R.E.G. 2001. The status of qualitative research as evidence, in *The Nature of Qualitative Evidence*, edited by J.M. Morse, J.M. Swanson and A.J. Kuzel, Thousand Oaks: Sage, 5–26.

Walsh, M. and Ford, P. 1989. *Nursing Rituals: Research, and Rational Action*. Oxford: Butterworth Heinemann.

Weiss, C.H. 1979. The many meanings of research utilization. *Public Administration Review*, Sept./Oct., 426–31.

White, J. 1995. Patterns of knowing: review, critique, and update. *Advances in Nursing Science*, 17(4), 73–86.

8 The risky business of birth

Frances Sheean and Jennifer M. Cameron

Exemplar 1

The obstetrician and the midwife left the woman's room. The woman was recovering from an emergency caesarean section performed for an episode of antepartum haemorrhage at 35 weeks gestation. This was her fifth baby. During the visit the obstetrician recommended that the woman have a CT pelvimetry before she embarked on another pregnancy. Outside the room the midwife asked the obstetrician why he was recommending a pelvimetry as the woman had previously, on four occasions, birthed vaginally and spontaneously, babies weighing between 3.9 kg and 5 kg. The midwife commented that as far as she could see there was no useful clinical information to be gained by this examination. The obstetrician agreed but said it was for medico legal reasons. As the woman was intending to have more children, she would be in a high risk category next time; that is, she would probably wish to birth vaginally and a pelvimetry is a reasonable examination to perform prior to a vaginal birth after caesarean section (VBAC). In most instances this is true but in this case the woman had proven that she had a more than adequate pelvis for birthing. Aside from the examination being a poor use of public money, the information obtained would not contribute to clinical decision making.

The discourse around risk related to childbirth has formed the modern day underpinnings of the historically strained relationship between obstetrics and midwifery. Whilst both groups of health professionals work closely in practice and with the well-being of the mother and baby as the agreed desired outcome, their paths diverge regarding the way in which this outcome is achieved (Darra and Norris 2008). In practice this often results in territorial behaviour, tension and competition between the two groups, which is not surprising given the long history of philosophical difference between the two professions.

History of maternity care providers

Throughout history the woman giving birth was attended by women who learned their craft from other women. How these early midwives, and the care they gave to childbearing women, were perceived reflects in many ways the social conditions of the time. Midwives were alternatively lauded or reviled. At the time of Hippocrates and Socrates (circa 500 BC) midwives had social recognition and were an honoured class (Towler and Bramall 1986), but in the fourteenth and fifteenth centuries midwives were tried as witches and burned at the stake at the behest of the Church (Ehrenreich and English 1973).

In the eleventh century the first medical school in Christendom was established in Italy and in the thirteenth century learning centres were established at Oxford and Cambridge, but women were excluded from these early universities. The universities took over medical teaching from the Church and they set up medical schools for 'young men of means' (Towler and Bramall 1986). From such early times, there was a separation of the roles of healthcare workers along the lines of education, economic circumstances and gender. Prior to the seventeenth century care of childbearing women was almost exclusively provided by women (Donnison 1988), but in the 1730s the Chamberlen brothers introduced the obstetric forceps (Willis 1989). Since man-midwives were the only practitioners permitted to use the forceps, they began to replace midwives at births, with the result that there was a decline in the status of midwives. Man-midwives, who were the earlier versions of modern day obstetricians, saw the midwife as 'a social, political, and economic impediment to the development of obstetrics' and instituted a political programme to eliminate the midwife, who was perceived in terms of competition (Arney 1982: 3). As obstetrics became professionalized, obstetricians were able to use their power to exert occupational imperialism (Larkin 1983) by deciding what work would be done and by whom. According to Arney, 'obstetrics organized itself as a continuously hierarchical, ubiquitously present team' (1982: 8), and midwifery practice became defined by the economic and territorial needs of institutions and medical staff instead of the best interests of mothers and babies or society as a whole (Goodman 2007).

Since the time of Agnodice, the Greek woman who practised maternity care disguised as a man (Towler and Bramall 1986), medicine attempted to control midwives' work by ensuring that all changes to maternity care were introduced on the physicians' terms (Witz 1992). Medicine was happy for midwives to take over some of the technical tasks they consider menial, for example, siting of intravenous therapy, perineal suturing and ultrasounds, but as midwives took on these roles there was less time for the core midwifery skills of being 'with women'.

Hospitals

Midwives lost power because birth moved to lying-in hospitals and they were forbidden to use pharmacological pain control (Towler and Bramall 1986) and wealthier clients enlisted care from those who could. The numbers of women birthing in hospitals gradually increased until the 1950s when virtually all babies were born in hospital (Tew 1995). Hospitals became the venues where there was a concentration of medical officers and increasingly sophisticated technology, and obstetric departments in universities and hospitals grew rapidly. But with the increased emphasis on science, the interest was in the biochemical and physiological aspects of birth not the psychosocial components (Tew 1995). Normality in childbirth was redefined to include a range of interventions, and since obstetricians could never accurately predict complications, all 'patients' had to come under their care. Women accept the dominant discourse because they are in unfamiliar surroundings where medicine is obviously in control and so the existing social order is maintained.

The policy of hospital births was an effective means of reducing the power and status of midwives, as obstetricians gained a competitive edge over their professional rivals – midwives (Arney 1982). Obstetricians set out on a propaganda campaign, as they had in the past, to ensure that all confidence was centred in them. At the same time they undermined midwives and were highly successful in destroying women's belief in their own ability to birth (Mander 2002) as labour was induced, accelerated and otherwise actively managed. The effect of this pervasive power is that specialists caring for women experiencing medical problems during childbearing had control of the care of women experiencing no medical problems.

Ways of knowing

Both obstetrics and midwifery have unique bodies of knowledge and also shared knowledge, but it is how these bodies of knowledge are used that is the major interest. Despite having complementary roles in the care of childbearing women, the differences in outlook between the two professions are vast, with obstetricians claiming that maternal and foetal morbidity are very low due to current practices and midwives arguing that intervention rates are too high (Weaver et al. 2005). In part these views are associated with what is considered valid knowledge. When one form of knowledge is given power, other ways of *knowing of* are marginalized and the adherents are seen as retrogressive (Wagner 2001). For this reason, professions may claim a science base to their knowledge to gain legitimacy as science is seen to be superior knowledge (Jordan 1997).

Scientific knowing

In days gone by, when the midwife learnt her craft from her mother, one of the most valued forms of knowledge was experience. As men gained access to formal education, philosophers, for example, Socrates and Plato, wrote their ideas (Wickham 2007) and rejected the old ways of knowing. In their view true knowledge was abstract, therefore skilled activity did not constitute true knowledge (Davis 1995). In the seventeenth century Descartes' writings separated the mind and body which formed the basis of objectivity required in scientific research. Science was valued because it was written and since men decided what was written and how it was disseminated the subjugation of experience and women's ways of knowing was complete.

Medicine grew out of the scientific movement and today still proudly claims it is based on science. However, science was often given credit for treatments when in reality any improvement was simply due to the body's ability to heal itself or, in the words of Voltaire (1694–1778), '[T]he art of medicine consists in amusing the patient while nature cures the disease'. Modern medicine still practices under the guise of science even when there is no evidence. In the middle of the twentieth century medicine convinced governments that it was medical care that produced a marked fall in foetal, infant and maternal morbidity and mortality. This view was readily accepted by governments because of the symbiotic power relationships between the two groups to maintain legitimate power (Fahy 2008). The argument persisted until the 1970s when it was recognized that foetal and maternal health improved because of public health measures, for example, improved housing, sanitation and water supplies. However 'obstetric discourses are powerful because they have the sanction of society' (Fahy 2002: 12).

While the hierarchy of evidence in medicine privileges randomized controlled trials (RCT) because of their scientific strength, they are not always appropriate in maternity care. For example, the available information may not be applicable to a particular woman's needs or it may be unethical to conduct an RCT because social and psychological issues are not amenable to them. Sensitivity measures such as Confidence Intervals are being included in research analyses but the uncertainty is not translated into practice (Downe and McCourt 2008). Despite medicine's claim to a scientific base, much of its knowledge is founded in personal experience and opinion.

Some practices have been changed because research has demonstrated that they had little or no value, for example, routine enemas and shaving of the perineum. However, despite the emphasis on evidence-based medicine, medical practitioners have been slow to acknowledge the evidence that midwifery care results in decreased intervention and increased satisfaction (e.g. Hatem et al. 2008). The power of authoritative knowledge is not that it is correct but that it counts (Jordan 1997).

Technical knowing

The analogy of the 'body as machine' arose from the scientific movement. For pregnant women the implication is that even well running machines can break down and therefore women with 'low-risk' pregnancies must be watched closely. When the machine breaks down it is repaired from the outside, usually with more technology, and the cascade of interventions is commenced (Davis-Floyd 2001). Safety and security are determined by parameters measured by the machine not by clinician's expertise. Yet normal birth, among other issues, depends on confidence because physiological progress is dependent on the woman's psychological state, which is also influenced by the attitudes of her caregivers (Leap 2000, Odent 2008).

Unfortunately, with the emphasis on science, there is little attention to the art of medicine, that is, what happens when the technology produces information. Clinicians working with childbearing women must deal with uncertainty, but because the focus of midwifery is to accentuate the normal and obstetrics is to highlight the abnormal, invariably there will be differences when interpreting the same data (Stewart 2001). This is illustrated in Exemplar 1. The obstetrician saw only the possibility of problems with future births and acted on that belief; whereas the midwife took the woman's previous history and the current clinical data into account to come to a different conclusion.

Because obstetrics claims that birth can only be normal in retrospect, the woman must be placed under surveillance to identify potential risk factors, although this would be carefully cloaked in the discourse of safety. Surveillance is achieved with the use of the 'electronic belly hand', which is precise but captures fewer signals than the midwife's hand (Blaaka and Schauer 2008: 351), and the emphasis is on the machine not on the woman. Problems arise when the machine's readings take over as legitimate knowledge and have greater credence than the clinician's assessment. An example is in the use of the electronic cardiotocography (CTG) when foetal death is suspected, or indeed has occurred since the CTG was commenced. The machine will produce a trace whether the foetus is alive or not and delay the inevitable realization that the foetus is dead or delay lifesaving measures while there is time for resuscitation. A skilled midwife can use the technology intelligently, interpret the results and act accordingly. However, technology can and does control the midwife's work, because a technical rationality encroaches upon the midwifery view of birth as a physiological process because the machinery does not allow for trust in a woman's body to birth.

Technology is not inherently bad, but most technology has been introduced into practice without supporting research, yet those who forego the use of technology are considered by the medical profession to be remiss or even negligent (Wagner 1994). The expert practitioner needs to consider a range of information so that options for treatment may be offered to the woman.

Tacit knowing

While science relies on absolute truth, practice very rarely represents textbook cases, so clinicians must improvise with a 'kind of intuitive understanding' that enables them to manage the situation competently (Schön 1987: 5). Intuitive understandings are derived from practice and are based on experience and expertise, which can be considered hidden experiential knowledge. Polanyi (1966) used the term 'tacit knowing' to describe personal knowledge that is embedded in experience, and Benner (1984) argued that this form of knowing is based on experience and pattern recognition. Experienced clinicians are able to process a number of issues simultaneously but have difficulty explaining how they arrived at their decisions.

Midwives make decisions based on review of clinical assessments, technology outputs and knowing the woman. When a midwife has the opportunity to work with a woman for the duration of the childbearing experience, a deep knowing develops and trust results. The trust is mutual in that the woman trusts the midwife and the midwife trusts the woman's ability to birth her baby. Even when care is fragmented the midwife provides continuous care during labour, and she is able to consider spiritual and psychosocial issues when interpreting biophysical parameters. Often the obstetrician does not have access to this information, since his visits are intermittent and only biophysical measurements are recorded. What is not recorded is not considered important.

Tacit knowledge is not the antithesis of scientific knowledge practice. Tacit knowledge combines all ways of knowing so that the clinicians have a well-stocked 'tool box' of knowledge and skills into which they can delve when the need arises. Despite the purported differences in the ways of knowing between obstetrics and midwifery, in practice the differences are not real. What does become apparent when there are differences in interpretation is that the exercise of power and knowledge is always subject to politics.

Challenges to the status quo

The definitions of midwife and obstetrician create an immediate difference in the clinician's relationship with the woman – midwife to be 'with woman' and obstetrician to 'stand before' (Mander 2004). Midwives regard childbirth as a physiological, normal healthy social act and one which usually requires no intervention. For obstetrics healthy and normal translates as 'low risk'; complicated pregnancies are 'high risk', thus women are classified into a 'risk' category regardless of their health status. Not only have medical practitioners been able to control the political, social and economic factors that impinged on their practice as was befitting for the status of professional, they have also controlled the patient (Arney and Neill 2004). The knowledge of medicine is seen to be of 'higher value' because it is based on science and of course it has a long history of being written. Midwifery, on the other hand, has a long history of oral transmission of knowledge as information was handed from mother to daughter and women traditionally had no access to universities. When midwives were trained in hospitals they were taught by obstetricians who could control the midwives' knowledge (Pitt 1997). Midwives were indoctrinated in their training to accept the status quo because there was no mechanism to critique medical knowledge and practice. They became the operators of technology, which grew rapidly; in some places midwives were called obstetric nurses, while many of the traditional midwifery skills came to be ignored or abandoned.

Some of the obstetricians' power was eroded in the latter half of the twentieth century (Annandale et al. 2004). In part this was due to the rise of the Childbirth Education movement, a group of people who rebelled against the medicalization of childbirth and demanded and won changes to the provision of maternity care. Another factor was that hospitals were affected by 'marketisation, managerialism and consumerism' (Lane 2006: 342), which has had an impact on traditional professional boundaries. Health professionals are expected to form multidisciplinary teams to achieve market efficiencies, specifically, reduced costs in healthcare. However, even under the guise of interdisciplinary professional practice 'the veto power of decision making is retained by obstetricians' (Lane 2006, 342). Managerialism also reduced medicine's power in healthcare as the medical staff became accountable to hospital managers and governments (Lane 2006). Managerialism also affects midwives; once bureaucracy takes over, the risk management starts to be applied and the rules become much less woman-friendly and more institutionalized. It becomes harder to give women real choice as the midwife is expected to support the hospital's policy to care. However, the changes to the management of healthcare provided opportunities for midwives to take on traditional midwifery roles, but progress has been slow and opposition from obstetricians has been intense.

Foucault (1980) has argued that without resistance there is no need for power because it would simply be obedience. Midwives who were encouraged by the changes brought about by women/consumers exerted their agency and also demanded changes. The midwife's power depends on the presence or absence of medical staff. Even though the rhetoric in maternity services is about woman-centred care, in standard hospital care the doctor, regardless of experience, is perceived to be in charge in the birth room, although sometimes a senior midwife may have to play the 'doctor-nurse game' and plant the seed for what she wants to happen. Midwives also find a way to reduce medical interference without confrontation by shutting the birth room door or by advising the woman to stay at home until she is in established labour (Crabtree 2008).

It is inevitable that midwifery has been compared to obstetrics, and in the eyes of some will be seen in a less favourable light. However, midwives, recognizing that knowledge and power are inextricably linked (Foucault 1980), began recording their knowledge and creating new knowledge by conducting and publishing research. In the late 1980s midwives in Australia sought to regain control of midwifery education and practice by arguing for the transfer of midwifery education to the university sector and fighting for recognition of midwifery as a discipline separate from nursing. All formal, Australian midwifery education now takes place in university; most states have, or are about to start, undergraduate midwifery programmes and most registration authorities are known as the Nurses and Midwives Board. Midwifery practice is governed by *Midwifery Competency Standards*, a *Code of Professional Conduct for Midwives* and a *Code of Ethics for Midwives* (Australian Nursing and Midwifery Council 2006, 2008a, 2008b).

Risk in maternity care today

Traditionally risk was established after weighing up the positives and negatives but this has now been replaced with the view that risk equates to danger and uncertainty. As such, risk is seen as an objective hazard; that is, it is independent of the observer (O'Byrne and Holmes 2007). However, risk is not merely a matter of knowledge; it is a value-laden concept that is largely unquantified (Rigakos and Law 2009). Beck's thesis (1992) is that risk is a negotiation of discourses among the participants. He argues that risk is located in the individual, rather than a hypothetical future. 'Preoccupation with risk and the complexity of its nature, shape every interaction and procedure between women and their [caregivers] as they negotiate a safe and fulfilling path through pregnancy and childbirth' (Tracy 2006: 227). It may have a marked impact on the ability of the woman to have a normal birth because risk does not have to represent the most likely or even the most fearsome dangers faced during childbearing. Instead, risks are dangers that clinicians believe they ought to control, mostly because they have become visible through surveillance and, once identified, ways are found to quantify and treat it (Cartwright and Thomas 2001). The media become major players because they are a key source of information about risk and the way in which information is presented in the media, including comments by experts, fuels public paranoia and creates the culture of fear (Beck 1992, Furedi 2002, Lupton 1999).

In the childbirth arena obstetricians hold positions in policy making at the highest level and they define risk and control the introduction of new procedures. Medicine extended its boundaries by developing the concept of risk to ensure childbearing was maintained as a medical problem and expanded to include potential problems (Ehrenreich and English 1973, Tracy 2006). Once people focus on the problems, the mindset of fear prevails, possibilities are overlooked and there is a preoccupation with danger. Armstrong (2004: 137) argues that the ability to see inside the body was the beginning of 'problematizing the normal'. When caring for pregnant women the women and her foetus become visible through regular visits, ultrasounds and blood tests, and it means that she can be regulated in new and different ways. As with the introduction of technology in the past, for example, the use of obstetric forceps and obstetric analgesia, obstetricians were able to convince even 'low risk' women that surveillance 'is good for your baby' and would provide reassurance of foetal health. As women place great emphasis on the health of their unborn babies they acquiesce to the intervention. Despite this level of control of the pregnant body, risk remains a possibility and there is an increase in the number of women considered to be of high risk status. The social determinants of health are often excluded in the examination of risk yet these are likely to be the most prevalent and the issues about which the woman can do little. Still, women are told to reduce risky behaviour and surveillance is increased. Health is seen as 'medical product' and as such is seen through a 'sick lens' that is, prevention of disease (Tracy 2006). Obstetric control of childbirth is complete as the woman is subjected to the medical gaze. The midwife becomes the protagonist and the antagonist of risk. She must denounce risky behaviour but she must also advocate for the woman who chooses to place a different emphasis on risk.

The emphasis on managing risk in healthcare today came about largely because of expensive litigation claims and none were more expensive than those linked to cerebral palsy. However, in spite of a fourfold increase in the rate of caesarean section, the introduction and liberal use of electronic foetal monitoring, the rate of cerebral palsy has remained constant over the last 40 years (MacLennan et al. 2005). The legacy of this has been that the interventions, for example, the use of surveillance techniques, thought to improve the outcomes of labour and births have, in spite of a lack of supporting evidence, remained in practice. As their use increases, health professionals and the public accept that the technology provides benefits to care. It is interesting to note that regardless of the precautionary principle of not taking risks until the outcome can be predicted (Furedi 2002: 9), technologies are introduced into maternity care with very little evidence or assessment of their usefulness. For example, the cardiotocograph (CTG) was designed to be used in situations where the foetus is compromised, but now, in some quarters, there is an expectation that it will be useful in assessing all foetuses, despite the fact that it records only a particular moment in time.

Increased knowledge is associated with better risk identification however many of the claims of risk are unsubstantiated or poorly researched (Beck 1992, Furedi 2002). When medical practitioners make statements about the risk of birth, even though there is little or weak evidence for their stance, it may be seen as means of establishing a professional power base (DeVries 1996, Mander 2001). The medical profession is deemed to speak with more authority, and once they raise the spectre of risk the woman becomes anxious and loses trust in her body's ability to birth (Linell et al. 2002). The allocation of risk is seemingly based on scientific evidence, however women will not necessarily ascribe the same level of risk. For example, a woman with her sixth pregnancy understands the normality of birth, but medicine labels her as a *grande multipara* who needs careful observation. Despite this, medicine uses disciplinary power in the form of rewards (promises of safety) and punishment (death or damage to the woman and/or her baby) to gain compliance (Fahy 2002). Power relations in healthcare make it very difficult to dispute medical claims and for women to offer their own interpretation of the literature. The majority of women should birth without intervention and while there has been some attempt to assess the risk using scoring systems, they generally lack precision, with many women who were classified as 'high risk' having a normal birth and some women who were classified as 'low risk' developing complications (Saxell 2000, Tracy 2006, World Health Organization 1996). O'Byrne (2008) argues that if risk is to be a social regulator it must have mechanisms by which it can be enforced, and the woman must believe the risk is real. This can be achieved when scare tactics are used, such as presenting hospital policies as non-negotiable and not as a recommendation based on current best practice, as illustrated in Exemplar 2.

Hospitals respond to risk by developing protocols and guidelines to direct care and are designed to reduce risk, even though there may be little strong evidence to support their routine use (Cartwright and Thomas 2001). Protocols, while they claim to empower practitioners, become instruments of regulation (Furedi 2002) as they reduce the practitioner's decision making through minimizing critical thinking. Many of the guidelines produce a 'recipe' for care, and individualized care for the woman and her family becomes a casualty. Efforts to simplify the management of pregnancy and childbirth through standardized formulae or evidence-based protocols are failing because it is 'not simply the woman or the setting, the attendant or the policies that influence the outcome. Rather, it is the complex interrelationships among these separate elements' (Enkin et al. 2006: 268).

Exemplar 2

A woman pregnant with her fourth child presented to a maternity unit, having ruptured her membranes at term. The fluid was clear and she had not started contractions. All other aspects of her health status were normal. The obstetric resident medical officer (RMO) following the hospital's policy, advised intravenous (IV) antibiotic cover and induction of labour with Syntocinon infusion if labour did not commence after 12 hours of ruptured membranes. The woman agreed to the antibiotics, albeit reluctantly, but refused the IV Syntocinon as she was certain she would labour and birth spontaneously, as this was her preference. At this point the RMO contacted the consultant obstetrician who instructed the RMO to have the woman sign a disclaimer as follows:

> *I understand that I am putting myself at risk for postpartum haemorrhage [PPH] by not agreeing to be induced with IV Syntocinon infusion.*

The woman signed the disclaimer. Once she was left alone with her known midwife, she commenced labour and birthed a healthy infant within two hours of signing the disclaimer. This is a clear example of the application of unsubstantiated claims being used in a manner to intimidate a woman as there is no evidence to support the claim that induction with IV Syntocinon will prevent a PPH; in fact the reverse is true. There is evidence to link induction or augmentation with IV Syntocinon slightly increasing the risk of PPH (Sheiner et al. 2005).

Normal birth

Normal birth has been the remit of midwives for centuries, and in 2000 the definition of a midwife was amended to specifically include in the scope of practice of the midwife: 'the promotion of normal birth' (International Confederation of Midwives 2005). The meaning of normal birth has been in dispute since 1902, when the term was used to distinguish midwifery from medicine and medicine determined the boundary (Mander 2004, Witz 1992). Normal birth became problematic for obstetrics because when birth was uncomplicated it was the domain of other practitioners. The practice of obstetrics is the pathology of childbirth and to overcome the normality of birth they had to be able to anticipate problems because they could not rely on pathology being present (Arney 1982). Until recently there has been little robust discussion about the meaning of the term 'normal birth' and there appears to be little agreement. For some, normal birth includes epidermal and instrumental delivery, while for others, normal birth is one without 'surgical intervention, use of instruments, induction, epidermal or general anaesthetic' (Downe 2006: 353). What is evident is that normal birth is defined in relation to absence of pathology.

In the discourse of normal birth there are competing forces – 'midwives as guardians of vulnerable childbearing women versus physicians wishing to take over and medicalise pregnancy' (Carolan and Hodnett 2007: 144). The perinatologist Marsden Wagner argues that obstetricians' interest in maternity care is for economic reasons and that as birth rates fall the competition will increase, particularly in those countries where there is a private practice option (Wagner 1995). He argues that there is considerable pressure for obstetricians to conform to the status quo and maintain the practices that are sanctioned by the profession. Innovations requiring changes to practice were accepted on very little evidence, 'provided that it has the appearance of being scientific' (Arney 1982), with that only about 10 per cent of routine obstetric practices having an adequate scientific base (Wagner 1997). Despite this, obstetric knowledge is considered authoritative knowledge (Davis-Floyd and Sargent 1997) and the technologies of testing have altered women's perceptions that pregnancy is primarily a normal, physiological event to seeing pregnancy as inherently risky and therefore unable to be undergone without medical assistance.

Recent government policies support midwifery models of care, which have been shown not only to maintain the normality of birth, with fewer interventions and lower use of intra partum analgesia, but to increase client satisfaction and achieve considerable cost savings (Hatem et al. 2008, Hodnett 2000, Homer et al. 2001, Page et al. 1999). However medical practitioners believe they have overall responsibility until the birth is completed because something could go wrong, a view which is accepted because of the power they wield in healthcare. In normal birth it is a 'stereotypically masculine reaction' for an obstetrician's need to do something in an uncomplicated labour. This is for the benefit of the labouring woman and 'to diminish his own anxiety about a process over which he realises he has little or no control' (Mander 2004: 22). Because the obstetrician is the holder of authoritative knowledge he is able to convince the woman that he can reduce uncertainty. It is the willingness to interfere which results in the cascade of interventions for the women and increased costs to healthcare (Tracy and Tracy 2003).

In practice, medical surveillance is continued with the use of a chart called the partogram, which was developed from a small research project using first-time pregnant African women (Friedman 1954). The chart was designed for use in areas where there are doctor/midwife shortages so that women could be transferred to larger centres before complications occurred. In 1994 the World Health Organization (WHO) recommended universal application of the partogram. In circumstances where the midwife to woman ratio is 1:1 the partogram is unnecessary as the midwife is with the woman and can monitor the progress of labour by other means, for example, abdominal palpation, and behavioural changes. The midwife uses clinical judgement to decide when a vaginal examination is needed and discusses this with the labouring woman before proceeding.

Employing a policy of partogram use in all labouring women inevitably deskills practitioners. Midwives have traditionally used their ears, eyes, noses and hands to assess labour progress. An RCT conducted by Windrim et al. (2007) found that the use of the partogram, compared to charting the progress of labour as written notes, showed no difference in outcome measures in particular rates of caesarean section. Other studies have reported increased rates of intervention, such as caesarean section, particularly where a two hour action line is used, without demonstrable benefits to the woman or the baby (Lavender et al. 2006). Medicalization of birth is so widespread and pervasive that we no longer notice (Gould 2002), and birth in hospitals has become technocratic, that is, there is separation of mind and body, with the body seen as a machine and the woman as an object of care. In this reductionist view of childbearing the woman's individuality is given scant attention as she is 'measured' against a previously developed norm (Oakley 1986). When women do not follow medicine's view of normal, the language changes to bring in the concept of machine, that is, 'you need a little bit of xxx to get you going' or 'failure to progress'. Failure to progress usually means failure to adhere to the partogram alert line. Often all that is required is patience and a known midwife, since there is a connection between cervical dilatation and emotional confidence (Hodnett et al. 2003)

Knowledge in action

Exemplar 3

A young primigravid woman was to be induced at 42 weeks gestation; she had reluctantly agreed to this. However, she came into labour the evening prior to the scheduled induction. This pleased her as she had originally planned to birth at home but was late booking and unable to access a home birth midwife. The admitting midwife allowed the woman to use the low risk birth centre-style room as, other than being post dates, she had no other risk factors and this was requested by the woman. The shift changed at 0700 hours and a second midwife took over her care. She noticed the woman appeared to have a large baby and on questioning it was revealed that her family history was of large infants. Her female relatives had birthed 4–5 kg infants without difficulty. The midwife discussed the possibility of shoulder dystocia and the possible need for an episiotomy. The woman was accepting of the episiotomy if it was necessary.

Soon after, the woman ruptured her membranes and there was meconium stained liquor, not unusual at 42 weeks. A vaginal examination (VE) revealed a fully dilated cervix. At this point she had no urge to push. The foetal heart rate was satisfactory. A CTG had been performed on admission and was reassuring. The obstetric RMO was notified about the onset of second stage and the presence of meconium in the liquor. After about half an hour the woman commenced pushing with contractions. The hospital had time limits for second stage and the obstetrician was to be notified after 45 minutes of pushing for a first time mother. This was duly done and the RMO came back into the room and stood at the end of the bed. The woman found this made her ill at ease; the midwife sensed this and quietly asked the RMO to leave the room, which he did.

The woman progressed and after another hour and a half birthed a 4.6 kg baby with an episiotomy. There was no true shoulder dystocia. The baby was born in good condition. The next day the consultant obstetrician requested the midwife explain why a) the woman did not have a foetal scalp clip and CTG applied in the presence of meconium stained liquor and b) the RMO was asked to leave the room.

The midwife explained that the foetal heart rate was reassuring and there was no evidence suggesting applying a CTG with or without a scalp clip would have provided any useful clinical information or improved the outcome. She explained that the RMO was asked to leave the room as his presence was affecting the woman's ability to relax and push her baby out.

This did not satisfy the obstetrician, who was outraged that hospital protocol had not been adhered to.

In the example above, the midwife used her knowledge of the woman's history and her clinical judgement to assess the progress of the labour and to determine actions. She knew *that* meconium-stained liquor was a common occurrence after 41 weeks of pregnancy and generally indicated a mature foetus (Wiswell 2001). She knew *that* meconium in the liquor represents an event that happened in the past and, given that the woman had a reassuring CTG on admission and the foetal heart tones were reassuring, and the rate was normal, there was no evidence to suggest that applying a CTG would improve the outcome (Alfirevic et al. 2006). She knew *how* women birth and in particular, *how* to birth a big baby. Women need privacy to birth and time and lots of position changes to birth a big baby. Assessments are continuously made and midwifery actions are shaped and directed by the needs of the woman. Midwives inevitably take some personal risks in decisions that go against hospital protocol but all decisions are made in consultation with the woman and using the available evidence.

Conclusion

In childbirth there are competing discourses of risk and normality. Because discourses are social norms and individuals are bound by these, choice is restricted through powerful language and discourses of surveillance and control. The reasons for competition are historical and are compounded by a decline in normal birth, medicalization with concomitant use of technology, paternalism, shortage of midwives and obstetricians, fear of childbirth and mass hospitalization for birth. Midwives believe in normal birth, but the majority work in a healthcare system that values medicine. Any changes they achieve, for example midwife-led models of care, are hard fought for and a constant battle to maintain. Recent government support for midwifery models of care and greater participation of the consumer of healthcare will result in midwifery and obstetrics having to accept professional equality, promoting trust between the professions and true partnership between each other and the women in their care.

References

Alfirevic, Z., Devane, D., Gyte, G. 2006. Continuous cardiotocography (CTG) as a form of electronic fetal monitoring (EFM) for fetal assessment during labour. *Cochrane Database of Systematic Reviews*, issue 3. art. No.: CD006066. DOI: 10.1002/14651858.CD006066.

Annandale, E., Elston, A. and Prior, L. 2004. Medical work, medical knowledge and health care. Themes and perspectives, in *Medical Work,*

Medical Knowledge and Health Care, edited by M.A. Elston, L. Prior and E. Annandale. Oxford: Blackwell, 1–18.

Armstrong, D. 2004. The rise of surveillance medicine, in *Medical Work, Medical Knowledge and Health Care*, edited by M.A. Elston, L. Prior and E. Annandale. Oxford: Blackwell, 135–45.

Arney, W. 1982. *Power and the Profession of Obstetrics*. Chicago: University of Chicago Press.

Arney, W. and Neill, J. 2004. The location of pain during childbirth, in *Medical Work, Medical Knowledge and Health Care*, edited by M.A. Elston, L. Prior and E. Annandale. Oxford: Blackwell, 146–67.

Australian Nursing and Midwifery Council. 2006. *Midwifery Competency Standards*. Canberra: Australian Nursing and Midwifery Council.

Australian Nursing and Midwifery Council. 2008a. *Code of Professional Conduct for Midwives in Australia*. Canberra: Australian Nursing and Midwifery Council.

Australian Nursing and Midwifery Council. 2008b. *Code of Ethics for Midwives*. Canberra: Australian Nursing and Midwifery Council.

Blaaka, G. and Schauer, T. 2008. Doing midwifery between different belief systems. *Midwifery*, 24, 344–52.

Beck, U. 1992. *Risk Society: Towards a New Modernity*. London: Sage.

Benner, P. 1984. *From Novice to Expert: Excellence and Power in Clinical Nursing*. Menlo Park: Addison-Wesley Publishing.

Carolan, M. and Hodnett, E. 2007. 'With woman' philosophy: examining the evidence, answering the questions. *Nursing Inquiry*, 14(2), 140–52.

Cartwright, E. and Thomas, J. 2001. Constructing risk: maternity care, law and malpractice, in *Birth by Design: Pregnancy, Maternity Care and Midwifery in North America and Europe*, edited by R. DeVries, S. Wrede, E.R. van Teijligen and C. Benoit. New York: Routledge, 218–28.

Crabtree, S. 2008. Midwives constructing 'normal birth', in *Normal Birth: Evidence and Debate.* 2nd Edition, edited by S. Downe. Edinburgh: Churchill Livingston, 97–112.

Darra, S. and Norris, S. 2008. Risk and normality in birth: a question of philosophy. *MIDIRS Midwifery Digest*, 18(2), 179–84.

Davis, D. 1995. Ways of knowing in midwifery. *Journal of Australian College of Midwives Inc*, 8(3) 30–32.

Davis-Floyd, R. 2001. The technocratic, humanistic and holistic paradigms of childbirth. *International Journal of Gynecology and Obstetrics*, 75, S5–S23.

Davis-Floyd, R. and Sargent, C. 1997. Introduction: the anthropology of childbirth, in *Childbirth and Authoritative Knowledge: Cross Cultural Perspectives*, R. Davis-Floyd and C. Sargent. Berkeley: University of California Press.

DeVries, R. 1996. The midwife's place: an international comparison of the status of midwives, in *Midwives and Safer Motherhood*, edited by S.F. Murray. St Louis: Mosby, 159–74.

Donnison, J. 1988. *Midwives and Medical Men: History of the Struggle for the Control of Childbirth*. London: Historical Publications.

Downe, S. 2006. Engaging with the concept of unique normality in childbirth. *British Journal of Midwifery*, 1(6), 352–56.

Downe, S. and McCourt, C. 2008. From being to becoming: reconstructing birth knowledges, in *Normal Childbirth: Evidence and Debate*, 2nd Edition, edited by S. Downe. Edinburgh: Elsevier, 3–28.

Ehrenreich, B. and English, D. 1973. *Witches, Midwives and Healers: A History of Women Healers*. New York: Feminist Press.

Enkin, M.W., Glouberman, S., Groff, P., Jadad, A.R. and Stern, A. 2006. Beyond evidence: the complexity of maternity care. *Birth*, 33(4), 265–9.

Fahy, K. 2002. Reflecting on practice to theorise empowerment for women: using Foucault's concepts. *Australian Journal of Midwifery*, 15(1), 5–13.

Fahy, K. 2008. Power and the social construction of birth territory, in *Birth Territory and Midwifery Guardianship: Theory for Practice, Education and Research*, edited by K. Fahy, M. Foureur, M. and C. Hastie. Sydney: Books for Midwives Press, 3–10.

Foucault, M. 1980. Truth and power, in *Power/Knowledge: Selected Interviews and Other Writings 1972–1977*, edited by C. Gordon. New York: Pantheon.

Friedman, E.A. 1954. Graphic analysis of labor. *American Journal of Obstetrics and Gynecology*, 68, 1568–75.

Furedi, F. 2002. *Culture of Fear: Risk-Taking and the Morality of Low Expectation*. London: Continuum.

Goodman, S. 2007. Piercing the veil: the marginalization of midwives in the United States. *Social Science and Medicine*, 65, 610–21.

Gould, D. 2002. Subliminal medicalisation. *British Journal of Midwifery*, 10(7), 418.

Hatem, M. Sandall, J. Devane, D., Soltani, H. and Gates, S. 2008. Midwife-led versus other models of care for childbearing women. *Cochrane Database of Systematic Reviews*, issue 4. art. no.: CD004667. DOI: 10.1002/14651858. CD004667.pub2.

Hodnett, E.D. 2000. Continuity of caregivers for care during pregnancy and childbirth. *Cochrane Database of Systematic Reviews*, DOI: 10.1002/14651858.

Hodnett, E.D., Gates, S., Hofmeyr, G. and Sakala, C. 2003. Continuous support for women during childbirth. *Cochrane Database of Systematic Reviews*, issue 3, art. no.: CD003766. DOI: 10.1002/14651858.CD003766. pub2.

Homer, C., Matha, D., Jordan, L., Wills, J. and Davis, G. 2001. Community-based continuity of midwifery care versus standard hospital care: a cost analysis. *Australian Health Review*, 24, 85–93.

International Confederation of Midwives. 2005. *Definition of a Midwife*. The Hague: International Confederation of Midwives.

Jordan, B. 1997. Authorative knowledge construction, in *The Anthropology of Childbirth. Childbirth and Authoritative Knowledge: Cross Cultural Perspectives*, edited by R. Davis-Floyd and C. Sargent. Berkeley: University of California Press, 55–79.

Lane, K. 2006. The plasticity of professional boundaries: a case study of collaborative care in maternity services. *Health Sociology Review*, 15, 341–52.

Larkin, G. 1983. *Occupational Monopoly and Modern Medicine*. London: Tavistock Publications.

Lavender, T. Alfirevic, Z. and Walkinshaw, S. 2006. Effect of different partogram action lines on birth outcomes. *Obstetrics and Gynecology*, 108, 295–302.

Leap, N. 2000. The less we do, the more we give, in *The Midwife-Mother Relationship*, edited by M. Kirkham. Basingstoke: Palgrave Macmillan, 3–7.

Linell, P., Adelswärd, V., Sachs, L., Bredmar, M. and Lindstedt, U. 2002. Expert talk in medical contexts: explicit and implicit orientation to risks. *Research on language and social interaction*, 35(2), 195–218.

Lupton, D. 1999. Risk and the ontology of pregnant embodiment, in *Risk and Sociocultural Theory: New Directions and Perspectives*, edited by D. Lupton, Cambridge: Cambridge University Press, 59–85.

MacLennan, A., Nelson, K.B., Hankins, G. and Speer, M. 2005. Who will deliver our grandchildren? Implications of Cerebral Palsy litigation. *Journal of the American Medical Association*, 294, 1688–90.

Mander, R. 2001. Response to male appropriation and medicalization of childbirth; an historical analysis by H.A. Churchill. *Journal of Advanced Nursing*, 35(3), 390–91.

Mander, R. 2002. The midwife and the medical practitioner, in *Failure to Progress: the Contraction of the Midwifery Profession*, edited by R. Mander and V. Fleming, London: Routledge, 170–88.

Mander, R. 2004. *Men and Maternity*. London: Routledge.

Oakley, A. 1986. *The Captured Womb: A History of the Medical Care of Pregnant Women*. Oxford: Basil Blackwell.

O'Byrne, P. 2008. The dissection of risk: a conceptual analysis. *Nursing Inquiry*, 15(1), 30–9.

O'Byrne, P. and Holmes, D. 2007. The *micro-facism* of Plato's good citizen: producing (dis)order through the construction of risk. *Nursing Philosophy*, 8, 92–101.

Odent, M. 2008. Birth territory: the besieged territory of the obstetrician, in *Birth Territory and Midwifery Guardianship: Theory for Practice, Education and Research*, edited by K. Fahy, M. Foureur and C. Hastie, Sydney: Books for Midwives Press, 131–48.

Page, L., McCourt, C., Beake, S., Vail, A. and Hewison, J. 1999. Clinical interventions and outcomes of One-to-One midwifery practice. *Journal of Public Health Medicine*, 21(3), 243–8.

Pitt, S. 1997. Midwifery and medicine: gendered knowledge in the practice of delivery, in *Midwives, Society and Childbirth: Debates and Controversies in the Modern Period*, edited by H. Marland and A.M. Rafferty. London: Routledge, 218–31.

Polanyi, M. 1966. *The Tacit Dimension*. London: Routledge and Kegan Paul.

Rigakos, G. and Law, A. 2009. Risk, realism and the politics of resistance. *Critical Sociology*, 35(1), 79–103.

Saxell, L. 2000. Risk: theoretical or actual, in *The New Midwifery: Science and Sensitivity in Practice*, edited by L.A. Page. London: Churchill Livingston, 87–104.

Schön, D. 1987. *Educating the Reflective Practitioner*. London: Jossey Bass.

Sheiner, E., Sarid, L., Levy, A. Seidman, D.S. and Hallak, M. 2005. Obstetric risk factors and outcome of pregnancies complicated with early postpartum hemorrhage: a population-based study. *The Journal of Maternal-Fetal and Neonatal Medicine*, 18(3), 149–54.

Stewart, M. 2001. Whose evidence counts? An exploration of health professionals' perceptions of evidence based practice focusing on the maternity services. *Midwifery*, 17, 279–88.

Tew, M. 1995. *Safer Childbirth?: A Critical History of Maternity Care*. 2nd Edition. London: Chapman and Hall.

Towler, J. and Bramall, J. 1986. *Midwives in History and Society*. London: Croom Helm.

Tracy, S. 2006. Risk: theoretical or actual, in *The New Midwifery: Science and Sensitivity in Practice*, 2nd Edition, edited by L.A Page and R. McCandish. Philadelphia: Churchill Livingstone, 227–33.

Tracy, S. and Tracy, M. 2003. Costing the Cascade: estimating the cost of increased obstetric intervention in childbirth using population data. *BJOG*, 110(8), 717–24.

Wagner, M. 1994. *Pursuing the Birth Machine: The Search for Appropriate Birth Technology*. Camperdown: Ace Graphics.

Wagner, M. 1995. A global witch-hunt. *The Lancet*, 346(8981), 1020–22.

Wagner, M. 1997. Confessions of a dissident, in *Childbirth and Authorative Knowledge: Cross Cultural Perspectives*, edited by R. Davis-Floyd and C. Sargent. Berkeley: University of California Press, 366–96.

Wagner, M. 2001. Fish can't see water: the need to humanize birth. *International Journal of Gynaecology and Obstetrics*, 75, S25–S37.

Weaver, E., Clark, K. and Vernon, B. 2005. Obstetricians and midwives modus Vivendi for current times. *Medical Journal of Australia*, 82(9), 436–7.

Wickham, S. 2007. Feminism and ways of knowing, in *Pregnancy, Birth and Maternity Care: Feminist Perspectives*, edited by M. Stewart. Edinburgh: Elsevier, 157–67.

Willis, E. 1989. *Medical Dominance*. Sydney: Allen and Unwin.

Windrim, R., Seaward, P.G., Hodnett, E., Akoury, H., Kingdom, J., Salenieks, M.E., Fallah, S. and Ryan, G. 2007. A randomized controlled trial of a bedside partogram in the active management of primiparous labour. *Journal of Obstetrics and Gynaecology*, 29(1), 27–34.

Wiswell, T.E. 2001. Advances in the treatment of the meconium aspiration syndrome. *Acta Paediatrica Supplement*, 90(436), 28–30.

Witz, A. 1992. *Professions and Patriarchy*. London: Routledge.

World Health Organization. 1996. *Care in Normal Birth: A Practical Guide*. Geneva: World Health Organization.

9 Skills for person-centred care: health professionals supporting chronic condition prevention and self-management

Sharon Lawn and Malcolm Battersby

With the growing burden of chronic conditions and the sheer volume of expected demand for health services over the coming decades, it will become increasingly important for health service providers to work smarter and more collaboratively with one another and with service users. Building cooperative models of practice that overcome traditional turf sensitivities between professionals, and that overcome structural boundaries between services, will be challenging. Underpinning this, and arguably more important and elusive, is the challenge for health professionals to truly understand how their input impacts on service consumers. If we acknowledge the fact that many of us professionals do not adequately look after our own health or follow health professionals' advice (Vermeire et al. 2001) despite 'knowing what is good for us', there is clearly something else going on that we are failing to recognize about ourselves and the consumers we treat, who expect to follow our advice as part of our interaction with them. The central argument of this chapter is that solutions to these challenges can, in large part, be found through a return to placing the consumer voice at the centre of the process, a return to the core skills of engagement and person-centred care. Person-centred care regards the person receiving services as the focus of any healthcare provision. The focus is on the needs, concerns, beliefs and goals of the person rather than the needs of the systems or professionals. The person feels understood, valued and involved in the management of their chronic condition. People are empowered by learning skills and abilities to gain effective control over their lives versus responsibility resting with others (Michie et al. 2003). We will be examining the elements of knowledge in the practice of person-centred care as applied to supporting people to manage their chronic conditions. To help demonstrate this argument, we will summarize some of the findings of a recent national primary healthcare workforce project that determined the skills required to effectively support

161

chronic condition prevention and self-management. The focus of this project specifically included interprofessional practice and education, that is, how each health profession engaged with consumers as well as each other.

In 2007, as part of joint Australian Government Department of Health and Ageing and State and Territory Government funding of the Australian Better Health Initiative (ABHI), the Flinders Human Behaviour and Health Research Unit (FHBHRU) in conjunction with its project partners, the Australian General Practice Network (AGPN), the Australian Psychological Society (APS) and the Flinders University Department of General Practice investigated training and information options to support chronic condition prevention and self-management in Australian primary health care (PHC). This project built upon previous work by FHBHRU in the development of an undergraduate curriculum framework in chronic condition self-management support for future medicine, nursing and allied health professionals. The ABHI was developed to improve chronic disease prevention and self-management across Australia. A key element of the strategy is education and training of the current and future PHC workforce in chronic condition prevention and self-management (CCSM) support principles (Australian Institute of Health and Welfare [AIHW] 2004). Justifications for the strategy include the ageing population, workforce pressures, a need for cultural change in clinician attitudes and practices, inequities in access to services, inadequate coordination and integration of services and the need to enhance the quality of services. Full ethics approval was granted for the work.

The objectives of the project were to investigate:

- What knowledge and skills primary health care professionals need to be able to provide effective support
- Their current knowledge and skills base, perceptions, practice, enablers and barriers
- What professional development opportunities are currently available to meet these needs
- Where the gaps are in professional development opportunities currently available and which gaps are of highest priority
- What options are available to address these gaps.

The PHC sector comprises health workers drawn from medicine, nursing and allied health, but often complemented by a broad range of semi-professional and community support and health promotion groups. What they all share is a commitment to promoting health and well-being and improving basic quality of life for people in their community. PHC professionals play a pivotal role at the primary, secondary and tertiary level, working closely with a full range of other services and sectors.

The efficacy of chronic condition prevention and self-management support depends on the quality of the collaboratively developed, integrated plan of care across these areas, the quality of their professional working relationships and, most importantly, the quality of the care relationship with consumers and carers. What enables health professionals to support the needs of people they serve together is effective training and knowledge, underpinned by person-centred attitudes to care that facilitate engagement with consumers and sustain it effectively over time.

Chronic condition self-management: the central underpinning notion

The term chronic condition self-management ('self-management') has emerged as a concept to describe the tasks, roles and responsibilities of individuals as they cope with their chronic conditions from diagnosis to long-term management. The Stanford model of chronic disease self-management, developed by Lorig and colleagues from the 1970s (Lorig 1993) has been prominent. It is based on patient-perceived problems. Its goal is to build the person's confidence (self-efficacy) to perform the three tasks of disease, role and emotional management, with the end goal of improved health status and appropriate utilization of healthcare. It draws heavily from the ideas of Corbin and Strauss (1988) in their earlier work with people with chronic conditions.

More recently, definitions of self-management have been informed by the Chronic Care Model (Wagner et al. 2001). Self-management control rests with the person, is often shared with peers, and acknowledges that the person is the 'expert' of their experience. It challenges the professional expert view of knowledge exchange/transfer. Central to self-management is the notion of rights and responsibilities and how these are shared. Self-management requires the person to hold the belief that they can effectively self-manage their condition, or learn to do so, to have improved self-efficacy or confidence in their ability to self-care, involving cognitive, perceptual, behavioural and lifestyle change.

The national consultation in the PHC self-management skills project led to an agreed definition of self-management (NHPAC 2006, Lawn and Battersby 2009, p. 7):

Self-management is a process that includes a broad set of attitudes, behaviours and skills directed toward managing the impact of the disease or condition on all aspects of living by the person with a chronic condition. It includes, but is not limited to, self-care and it may also encompass prevention. The following are considered to contribute to this process:

- Having knowledge of the condition and/or its management
- Adopting a self-management care plan agreed and negotiated in partnership with health professionals, significant others and/or carers and other supporters
- Actively sharing in decision making with health professionals, significant others and/or carers and other supporters
- Monitoring and managing signs and symptoms of the condition
- Managing the impact of the condition on physical, emotional, occupational and social functioning
- Adopting lifestyles that address risk factors and promote health by focusing on prevention and early intervention
- Having access to, and confidence in, the ability to use support services. (Lawn et al. 2007)

Self-management support is what health professionals, carers and the health system do to assist the person to manage their disease or condition.

Justification for chronic condition self-management

Lifestyle is recognized internationally as the major remedial cause of ill health. Chronic conditions are recognized as being among the most common and costly to the health system and among the most preventable, with an estimated 6.8 million Australians who have a chronic condition (AIHW 2004). Early detection and treatment can delay complications and disability, but it is crucial that this occurs within an integrated system (Lawrence 2005, Best et al. 2003a) and supports self-management by the person. There is a growing body of evidence regarding the efficacy of CCSM and CCSM support for improving health outcomes for various conditions, and its use within various PHC professions (Department of Health Australia 2007). The World Health Organization (WHO) recently identified a range of competencies required to deliver effective care for those with chronic conditions, including patient-centred care and partnering and adopting a public health perspective. Empowering individuals towards adopting self-management strategies, where appropriate, features significantly in these competencies (World Health Organization 2005a). Yet, many health professionals continue to find it difficult to provide truly patient-centred care. Many claim to do so yet merely serve the rhetoric of their organizations, and others openly deny the person's collaborative involvement in the process. Paterson and Hopgood (Battersby et al. in press) discuss this phenomenon in the context of the rise of 'healthism', especially within Western neoliberal economies. Individual behaviour, attitudes and emotions are viewed as factors that need attention in order to realize health. Solutions to preventing or managing illness are perceived to lie in the realm of individual choice. Within this view, personal responsibility is paramount. Behaviours, attitudes and emotions are medicalized and people become morally accountable for their health choices and are at risk of being blamed and stigmatized for their choices. The wholesale, arguably simplistic, adoption of the Stages of Change model (Prochaska and DiClemente 1983) by health professionals, in the absence of critical analysis, has done little to alleviate this problem. Our understanding of 'precontemplation' (that is, those not thinking of change at this stage) continues to be little understood and yet it is at the heart of understanding why people do not change despite often clearly displaying poor health choices. And people deemed to be in this group are not the minority of our clients; they often clog our health systems and disproportionately use service resources. The Stages of Change model has been criticized on a number of fronts (West 2005). Largely, it fails to acknowledge the social determinants of health that need to be understood in order to understand the problem from the person's perspective and why compliance and adherence to health professionals' advice is such a problem. We are repeatedly drawn back to asking whose agenda is ultimately being considered and is the person genuinely engaged in the first place.

Education and training of PHC professionals is influenced by many factors, including location, population profiles and contexts, government policies, healthcare trends, organizational needs and professional requirements. Opportunities and constraints for training arise from organizational factors such as their vision, values and strategic directions, which influence the structure and culture of the organization and its service objectives. These factors may encourage or inhibit changes in the overall practice of health professionals and expectations of consumers about the service. Informed, engaged, patients need proactive practice teams and agencies that together need collaborative social, economic and political systems to address the social determinants of health through effective education and training systems, resource management and social policy. Yet, arguably, the needs of service consumers are a common thread through all health service organizations regardless of how we may try to shape them to fit our service entry requirements, diagnostic criteria and boundaries. Consumers should not be made to navigate through each service receiving largely fragmented and superficial support and understanding of their needs. Rather, we professionals could do more to come together with the person and one another to know how we each contribute to the larger picture of care for the person. Much of this skill and knowledge can be seen implicitly in what we call practice experience.

The primary health care workforce skills project

The work was undertaken in five stages from June 2007 to January 2008. The first two stages involved establishing a national reference group to guide the work and undertaking an extensive literature review to guide the construction and parameters for surveys and other data collection tools. The latter three stages produced the findings for the project. They included an electronic survey of the national PHC workforce to assess their training needs in this area, an audit of existing training programmes in this regard, focus groups across the PHC sector, and a gaps analysis, involving the national reference group and a national stakeholder workshop to test, refine and validate recommendations that emerged from data analysis. Reference group members and stakeholders included representatives of national peak bodies representing relevant primary healthcare professionals (such as nursing, physiotherapy, occupational therapy, dietetics, diabetes education, medicine, general practice, psychology, pharmacy, exercise physiology), experts in continuing professional development and delivery, experts in chronic condition prevention and self-management, consumer and carer peak organizations, and Department of Health and Ageing and state government representatives. Details of methods used can be found elsewhere (Lawn et al. 2009).

Based on a multifaceted research strategy of online and mailed surveys to the workforce and training organizations, focus groups and key informant interviews with a broad range of stakeholders, the PHC workforce project identified a broad range of training needs specific to CCPSM support. These are presented with a caveat. Of the more than 120,000 primary health professionals in Australia and of the 83,000 who were within the scope of the project, those who responded (1,168 to PHC workforce survey and 73 in focus groups) represent a limited and potentially biased sample, skewed towards those who are aware of and have participated in CCPSM support training. Survey respondents were also largely nurses and allied health professionals. General Practitioners (GPs) were engaged largely through focus groups, given their poor response to the online survey. However, given this bias towards those with some awareness of CCPSM support, the argument becomes even stronger for potential needs and gaps in knowledge and skills within the overall PHC workforce. That is, issues and needs that are identified for these participants will equally hold for others; arguably even more so.

The needs assessment and subsequent gaps analysis that considered all data sources from the project found that:

- There is an overall lack of understanding, competence and practice of CCPSM support among PHC professionals.

- Translation of training into practice is a major problem and more quality control of training programmes is needed.
- The PHC workforce appears not to have the full set of skills needed to support consumers' behaviour change and, in particular, the workforce needs more psychosocial skills and understanding.

The needs assessment also found that, although a prescriptive approach to healthcare delivery still tends to dominate practice, the workforce is keen to develop more skills in behaviour change techniques and to undertake more multidisciplinary training that is translatable to practice.

Interestingly, in their perception of receiving services, consumers and carers reported that health professionals:

- Often do not listen or ask the patient their views or perspectives
- Often have little knowledge of community resources available to support the person, largely because they continue to work within their own narrow frame of reference and service provision
- Rarely work from a position of identifying consumers' strengths and current capacities
- Need to be more collaborative with consumers, carers and particularly each other.

Consumer-driven training and more involvement overall was endorsed as needed, from accreditation through to development, delivery and evaluation of training and education.

What these broad findings tell us is that there is a significant discrepancy between the content and quality of what health service providers perceive they are providing and what service users experience as recipients of support from health services. Little wonder that we have such challenges with compliance and adherence to health professionals' advice.

The PHC workforce appears not to have the full set of skills needed to support consumers' behaviour change. This is perceived by their responses to the workforce training needs (see Table 9.1) survey in which they were asked to rate the usefulness of a range of core elements of training known to be essential for supporting behaviour change, as determined by an extensive literature review of existing evidence. Their responses indicate that there is still a substantial percentage of the PHC workforce that do not realize that these elements are essential to the process, despite the evidence. This was also reiterated in focus groups. It is also unclear if, how and in what context the PHC workforce integrates what it has learned and applies it effectively to the field, post training. An example of this is whether they are integrating motivational interviewing and stages of change by recognizing that one

Table 9.1   The percentage of health professionals reporting on the usefulness of prevention and CCSM training topics

Topic area	Not useful				Very useful	Not useful				Very useful
Health promotion approaches	1.0	10.7	31.4	30.8	26.0	1.6	11.9	32.8	30.2	23.4
Communication skills	.9	7.2	18.3	34.7	39.0	.8	5.3	20.6	33.8	39.5
Stages of change	1.0	7.7	20.1	34.7	36.5	1.0	8.0	20.5	34.5	36.1
Motivational interviewing	2.2	7.4	19.2	29.5	41.7	2.2	6.5	16.9	31.4	43.1
Assessment of risk factors	.4	5.9	22.7	34.6	36.4	1.0	6.5	22.9	35.6	34.0
Assessment of self-management capacity	.9	7.8	23.5	33.6	34.1	1.1	4.7	21.5	33.5	39.3
Goal setting	.9	4.7	18.1	33.8	42.5	.5	4.2	19.2	31.3	44.7
Structured problem solving	.9	6.6	28.4	33.3	30.8	1.3	6.3	26.8	31.5	34.2
Behavioural techniques	1.1	9.1	27.5	34.8	27.5	1.3	8.5	25.8	33.9	30.5
Working in multidisciplinary teams	.8	5.4	20.1	32.7	41.0	.9	6.4	20.8	31.6	40.3
Electronic recall systems	8.0	17.2	31.9	26.4	16.6	7.5	19.0	39.1	18.4	16.1
Organizational change techniques	6.7	14.6	39.8	26.4	12.6	6.6	23.0	34.6	21.4	14.4
Health coaching	3.3	9.6	28.1	26.2	32.8	3.7	10.8	29.3	26.9	29.3
Evidence based guidelines	1.2	8.9	21.6	29.4	38.9	.2	9.9	26.0	29.4	34.5
Conducting practice based research	3.5	17.0	28.5	26.5	24.5	3.2	15.5	29.0	29.0	23.3
Use of peer support	1.8	12.2	25.0	34.7	26.3	1.2	11.0	26.4	35.4	25.9
Cultural awareness	1.8	12.3	25.9	32.1	27.9	1.5	13.2	26.2	32.3	26.7

facilitates the other, rather than learning about them in isolation from each other and therefore perceiving them as separate entities or skill sets. The quality of this integration of concepts is also not clear from the survey of training organizations.

Likewise, training organizations gave mixed and concerning responses when asked about the coverage of these important core elements of CCPSM support within their CCPSM training. For example, approximately one-third of training providers reported that assessment of self-management capacity is covered only some, minimally or none of the time. Likewise, 25.7 per cent of training in CCSM does not cover motivational interviewing at all and 79 per cent of training provides some, minimal or no coverage of health coaching.

Cultural awareness and competence in culturally sensitive practice appears to be largely neglected as a priority by both the workforce and training organizations. In focus groups it was only discussed when facilitators were proactive in raising it within the larger discussion.

In general, participants believed that it would be difficult to implement CCPSM support into their practice without support from professional bodies and requisite organizational change. Despite these barriers, the importance of an interdisciplinary approach to CCPSM support was recognized by participants. They stated that it would motivate them to participate in training programmes, enabling them to effectively implement CCPSM into their current practice.

Training content

There was an overall consensus that current training programmes were limited in their scope, focus and longevity. Although current programmes provide solid theoretical background and are effective for mainstream and well-functioning individuals, participants believed that they had limited suitability for other populations due to the lack of recognition of psychosocial factors and social determinants of health generally. Current training programmes appeared to have limited practitioner focus in that they lacked directive guidelines to inform professionals how to meet the specific needs of the patient in practice. Identified opportunities in current training models included emphasis on interdisciplinary support and shared respect between health professionals. The main areas of training requested by at least one-third of participants were structured problem solving, health promotion approaches, behaviour change techniques, assessment of self-management capacity, health coaching, and dealing with symptoms of anxiety and depression. These preferences were part of, and in addition to, a number of broader training needs identified as follows:

- Interdisciplinary knowledge and collaboration. Health professionals need to be encouraged to 'break down the professional barriers'. They are perceived to be inflexible and territorial and often are not trained to consider issues that are beyond their primary focus.
- Flexibility to allow for patient-specific variables. This involves acknowledging that a spectrum of self-management support is needed that clearly matches the stage of self-management activation the person is at. Central to this is educating health professionals about assessment skills in order to ascertain the most important strategies for the client using 'a best practice guidelines pathway' focusing on the processes taken with the client.
- Review of professionally defined roles of health professions, with consumer engagement, self-management support and inter-professional practice expectations beginning at training, whether it is university or institution delivered.
- Consideration of language. The terminology used is very important and needs to be more positively framed. The word 'chronic' held negative connotations for many participants.

Training characteristics

A number of needs and recommendations arose from the data:

- Continued training is needed to enable effective and sustained transfer into practice, and to provide feedback to training providers so that programmes can regularly be modified and developed.
- Multimodal delivery is seen as particularly important for health professionals in rural or remote regions who face difficulties in accessing training programmes due to distance, limited resources and lack of commitment from organizational management (for example, more CD- or DVD-based resource systems and e-learning platforms).
- A systematic approach to training with some form of oversight by government would be preferred.
- Training programmes would most effectively be delivered through educational providers as they have 'the engine room to do this and do it all day long'.
- The lack of a central source of information that enables health professionals to locate other services.
- The development of networks in practice education and training, including an online database, online discussion forums, peer supervision groups, and libraries and community centres set up to support health professionals to access resources.

- The importance of interdisciplinary training opportunities as well as the need for discipline-specific groups that are tailored to each profession, including appropriateness for different levels of competencies and using discipline-specific examples.
- Training should be largely interactive and experiential, to assist with engaging the health professionals and to enhance transfer from training into practice.

Particular needs were identified for GP practices with recommendations that workforce training be:

- Directed at the whole of practice, with a particular focus on skills development for practice nurses and Aboriginal health workers and with information directed at General Practitioners (GPs) and community pharmacists to ensure their support and understanding
- Delivered locally, after hours, offered more than once, and with ongoing support to embed learning
- Scheduled to avoid clashing with other major training initiatives
- Free or of low cost
- Offered in alternative formats such as one-on-one, small group and online to account for different access requirements.

Audit of CCPSM training to the PHC workforce

A survey of training organizations was undertaken to complement the information received from other methodologies. This survey produced responses of 57 providers of training covering 76 different courses. Participants were asked whether the training they deliver covers various aspects of chronic condition prevention and self-management support, rating each on a scale of 1 (none) to 5 (extensive).

The overwhelming mode of delivery of training was by workshop and the majority of training was delivered over two days and away from the practice field. By contrast, this length and style of training may be a barrier to access, given the workforce have clearly indicated that they do not always have time, financial resources or management commitment for other staff to be available to backfill their positions whilst they attend training.

Goal setting and structured problem solving are relatively straightforward to teach. However, it is how they are incorporated and integrated into overall course objectives that is important. It is not possible to determine from survey responses whether these skills are integrated into training courses or are provided as an addition to training with little integration into the overall needs of people receiving support. Similar concerns exist for how the Stages of Change model is incorporated into training and whether it is taught as a distinct model in isolation or integrated with an understanding of other skills, such as motivational interviewing and an understanding of the social determinants of health that may influence if and how consumers engage with services in the first place.

The extent to which training is translated into practice is also unclear, given the overwhelming identification by the workforce and key informants of problems with this for most available training. These views contrast with the self-reported responses of training providers: 63.2 per cent selected a 4 or 5 when asked to what extent their prevention training covers 'translating training into practice' and 65.4 per cent selected a 4 or 5 for self-management training. Discussing translation into practice in a training session may well be different and less effective than giving people practical tools for implementation into practice.

Areas reported to be well covered included:

- Communication skills (contrary to the feedback from consumers and carers)
- Goal setting
- Structured problem solving
- Use of evidence-based guidelines
- Working in a multidisciplinary team
- Translation of training into practice.

Training in practice-based research was reported as receiving poor coverage by most providers, with approximately 75 per cent of providers covering this aspect between 'some' of the time and 'not at all'. Given the importance of innovation and uptake by the field, we suggest that this needs increased emphasis in view of the role the field plays in the development and then the translation of evidence-based guidelines into practice. Focus on multidisciplinary work was better for training in CCSM support than for prevention training; however, that it is arguably of greater importance for the management of complex and often multiple chronic conditions also suggests room for improvement in building this component of training.

A range of effective adult learning principles are being applied as part of the delivery of training to the PHC workforce. Small group learning is the dominant learning format. Other commonly reported approaches included:

- Didactic presentations
- Case studies
- Skills rehearsal/role plays
- Evidence for CCSM support

- Resources to assist implementation of training, for example, worksheets, tools.

Case studies are being used extensively in training. However, no information is available as to their relevance to the specific groups receiving training or whether there is any capacity for case studies to be tailored to different locations, professions, conditions or contexts, or special needs groups. Table 9.2 details training organizations' responses to a range of approaches determined to be important from a review of existing literature of the variables that constitute best practice in training for this area.

Table 9.2   Does your training use the following approaches?

Type of training approach	Responses		
Didactic presentations	Not at all – 1	2	4.1
	2	2	4.1
	Some – 3	23	46.9
	4	14	28.6
	Extensively – 5	8	16.3
Problem-based learning	Not at all – 1	1	1.9
	2	5	9.6
	Some – 3	18	34.6
	4	20	38.5
	Extensively – 5	8	15.4
Small group learning	Not at all – 1	2	4.0
	2	3	6.0
	Some – 3	13	26.0
	4	15	30.0
	Extensively – 5	17	34.0
Case studies	Not at all – 1	6	12.0
	2	4	8.0
	Some – 3	12	24.0
	4	17	34.0
	Extensively – 5	11	22.0
Skills rehearsal/role plays	Not at all – 1	8	15.7
	2	3	5.9
	Some – 3	12	23.5
	4	14	27.5
	Extensively – 5	14	27.5

Table 9.2 cont'd

Type of training approach	Responses		
Workplace training	Not at all – 1	16	32.0
	2	7	14.0
	Some – 3	11	22.0
	4	10	20.0
	Extensively – 5	6	12.0
Academic detailing	Not at all – 1	24	52.2
	2	6	13.0
	Some – 3	5	10.9
	4	9	19.6
	Extensively – 5	2	4.3
Evidence for prevention	Not at all – 1	6	12.2
	2	4	8.2
	Some – 3	15	30.6
	4	15	30.6
	Extensively – 5	9	18.4
Evidence for CCSM	Not at all – 1	6	12.2
	2	4	8.2
	Some – 3	9	18.4
	4	16	32.7
	Extensively – 5	14	28.6
Follow-up by trainers	Not at all – 1	11	22.4
	2	6	12.2
	Some – 3	13	26.5
	4	15	30.6
	Extensively – 5	4	8.2
Resources to assist implementation of training e.g. worksheets, tools	Not at all – 1	6	12.8
	2	1	2.1
	Some – 3	21	44.7
	4	5	10.6
	Extensively – 5	14	29.8
Other e.g. manuals, DVDs, CDs, website, newsletter	Not at all – 1	5	55.6
	2	0	0.0
	Some – 3	0	0.0
	4	1	11.1
	Extensively – 5	3	33.3

National stakeholder workshop

The project consortium convened a national stakeholder workshop in Melbourne in December 2007 to test, refine and validate recommendations that emerged from the analysis of data collection undertaken with the PHC workforce and training organizations. The 40 workshop participants from nursing, allied health and medical professional organizations, training and accreditation organizations, consumer and carer advocacy groups, and Commonwealth, State and Territory governments were provided with a brief summary of findings from the data collection stages of the project and asked for their comments. This discussion document summarized the findings of the literature review and consultation process and the 19 recommended areas of knowledge and skills arising (see Table 9.3) from these processes. Workshop participants were then asked to consider the 19 core skills identified from the project as part of their group discussions. A series of case studies were also developed by the consortium and used to provide structure and context for the conversations. A variety of scenarios were deliberately chosen that could match the needs and interests of each discussion table, with a series of prompt questions used to support group discussions.

The skills deemed by consumers to be necessary core aspects of all training for health professionals, as determined by the existing literature, focus group and key informant interviews included:

- Interviewing skills
- Assessment of consumers' needs
- More person-centred approaches
- Communication skills
- Collaboration with consumers and acknowledging their self-management role
- Raising issues ('learn how to ask')
- Developing rapport
- Understanding stages of change
- Goal-setting
- Understanding how to use community resources more effectively
- Helping consumers navigate the system
- Identifying consumers' strengths and supporting self-efficacy
- Meeting culturally and linguistically diverse (CALD) groups' needs and delivering culturally appropriate practice.

Workshop participants supported all 19 core skills. They were unanimous that knowledge and values supporting CCPSM should be the same for all;

however, it is the skill levels and emphases that may vary by profession, location and context. Examples of this are:

- Organizational change techniques that include business model skills will be important for GPs, practice nurses, and private providers, but may not be as important for PHC workers in other settings. However, understanding how to conduct and be part of Plan, Do, Study, Act (PDSA) cycles will be relevant to all as part of team approaches to organizational change.
- Personal trainers and others in the broader 'health and well-being' industry sector on the periphery of formal healthcare provision will also need skills in CCPSM, especially considering their role and opportunity in prevention. Concern that they generally target white collar groups in the community may mean that they need more skills in health promotion approaches and the social determinants of health that underlie them, with implications for improving access to their services by the lower socioeconomic groups in the community.

Table 9.3   Core skills for the PHC workforce

General patient-centred capabilities	Behaviour change capabilities	Organizational/systems capabilities
1. Health promotion approaches	9. Models of health behaviour change	14. Working in multidisciplinary teams/inter-professional learning and practice
2. Assessment of health risk factors	10. Motivational interviewing	15. Information, assessment and communication management systems
3. Communication skills	11. Collaborative problem definition	16. Organizational change techniques
4. Assessment of self-management capacity (understanding strengths and barriers)	12. Goal setting and goal achievement	17. Evidence-based knowledge
5. Collaborative care planning	13. Structured problem solving and action planning	18. Conducting practice based research/quality improvement framework
6. Use of peer support		19. Awareness of community resources
7. Cultural awareness		
8. Psychosocial assessment and support skills		

In summary, workshop participants confirmed that all health professionals need to:

- Communicate a clear assessment of the person's health risks and be able to perform a holistic assessment of needs, strengths, capacities, and goals
- Understand the pathology of disease and life stages and varying impacts on the person at different stages. This will include understanding influences on the person's capacity or willingness to change their behaviour and recognition that one size will not fit all, for example, CALD and Indigenous influences.
- Understand core principles of self-management and prevention, including the benefits of these and what they involve. This must include the need for a clear rationale for CCSM and the health professional's place within it, as well as what is in it for them.
- 'Walk the talk' as part of deconstructing the power relationship/ differential between 'professional' and 'patient, that is, be aware that this relationship can be inherent in the process of help-seeking, and take active steps to acknowledge it and minimize its impact on the engagement and treatment process.
- Have effective communication skills and family and carer involvement skills that acknowledge the 'team' as also involving carers and other informal supports.
- Understand that multidisciplinary team skills mean understanding the role and function of all members. Multidisciplinary understanding also needs to be understood in the broader sense of being across systems, sectors and agencies, not just within organizations.

In order for these core skills to be acknowledged by health professionals, workshop participants concluded that:

- Endorsement of these skills will require the support and leadership of professional bodies
- Core skills will need to be integrated with each other as part of delivery of training
- Community education regarding self-management will be necessary to raise awareness among recipients of CCPSM support
- Core skills will need to be defined by consumer needs, that is, CCPSM core skills should not be considered by individual professions; it is role and context that determine what skills are needed
- Management will have a pivotal role in initiating, driving and sustaining change. An organizational response that covers structural aspects must also be included. Managers must clearly understand the benefits of CCPSM

- Consumers are integral to the success of training and should be involved in the development, delivery, evaluation and accreditation of training.

Training delivery

In summary, workshop participants confirmed that training providers need to ensure:

- Multiple modes for delivery of training to ensure accessibility for the widest possible group of PHC professionals
- Training is delivered in modules, over time, in several sessions so that skills are delivered in a manageable manner, and with proper support mechanisms and follow-up to allow for reflection and practicing of skills during the training process
- Different levels of training are offered for different people both within and across different professions, some highly skilled, others with only basic skills and awareness
- Consideration about how training is joined up with existing programmes (otherwise a 'Rolls Royce' course that nobody comes to could eventuate)
- That they address issues for training delivery to GPs and allied health together, given that Divisions of General Practice are not funded to deliver to other professions
- Involvement by consumers to help drive training, with increased support given to consumer bodies and use of networks
- That they engage with employers and managers who need to be involved, convinced and committed to training delivery
- Consideration of specific PHC workforce groups, for example, Aboriginal Health Workers in remote areas who may not want to leave their communities to attend training and for whom online learning is problematic
- Accountability to the field, including greater scrutiny of the content of training via improved evaluation of its impact on the workforce in their attempts to translate what they learn in training to their practice. It also considers the need for a continuum of skills transfer from undergraduate training to practice to address organizational cultural barriers to CCPSM practice.

Recommendations

The National Reference Group confirmed the recommendations of an earlier consultation (Martin et al. 2007) undertaken in August 2007 with representatives from:

- Tertiary education providers from the disciplines of medicine, nursing and allied health
- The Medical Deans of Australia and New Zealand
- The Council of Deans of Nursing and Midwifery
- The Australian Council of Pro-Vice Chancellors and Deans of Health Science
- The Australian Nursing and Midwifery Council
- Allied Health Professions Australia
- The Consumers' Health Forum
- Representatives with recognized relevant expertise in the application of a variety of self-management approaches in clinical and community settings in Australia
- Representatives from a range of States and Territories across Australia.

These representatives developed a vision and philosophy to underpin self-management capabilities of the future and existing primary healthcare workforce. They emphasized that all Australians with chronic conditions and their carers should receive care from health professionals competent in providing self-management support.

Core principles

Adoption of the following principles is recommended by representatives from both national reference groups to ensure a seamless transition from the student experience of CCSM to practice by health professionals in the field and the culture of health organizations. The core principles are:

1. All PHC professionals will be competent in supporting people to maintain wellness and prevent the development of chronic conditions, identify and mitigate the effects of risk factors on the development of chronic conditions, and self-manage their existing chronic condition(s).
2. Health professional education will ensure that the workforce are equipped to:
   - Conduct their practice so that the person receiving support and their carers are central to the process of care, ensuring they feel

understood, valued and involved in efforts to support their self-management

- Work in interprofessional teams that support chronic condition prevention and self-management
- Understand and base their chronic condition prevention and self-management support on the bio-psychosocial, cultural and economic context of the person and their carers.

Operational principles

The operational principles to develop strategies to achieve the above include:

1. Consumers' involvement in the design, conduct and evaluation of chronic condition prevention and self-management support training
2. Agreed national prevention and chronic condition self-management definitions and terms
3. Exposure of PHC workers to a range of self-management models that support consumer education and behaviour change
4. Understanding by workers of the influence of the healthcare system on CCPSM
5. CCPSM support training incorporating interprofessional learning
6. Worker learning of CCPSM support in interprofessional practice settings
7. Identified individuals competent in CCPSM support to champion development and delivery of CCPSM support training
8. CCPSM support training integrated across the career of PHC workers, with opportunities for further development of skills and specialization beyond the generic training offered to all PHC workers
9. Explicitly assessment of CCPSM support competencies
10. Evaluation of the effectiveness of CCPSM support training according to effectiveness of translation to practice and outcomes for patients/consumers and carers.

The following key areas are seen as priorities for improving the skills base of PHC health professionals in the area of CCPSM support:

- Shared/consistent definitions of prevention and CCSM and a conceptual framework to provide an overall vision for implementation (Royal Australian College of General Practitioners [RACGP] 2006, Greenhalgh et al. 2004, Zapka et al. 2003, Best et al. 2003b)
- Understanding the inherent relationship between prevention and CCSM as part of a population health/public health approach that

recognizes and incorporates the social determinants of health (WHO 2005b, RACGP 2005, Fraser 2005, WHO 2003)

- Patient education and communication techniques and tools that more collaboratively involve the person in planning, decision making and activities to promote better self-management (Marshal et al. 2005, Lorig and Holman 2003, Martin et al. 2004, RACGP 2006)
- Training that supports a cultural, philosophical and organizational shift towards placing the person at the centre of the collaborative care process, with an emphasis on inclusion, participation, quality of life and well-being for the person (Hibbard 2003, Lewin et al. 2001)
- Effective techniques to support behaviour change by the person that incorporate an understanding of self-efficacy, motivation, stages of change, effective problem solving, reasons for non-compliance/ adherence, goal setting, support systems and management of negative affect (Taylor and Bury 2007, Marks et al. 2005a, 2005b, Warsi et al. 2004)
- Recognition of the benefits of peer support (Copeland 2006, Deegan 2006, Glover 2005, Lawn et al. 2008)
- Understanding of organizational change and the need for a supportive organizational infrastructure to support implementation (Litt 2007, RACGP 2006)
- Multidisciplinary teamwork
- Maximizing information technology to underpin chronic disease prevention and self-management (Jimbo et al. 2006, Chaudhry et al. 2006, Wofford et al. 2005, Kawamoto et al. 2005, Bodenheimer and Grumbach 2003)
- Effective use of existing evidence-based guidelines and resources to support clinical decision making and planning of service delivery, including MBS items for prevention and CCSM (RACGP 2006, Buchan 2004, Grimshaw et al. 2004)
- Skills to support people with specific needs (for example, people with mental illness, young people, ATSI populations, and people with drug addictions) (Marmot 2005, Will et al. 2004, Health Inequalities Research Collaboration (HIRC) Primary Health Care Network 2004, Lawn et al. 2007)
- Effective use of other community resources, both formal and informal. (RACGP 2006, Flocke et al. 2006, Prilleltensky 2005, Glasgow et al. 2004, Bodenheimer et al. 2002).

This project has identified the core skills, knowledge and values underpinning health professional practice in general, not just in relation to CCPSM support. The process has also defined the core principles, components and practices of person-centred care. It also defined the issue in relation to training and integration of these skills into practice.

References

Australian Institute of Health and Welfare. 2004. *National Public Health Expenditure Report 2000–2001*. Series no. 18. Available at: http://www.aihw.gov.au/publications/index.cfm/title/10012 [accessed: 2008].

Bandura, A. 1977. Self-efficacy: toward a unifying theory of behavioral change. *Psychological Review*, 84, 191–215.

Battersby, M., Ask, A., Reece, M., Markwick, M. and Collins, J. 2003. The partners in health scale: the development and psychometric properties of a generic assessment scale for chronic condition self-management. *Australian Journal of Primary Health*, 9, 41–52.

Battersby, M., Lawn, S. and Pols, R.G. in press. Conceptualization of self-management, in *Translating Chronic Illness Research into Practice*, edited by D. Kralik, B. Paterson and V. Coates. Oxford: Wiley Blackwell, 155–201.

Battersby, M., Harvey, P., Mills, P.D., Kalucy, E., Pols, R.G., Frith, P., Mcdonald, P., Esterman, A., Tsourtos, G., Donato, R., Pearce, R. and Mcgowan, C. 2007. SA HealthPlus: a controlled trial of a statewide application of a generic model of chronic illness care. *Milbank Quarterly*, 85, 37–67.

Best, A., Moor, G., Holmes, B., Clark, P.I., Bruce, T., Leischow, S., Buchholz, K. and Krajnak, J. 2003a. Health promotion dissemination and systems thinking: towards an integrated model. *American Journal of Health Behavior*, 27, S206–16.

Best, A., Stokols, D., Green, L., Leischow, S., Holmes, B. and Buchholz, K. 2003b. An integrative framework for community partnering to translate theory into effective health promotion strategy. *American Journal of Health Promotion*, 18, 168–76.

Bodenheimer, T. and Grumbach, K. 2003. Electronic technology: a spark to revitalize primary care? *Journal of the American Medical Association*, 290, 259–64.

Bodenheimer, T., Wagner, E.H. and Grumbach, K. 2002. Improving primary care for patients with chronic illness: the Chronic Care Model, Part 2. *Journal of the American Medical Association*, 288(15), 1909–14.

Braithwaite, J. and Travaglia, J. 2005. Inter-professional learning and clinical education: an overview of literature. Canberra: Braithwaite and Associates and ACT Health Department.

British Association of Behavioural and Cognitive Psychotherapies 2005. *Mapping Psychotherapy – What is CBT? What are the Cognitive and/or Behavioural Psychotherapies?* Available at: http://www.babcp.com/silo/files/what-is-cbt.pdf.

Buchan, H. 2004. Gaps between best evidence and practice: causes for concern. *Medical Journal of Australia*, 180, S48–S49.

Centre for Cultural Diversity in Ageing 2008. *Cultural Awareness*. Available at: http://www.culturaldiversity.com.au/Resources/ServiceProviderRes ources/CulturalAwareness/tabid/81/Default.aspx [accessed: 2008].

Chaudhry, B., Wang, J., Wu, S., Maglione, M., Mojica, W., Roth, E., Morton, S.C. and Shekelle, P.G. 2006. Systematic review: impact of health information technology on quality, efficiency, and costs of medical care. *Annals of Internal Medicine*, 144(10), 742–52.

Copeland, M.E. 2006. *Wellness Recovery Action Plan and Peer Support*. Available at: http://www.mentalhealthrecovery.com [accessed: 2007].

Corbin, J.M. and Strauss, A. 1988. *Unending Work and Care: Managing Chronic Illness at Home*. San Francisco: Jossey-Bass Inc.

Deegan, P. 2006. *Recovery and the Conspiracy of Hope*. Available at: http://www.patdeegan.com [accessed: 2008].

Department of Health Australia 2007. *Research Evidence on the Effectiveness of Self Care Support*. Available at: http://www.dh.gov.uk/en/Publicationsandstatistics/Publications/PublicationsPolicy AndGuidance/DH_080689 [accessed: 2008].

Flocke, S.A., Gordon, L.E. and Pomiecko, G.L. 2006. Evaluation of a community health promotion resource for primary care practices. *American Journal of Preventive Medicine*, 30(3), 243–51.

Fraser, J. 2005. Population and public health in Australian general practice – changes, challenges and opportunities. *Australian Family Physician*, 34(3), 177–9.

Glasgow, R.E., Davis, C., Funnell, M.M. and Beck, A. 2003. Implementing practical interventions to support chronic illness self-management. *Joint Commission Journal on Quality and Safety*, 29(11), 563–74.

Glasgow, R.E., Goldstein, M., Ockene, J.K. and Pronk, N.P. 2004. Translating what we have learned into practice: principles and hypotheses for addressing multiple behaviors in primary care. *American Journal of Preventive Medicine*, 27(2), 88–101.

Glover, H. 2005. Recovery based service delivery: are we ready to transform the words into a paradigm shift? *Australian e-Journal for the Advancement of Mental Health*, 4(3) 1–4. Available at: http://auseinet.flinders.edu.au/journal/.

Greenhalgh, T., Robert, G., Macfarlane, F., Bate, P. and Kyriakidou, O. 2004. Diffusion of innovations in service organisations: systematic review and recommendations. *Milbank Quarterly*, 82(4), 581–629.

Grimshaw, J., Thomas, R., Maclennan, G., Fraser, C., Vale, L. and Whitty, P. 2004. Effectiveness and efficiency of guideline dissemination and implementation strategies. *Health Technology Assessment*, 8(6), 1–72.

Hibbard, J. 2003. Engaging health care consumers to improve quality of care. *Medical Care*, 41(4), 161–70.

Huni, N.M. 2005. Enhancing psychosocial support of children affected by HIV/AIDS: a special focus on memory work. *Bulletin of Medicus Mundi*, 97, June 2005.

Jessup, R.L. 2007. Interdisciplinary versus multidisciplinary care teams: do we understand the difference? *Australian Health Review*, 31(3), 330–1.

Jimbo, M., Nease, D.E., Ruffin, M.T. and Rana, G.K. 2006. Information technology and cancer prevention. *CA: A Cancer Journal for Clinicians*, 56, 26–36, doi:10.3322?canjclin.56.1.26.

Johnson, A. and Paton, K. 2007. *Health Promotion and Health Services: Management for Change*. Australia and New Zealand: Oxford University Press.

Katon, W., Russo, J.E., Von Korff, M., Lin, E.H.B., Ludman, E. and Ciechanowski, P. 2008. Long-term effects on medical costs of improving depression outcomes in patients with depression and diabetes. *Diabetes Care*, 31(6), 1155–9.

Kawamoto, K., Houlihan, C., Balas, A. and Lobach, D. 2005. Improving clinical practice using clinical decision support systems: a systematic review of trials to identify features critical to success. *British Medical Journal*, 330(765), doi:10.1136/bmj.38398.500764.8F.

Lawn, S. and Battersby, M.W. 2009. *Capabilities for Supporting Prevention and Chronic Condition Self-Management: A Resource for Educators of Primary Health Care Professionals*. Flinders University, Adelaide: Australian Government Department of Health and Ageing.

Lawn, S., Smith, A. and Hunter, K. 2008. Mental health peer support for hospital avoidance and early discharge: an Australian example of consumer driven and operated service. *Journal of Mental Health*, 17(5), 498–508.

Lawn, S., Battersby, M., Pols, R.G., Lawrence, J., Parry, T. and Urukalo, M. 2007. The mental health expert patient: findings from a pilot study of a generic chronic condition self-management programme for people with mental illness. *International Journal of Social Psychiatry*, 53(1), 63–74.

Lawn, S., Battersby, M., Lindner, H., Matthews, R., Morris, S., Wells, L., Litt, J. and Reed, R. 2009. What skills do primary health care professionals need to provide effective self-management support? Seeking consumer perspectives. *Australian Journal of Primary Health*, 15(1), 37–44.

Lawrence, D.M. 2005. A comparison of organized and traditional health care: implications for health promotion and prospective medicine. *Methods of Information in Medicine*, 44(2), 273–7.

Lewin, S., Skea, Z., Entwistle, V., Zwarenstein, M. and Dick, J. 2001. Interventions for providers to promote a patient-centred approach in clinical consultations. *Cochrane Database of Systematic Reviews*, issue 4. art. no.: CD003267. doi: 10.1002/14651858.CD003267.

Litt, J. 2007. *Exploration of the Delivery of Prevention in the General Practice Setting*. Adelaide: Flinders University.

Locke, E.A. and Latham, G.P. 1990. *A Theory of Goal Setting and Task Performance*. Englewood Cliffs: Prentice Hall.

Lorig, K. 1993. Self-management of chronic illness: a model for the future. *Generations*, 17(3), 11–14.

Lorig, K.R. and Holman, H.R. 2003. Self-management education: history, definition, outcomes, and mechanisms. *Annals of Behavioral Medicine*, 26(1), 1–7.

Marks, R., Allegrante, J. and Lorig, K. 2005a. A review and synthesis of research evidence for self-efficacy-enhancing interventions for reducing chronic disability: implications for health education practice (Part I). *Health Promotion Practice*, 6, 37–43, doi:10.1177/1524839904266790.

Marks, R., Allegrante, J. and Lorig, K. 2005b. A review and synthesis of research evidence for self-efficacy-enhancing interventions for reducing chronic disability: implications for health education practice (Part II). *Health Promotion Practice*, 6, 148–56, doi:10.1177/1524839904266792.

Marmot, M. 2005. Social determinants of health inequalities. *The Lancet*, 365(9464), 1099–104.

Marshall, S., Haywood, K. and Fitzpatrick, R. 2005. *Patient Involvement and Collaboration in Shared Decision-making: A Review*. Report from the Patient-Reported Health Instruments Group, Department of Public Health, University of Oxford.

Martin, A., Hood, C., Lawrence-Wood, E. and Battersby, M. 2007. *Allied Health Professions and Chronic Condition Self-management: Final Report*, submitted to the Commonwealth Department of Health and Ageing. Adelaide: Flinders University.

Martin, J.C., Avant, R.F., Bowman, M. Bucholtz, J., Dickinson, J., Evans, K. and Al, E. 2004. The future of family medicine: a collaborative project of the Family Medicine Community. *Annals of Family Medicine*, 2, S3–S32, doi:10/1370/afm.130.

McDonald, J., Harri, E., Kurti, L., Furler, J., Apollini, L. and Tudball, J. 2004. *Action on Health Inequalities: Early Intervention and Chronic Condition Self-Management*. Sydney: The Health Inequalities Research Collaboration (HIRC), Primary Health Care Network, University of NSW.

Michie, S., Miles, J. and Weinman, J. 2003. Patient-centredness in chronic illness: what is it and does it matter? *Patient Education and Counseling*, 51(3), 197–206.

Miller, W.R. and Rollnick, S. 1991. *Motivational Interviewing Preparing People to Change Addictive Behavior*. New York: The Guilford Press.

Muir, G. 1997. *Evidenced-Based Healthcare – How to Make Health Policy and Management Decisions*. New York and Melbourne: Churchill Livingstone.

National Health Priority Action Council (NHPAC). 2006. *National Chronic Disease Strategy*. Australian Government Department of Health and Ageing, Canberra.

Pender, N.J., Murdaugh, C.L. and Parson, M.A. 2006. *Health Promotion in Nursing Practice*. 5th Edition. New Jersey: Pearson/Prentice Hall.

Prilleltensky, I. 2005. Promoting well being: time for a paradigm shift in health and human services. *Scandinavian Journal of Public Health*, Supplement 66, 53–60.

Prochaska, J. and DiClemente, C. 1983. Stages and processes of self-change of smoking: towards an integrated model of change. *Journal of Consulting and Clinical psychology*, 51(3), 390–95.

Prochaska, J. and Velicer, W.F. 1997. The transtheoretical model of health behavior change. *American Journal of Health Promotion*, 12(1), 38–48.

Royal Australian College of General Practitioners (RACGP). 2005. *Guidelines for Preventive Activities in General Practice*. Melbourne: RACGP.

RACGP. 2006. *Putting Prevention into Practice. Guidelines for the Implementation of Prevention in the General Practice Setting*. 2nd Edition. Melbourne: RACGP.

Smith, D. 2005. *Educating to Improve Population Health Outcomes in Chronic Disease*. Darwin: Menzies School of Health Research.

Solomon, P. 2004. Peer support/peer provided services: underlying processes, benefits and critical ingredients. *Psychiatric Rehabilitation*, 27(4), 392–401.

Taylor, D. and Bury, M. 2007. Chronic illness, expert patients and care transition. *Sociology of Health and Illness*, 29(1), 27–45.

Vermeire, E., Hearnshaw, H., Van Royen, P. and Denekens, J. 2001. Patient adherence to treatment: three decades of research. A comprehensive review. *Journal of Clinical Pharmacy and Therapeutics*, 26(5), 331–42.

Victorian Quality Council. 2005. *Better Quality, Better Health Care: A Safety and Quality Improvement Framework for Victorian Health Services*. Melbourne: State Government of Victoria.

Von Korff, M., Gruman, J., Schaefer, J., Curry, S.J. and Wagner, E.H. 1997. Collaborative management of chronic illness. *Annals of Internal Medicine*, 127(2), 1097–102.

Wagner, E.H., Austin, B.T. and Von Korff, M. 1996. Improving outcomes in chronic illness. *Managed Care Quarterly*, 4(2), 12–25.

Wagner, E.H., Austin, B.T., Davis, C., Hindmarsh, M., Schaefer, J. and Bonomia, E. 2001. Improving chronic illness care: translating evidence into action. *Health Affairs*, 20(6), 64–78.

Warsi, A., Wang, P.S., Lavalley, M.P., Avorn, J. and Solomon, D.H. 2004. Self-management education programs in chronic disease: a systematic review and methodological critique of the literature. *Archives of Internal Medicine*, 164(15), 1641–9.

West, R. 2005. Editorial: Time for a change: putting the transtheoretical (stages of change) model to rest. *Addiction*, 100(8), 1036–9.

Will, J., Farris, R., Sanders, C., Stockmyer, C. and Finkelstein, E. 2004. Health promotion interventions for disadvantaged women: overview of the Wisewoman Projects. *Journal of Women's Health*, 13(5), 484–502.

Wofford, J., Smith, E. and Miller, D. 2005. The multimedia computer for office-based patient education: a systematic review. *Patient Education and Counselling*, 59(2), 148–57.

World Health Organization (WHO). 1986. Ottowa Charter for Health Promotion. Available at: http://www.euro.who.int/aboutwho/policy/20010827_2 [accessed 29 June 2009].

WHO 2003. *Primary Health Care: A Framework for Future Strategic Directions*. Geneva: WHO.

WHO 2005a. *Preparing a Health Care Workforce for the 21st Century. The Challenge of Chronic Conditions*. Geneva: WHO.

WHO 2005b. *Preventing Chronic Disease. A Vital Investment*. Geneva: WHO.

Zapka, J., Taplin, S., Solberg, L.I. and Manos, M. 2003. A framework for improving the quality of cancer care: the case for breast and cervical cancer screening. *Cancer Epidemiology Biomarkers and Prevention*, 12(January), 4–13.

Appendix: Definitions of core skills for self-management support

Person-centred skills	Definition
1. Health promotion approaches	Any work which actively and positively supports people, groups, communities or entire populations to be healthy. It does not focus on sickness, but on building capacity. It includes building healthy public policy, creating supportive environments, strengthening community action, developing personal skills and re-orientating health care services toward prevention of illness and promotion of health (WHO 1986). It involves working with people and communities as they define their goals, mobilize resources and develop action plans for addressing problems they have collectively identified (Smith 2005).
2. Assessment of health risk factors	Awareness and effective identification of predisposing factors (smoking, nutrition, alcohol, physical activity, stress) that may lead to future health problems for the patient. Further factors within the patient or part of their environment may increase their chances, or make it more likely, that they will develop a disease or other health condition (Royal Australian College of General Practitioners 2006).
3. Communication skills	Effective communication involves the ability to establish and develop mutual understanding, trust, respect and cooperation. It is the ability to express oneself clearly so the other person understands, and to listen and interpret effectively to understand what the other person is trying to express. In this context, it includes communication between patients and PHC workers, as well as communication between staff in PHC teams and with other service providers.
4. Assessment of self-management capacity	Assessment of the patient's health beliefs, knowledge, attitudes, behaviours, strengths, barriers, readiness to change (motivation), confidence (self-efficacy) and the importance they place on their health (priority). This will be interpreted by the patient through the lens of social, cultural, economic, political and spiritual influences. It may also include an assessment of the capacity of carers/family to support self-management (Battersby et al. 2003).

5. Collaborative care planning — The process in which all those involved in the organizing, provision and receipt of care for a given patient are actively involved in the planning and decision-making surrounding what that care involves over a given time period (Battersby et al. 2007).

6. Use of peer support (within chronic condition self-management context) — Peer support is provided by people with a 'lived experience' of effectively self-managing chronic conditions who can therefore act as positive role models for others with chronic conditions. Supportive cultural values held by the organization or setting in which they are utilized are important (Solomon 2004).

7. Cultural awareness / interpreter service utilization — Cultural awareness entails an understanding of how a patient's culture may inform their values, behaviour, beliefs and basic assumptions (Centre for Cultural Diversity in Ageing 2008). It involves understanding the local community and its needs, and specific communication skills that are culturally respectful. This may involve the effective use of interpreters to accurately relay and receive what is communicated between the worker and the patient and their carers / family.

8. Psychosocial assessment and support skills / skills enhancement — The ability of health professionals to identify, build and sustain positive aspects of psychosocial health such as resilience, strengths and coping skills with the patient and their carers. Psychosocial support by health professionals and others are 'interventions and methods that enhance [patients'], families', and communities' ability to cope, in their own context, and to achieve personal and social well-being; enabling [them] to experience love, protection, and support that allow them to have a sense of self-worth and belonging' (Huni 2005).

Behaviour change skills	Definition
9. Models of health behaviour change	Frameworks which help us to understand human behaviour and how to change it. This involves theoretical understanding of the mechanisms involved in the choices people make in their lives and how to engage them in the process of change. Various models exist, including: Health Belief Model (Pender et al. 2006); Theory of Reasoned Action and Theory of Planned Behaviour (Pender et al. 2006); Social Learning Theory (Bandura 1977); Transtheoretical (Stages of Change) Model (Prochaska and DiClemente 1983, Prochaska and Velicer 1997); Relapse Prevention Model (Miller and Rollnick 1991); Health Promotion Model (Pender et al. 2006); 5As Model (Glasgow et al. 2003); and Cognitive Behavioural Therapy (British Association of Behavioural and Cognitive Psychotherapies 2005).
10. Motivational Interviewing	A process undertaken with a person to support their behaviour change. The sequence in Motivational Interviewing involves encouraging the person to talk, generate self-motivational statements, deal with resistance, develop readiness to change and negotiate a plan, developing determination and action. The five principles underlying the process are expressing empathy, developing discrepancy, avoiding arguing, rolling with resistance and supporting self-efficacy. Motivational Interviewing embodies cognitive change skills (Miller and Rollnick 1991).
11. Collaborative problem definition	Having an open dialogue with the patient about what they see as their main problem, what happens because of the problem, and how the problem makes them feel (Von Korff et al. 1997).
12. Goal setting and action planning	The process of deciding on what one wants, planning how to get it, and then working towards the objective of achieving it, usually by ensuring that it is SMART (specific, measurable, achievable, realistic, and timely). In the health context, goal setting can be done by the patient alone or with the support of others to help formulate the goal and help the patient to remain motivated to achieve it, i.e. involving collaborative goal setting, problem-solving and other goal attainment skills (Locke and Latham 1990).
13. Structured problem solving	The ability to systematically assist a patient to learn the skill of problem solving, i.e. identify and analyse practical issues arising in a situation and to determine options for a practical solution, making effective use of time and resources available (Katon et al. 2008).

Organizational/ systems skills	Definition
14. Working in multidisciplinary teams/inter-professional learning and practice	The ability to establish working relations with others of a different profession or discipline, to interact effectively, and to promote productive cooperation, collaboration and coordination. It involves understanding and respecting the role and function of all members, and integrating care by recognizing and actively engaging service providers across systems, sectors and agencies, not just within organizations. It involves communication skills together with the timeliness of those communications. 'Inter-professional education occurs when two or more professions learn with, from and about each other to improve collaboration and the quality of care' (Jessup 2007, Braithwaite and Travaglia 2005).
15. Information, assessment and communication management systems	A systematic approach to proactive use of clinical data to screen, monitor and provide self-management support to patients. This may include use of electronic (or other) recall and reminder systems to enable health service providers to become pro-active in providing support to patients and alerting them to the need for a review of their health condition(s). These information system management skills also include use of systems for sharing of health records and coordination of communication and support between PHC service providers within the patient's community (Wagner et al. 1996).
16. Organizational change techniques	Change in the structure of service delivery in order to impact on the way work is delivered to the population served. Various techniques are used within health care settings, each based on theories of organizational structure, culture and models of change, group behaviour and values. The Plan, Do, Study, Act (PDSA) cycle is one mechanism for mobilizing staff for incremental organizational change (Johnson and Paton 2007).

Organizational/ systems skills	Definition
17. Use of evidence-based knowledge	An explicit approach to health care practice in which the health professional is aware of the evidence that bears on their practice, and the strength of that evidence. This includes the risks and benefits of any intervention including self-management support. This approach to decision making involves the health professional using the best evidence available, in consultation with the patient, to decide upon the option which suits that patient best (Muir 1997). Most evidence-based guidelines are disease specific. However, co-morbidity is common among people with chronic conditions. Therefore, it is important for evidence-based knowledge and practice to acknowledge this complexity.
18. Conducting practice based research/quality improvement framework	Undertaking practical research or evaluation in the field that can be used to inform everyday practice and improve the delivery of service to patients. Measures may include patient or health professional rated self-efficacy, self-management behaviours, patients' health-related quality of life, health service utilization, patient/carer satisfaction with the service, service costs, or specific disease measures. This practice-based research provides services with a strategic overview of the key principles and practices necessary for the effective monitoring, management and improvement of their health services. The Plan, Do, Study, Act (PDSA) cycle is one mechanism for undertaken this research in practice (Victorian Quality Council 2005).
19. Awareness of community resources	Broad understanding of available resources, supports, services and activities within the patient's community that would be useful in supporting them and their carers/ family. This involves an understanding of what the services involve, how to access them and their appropriateness in being able to meet the patient's and their carer's identified needs (Wagner et al. 2001).

10 Knowledge and reasoning in practice: an example from physiotherapy and occupational therapy

Megan Smith, Sylvie Meyer, Karen Stagnitti and Adrian Schoo

Introduction

In this chapter we describe the nature and sources of knowledge used by physiotherapists and occupational therapists in their daily clinical work. We have chosen to integrate our discussion of knowledge with a discussion of clinical reasoning reflecting the current understanding that knowledge and reasoning are inherently related in clinical practice (Higgs and Jones 2008). To illustrate the nature of knowledge and clinical reasoning used by these caring professions, we present an example of a client following a stroke. We conclude that the knowledge and reasoning processes used by these professions include shared and distinctive elements reflecting a close relationship between two professions that maintain defined and separate roles in health practice.

Physiotherapy (or physical therapy) is a healthcare profession which focuses on the restoration of movement. The World Confederation of Physical Therapists (WCPT) has defined physiotherapy in the following manner.

> Physical therapy provides services to individuals and populations to develop, maintain and restore maximum movement and functional ability throughout the lifespan. This includes providing services in circumstances where movement and function are threatened by ageing, injury, disease or environmental factors. Functional movement is central to what it means to be healthy.
>
> Physical therapy is concerned with identifying and maximising quality of life and movement potential within the spheres of promotion, prevention, treatment/intervention, habilitation and rehabilitation. This encompasses physical, psychological, emotional, and social well being. Physical therapy involves the interaction between physical therapist, patients/clients, other health professionals, families, care givers, and communities in a process where

movement potential is assessed and goals are agreed upon, using knowledge and skills unique to physical therapists. (WCPT 2009)

Occupational therapy is a healthcare profession that focuses on using purposeful activity to assist people to restore function. The World Federation of Occupational Therapists (WFOT) defines occupational therapy in the following way:

> Occupational Therapy is a healthcare profession based on the knowledge that purposeful activity can promote health and well-being in all aspects of daily life. The aims are to promote, develop, restore and maintain abilities needed to cope with daily activities to prevent dysfunction. Programs are designed to facilitate maximum use of function to meet demands of the person's working, social, personal and domestic environment. The essential feature of occupational therapy is the active involvement of the person in the therapeutic process. Occupational therapists receive education in social, psychological, biological and medical sciences, professional skills and methods. Fieldwork studies form an integral part of the course. (WFOT 2008)

Occupational therapists work with a wide range of people, in both the physical and psychosocial areas of health and well-being. Occupational therapy process is based on assessment of the person's abilities, social support, environment and any issues that hinder the person in their daily life. The intervention process is person orientated as well as environmentally orientated (WFOT 2008).

A case study from clinical practice

Throughout this chapter we refer to the story of Albert during his rehabilitation journey following a stroke. Physiotherapists and occupational therapists (OT) work independently with Albert and also collaborate as team members sharing in his care.

Albert is 63 years old and has suffered a stroke affecting the left side of his body. In the first two weeks after the stroke he had low tonus with little movement on his affected side. His state of consciousness was poor. He felt very tired and weak and was not able to move independently in his bed. He recognized his wife and could answer simple questions but was too confused to have a conversation. He was not aware of his health condition. During this time his neurological problems were compounded by the development of pneumonia. He was at risk of dying and his family was afraid.

At the end of this acute phase his level of consciousness had improved, he was no longer confused and his pneumonia had resolved. He understood he had had a stroke but he didn't comprehend what it meant. He expressed a need to move in his bed, to be able to sit in the bed and to go to the toilet, and expressed his frustration at being unable to independently complete these activities. The nurses, physiotherapists and occupational therapists involved in his care suspected that he had unilateral special neglect because he had difficulties perceiving the left side of his body and the left side environment. After two weeks he was transferred to a rehabilitation unit.

On arrival at the rehabilitation unit Albert was evaluated by the OT and physiotherapist. Assessments used were observational assessment of mobility, tone, position, upper limb, use of wheelchair and visual perceptual assessment. This assessment determined that he was able to mobilize with the maximal assist of two, he could sit independently, sit to stand with the assistance of one and could stand unaided for five seconds. His left arm remained flaccid and he was unable to reach, grasp or hold objects.

The final goal of rehabilitation was to return Albert to his home. Albert had been a truck driver for a local firm and was intending to retire soon. He had worked with the firm for ten years and drove within set regional boundaries. He lives with his wife in a regional city. His wife is 60 years old and suffers from arthritis in her hands, knees and feet. He has three adult children and four grandchildren. His adult children live within a radius of a one hour drive of his home. His social life is centred on his workmates. He spends his lunch hours playing cards and talking to workmates and goes to the pub with his workmates every Friday evening. He has no other friends outside work. Albert lives in a two-storey home with ten external stairs and seven internal stairs. The kitchen, lounge area and garage are downstairs. There is a yard with front and back garden. The home is in walking distance to a local shopping centre, bus and train stops. Albert previously spent his time outside of work hours with his family and/or watching TV. He tends a small vegetable garden in his backyard at home with his wife.

Albert spent four months in the rehabilitation unit. He was discharged home. On discharge he was able to walk inside his home without falling but could only walk outside if the ground was flat. He could not use his left arm efficiently and could not drive because of some remaining perceptual impairments.

Physiotherapy knowledge and clinical reasoning

Physiotherapy practice in Albert's care would begin in the acute care setting with a focus on his respiratory health as affected by pneumonia, as well as the variations to his movement ability. Once Albert recovered from this acute phase and entered the rehabilitation phase the physiotherapy emphasis would shift to his movement function. His rehabilitation would typically involve an initial comprehensive assessment of his movement ability. For example, is he able to move himself from lying in bed to sitting independently on the side of the bed, walk independently and reach for and manipulate an object such as a cup? Physiotherapists interpret assessment findings against their knowledge base to diagnose any movement abnormalities and select rehabilitation strategies to facilitate the optimal recovery of movement activities needed for quality of life.

Research investigating clinical decision making by physiotherapists in acute care settings indicates that practitioners use a knowledge base that is multidimensional in nature, consisting of multiple knowledge types derived from multiple sources (Smith et al. 2007). Building on the work of Vico, an approach was presented by Higgs and Titchen (2001) on the categorization of knowledge that differentiated between propositional and non-propositional forms of knowledge used in healthcare practice. *Propositional knowledge* refers to knowledge arising from theory and research. In the case of Albert this would refer to knowledge of areas of the brain responsible for particular movement functions and the implications of impaired blood supply to this region. Propositional knowledge can consist of facts and concepts, knowledge of theories underpinning their practice, and knowledge of published clinical research. It is apparent that this knowledge is not drawn from a body of knowledge confined to the discipline of physiotherapy; rather, physiotherapists draw upon a collective knowledge base relevant to all health professionals. How physiotherapists interpret and incorporate this knowledge into their clinical reasoning processes may, however, be distinct to their profession.

Non-propositional knowledge refers to experiential knowledge. Higgs and Titchen (2001) differentiated this type of knowledge into professional craft knowledge and personal knowledge. *Professional craft* knowledge refers to knowledge arising from professional experience while *personal knowledge* is knowledge that an individual acquires from personal life experience. In the case of Albert, the physiotherapists involved in his care could have knowledge of characteristic features of unilateral spatial neglect and how that manifests itself in individual clients and their response to physiotherapy rehabilitation strategies. Personal knowledge would refer to the knowledge an individual physiotherapist might hold about what it is to experience fear for a loved one who is ill.

Research conducted in acute care settings (Hedberg and Sätterlund Larsson [2004] studying nurses and Smith [2006] studying physiotherapists) has found that professionals have knowledge that is applied for different reasoning purposes. These different types of knowledge include procedural knowledge (or how to perform certain skills), comparative and predictive knowledge, situational or contextual knowledge, and social and interpersonal knowledge. This knowledge allows them to manage the particular context in which they work. Applying this to Albert's case reveals that physiotherapists could draw upon:

- Procedural knowledge, which would inform physiotherapists how to transfer Albert from bed to chair safely by providing appropriate support and instructions and knowledge of the optimal placement of a chair. This knowledge could be constructed from knowledge of the mechanics of normal movement but also experience of how to organize optimally the task to ensure a safe and efficient transfer.
- Comparative and predictive knowledge would refer to knowledge used to compare Albert's presentation with other clients following stroke and to determine his likely progress. Practitioners would have a sense of how Albert related to 'normal'. This type of knowledge could also be used to predict Albert's likely response to particular interventions.
- Situational or contextual knowledge could involve knowledge of the location of resources that could be used in therapy and the optimal timing of therapy in relation to other activities being undertaken in the rehabilitation unit. This would also involve knowledge of others who work in their context.
- Social knowledge would refer to knowledge of other team members as people and also health professionals, their roles and responsibilities and how to interact and work effectively together to achieve effective outcomes. This knowledge and its application is important for occupational therapists and physiotherapists collaborating effectively together.
- Interpersonal knowledge would relate to understanding Albert and his family and their response to his condition and how it might impact on his life.

The literature also makes reference to intuitive and tacit knowledge as types of knowledge relevant to healthcare practice. Some argue strongly for the presence of intuitive knowledge and judgement, defining intuition as 'understanding without rationale' (Benner and Tanner 1987: 2) where this understanding is a 'gut feeling' (Titchen and Errser 2001: 36). Others refute the idea of intuition being simply labelled inexplicable, suggesting, rather, that it is knowledge of which practitioners are currently unaware, as it has become deeply integrated into practice and professional judgement (Higgs and Titchen 2001). A related term is tacit knowledge, which refers to Polyani's idea that 'we know more than we can tell' (Polanyi 1958: 27). It is possible that in Albert's case practitioners used a high level of these subconscious or unarticulated types of knowledge to inform their practice.

The discussion so far has alluded to the dimensions of physiotherapy clinical reasoning. In this section we specifically review the current understanding of physiotherapy reasoning as relevant to Albert. Research investigating physiotherapy clinical reasoning indicates that physiotherapists use a range of reasoning strategies that vary according to the nature of the task and context (Edwards 2004, Smith 2007). Edwards (2004) portrays these categories as reasoning about diagnosis and reasoning about management. Reasoning about diagnosis includes diagnostic reasoning and narrative reasoning. In the case of Albert, this would involve a diagnosis about the nature of his physical and functional impairments. This aspect of reasoning would draw on propositional knowledge such as the impact of his neurological pathology on function, and comparisons between Albert's movement ability and movement function under normal circumstances. Narrative reasoning relates to developing an understanding of the client's illness and disability experience. As we have noted in the case, this is expressed by Albert in terms of his frustrations and goals. Edwards and Jones (2007) also describe physiotherapy reasoning as dialectical in nature, as practitioners move between biomedical aspects of clients' condition and situations and narrative aspects. As we will note later, narrative reasoning is an aspect of reasoning shared by both physiotherapists and occupational therapists, as is this notion of a dialectical process in reasoning.

Physiotherapy reasoning has been found to involve the cognitive processes of hypothetico-deductive reasoning and pattern recognition. These processes of reasoning are underpinned by a knowledge base organized for practice that enables practitioners to recognize and interpret the nature of the presenting problem and its meaning for the client and their outcome. The source of this knowledge can be propositional in nature but is also dependent on professional craft knowledge critically derived from experience. Jones (2008) also highlighted physiotherapy as a collaborative process involving clients, where clients' reasoning about their own condition is incorporated with the physiotherapist's. Undertaking this collaborative process would require practitioners to access their body of personal knowledge to inform their relationships with people and to understand clients' experience of their illness and loss of function.

The second major aspect of reasoning identified by Edwards (2004) was reasoning about management, where this encompasses reasoning about procedure, interactive reasoning, collaborative reasoning, reasoning about teaching, predictive reasoning and ethical reasoning. These many aspects of reasoning are integrated by physiotherapists as they make and implement decisions to bring about changes in movement function and support clients' skills of self-management and understanding of their condition. In the case of Albert this aspect of physiotherapy reasoning would be seen in the practice of structuring therapy activities to address his difficulties with functional activities such as standing up from a chair and walking.

Physiotherapy reasoning is affected by factors in the context in which it occurs and by factors that are related to physiotherapists themselves (Smith 2006). Smith found that physiotherapists in acute care settings were affected by physical, social and organizational factors. Clinical decision making by acute care physiotherapists was unable to be separated from the context in which it occurred. Indeed clinical reasoning involved the incorporation of contextual features as an integral component of the reasoning process. For example, in the case of Albert decisions about activities such as which therapy activities to use could require consideration of contextual factors such as the physical environment and equipment available, social factors such as other health professionals and clients and their actions, and organizational factors, such as workload and priorities. Smith (2006) also found that decision making was affected by factors relating to the practitioner based on their unique frames of reference.

Occupational therapy knowledge and reasoning

Occupational therapists have formal knowledge about the diagnosis and its potential impact on skills and functions and can describe the client's assets and limitations in relation to the diagnosis (Rogers 1983). In Albert's case, during the acute phase, information required by the occupational therapist would be obtained through observation and concrete techniques or procedures. For example, consideration would be given to Albert's bed mobility, sitting, eating, and bowel and bladder control.

In the rehabilitation phase, the occupational therapist undertakes assessments to measure motor, sensation, visual perceptual skills and performance in basic or instrumental activities of daily life. These assessments, for example, the Canadian Occupational Performance Measure (Law 1998b), assist the therapist to set goals and objectives, to measure progress and to decide the best treatment options. These goals centre on restoring or modifying the occupations that are identified by Albert as meaningful to him. Through this collaboration between the occupational therapist and Albert, the therapist is working in a client-centred approach (Law 1998a). In conjunction with the client, the therapist identifies the client's limitations and resources, and this leads to the setting of specific, measurable, achievable, realistic and timely objectives. These objectives can be set according to the occupational therapist's knowledge about stroke and its impact, for instance, how to move in one's bed, then to dress oneself with a one-hand technique, or to perceive one's environment on the left side, and to prepare a sandwich.

The occupational therapist also uses knowledge about frames of reference, models and methods recommended to remediate or to compensate for limitations due to stroke. The occupational therapist's unique contribution is, according to a classical operative principle, to work with clients on tasks that encourage them to use personal factors (skills, performance components, functions) that must be trained or recovered (Crepeau 2003, Meyer 2007). These tasks are often clients' occupations in daily life, for instance, in Albert's case, to deal out playing cards, to pick the cards off the table, then hold them in the left hand and manage his left visual field neglect (Wilby 2007). These tasks must meet the client's volitional needs otherwise the motivation to engage in them will be low. These tasks can also assist the client by progressive re-training of skills, for instance skills involving the mobility of the left arm. From one session to another, exercises requiring higher levels of functioning (for example, global grasp, then fine grasp) or combinations of skills are offered (for example, to bend, to seize, to lift, to manipulate with both hands). In the end they lead to performances in activities (for example, to fill a cup of tea, to answer a phone call). The approach is called 'bottom-up' when successive functions are trained in order of complexity to achieve functioning in the performance of activities or occupations. It is named 'top-down' when functional activities are used to train functions or skills (Schell 2003).

After discharge, Albert's intervention includes home visits and modifications to fit out the home environment so it is more suitable for Albert's needs, choosing, buying and learning how to use technical aids that assist in daily occupations, as well as modifications or reorganization of everyday occupations. Usually this stage of recovery requires a home visit to decide on modifications that are essential if the client is to return home. The basis of these actions is influenced by the occupational therapist's formal medical and professional knowledge of stroke, assistive technology, environmental adaptation for safety and accessibility, task organization, and social participation because this knowledge assists the client to understand and face up to the impact of the disability in his or her occupational performances. The occupational therapist also discusses problems with the client and his family and decisions are negotiated with them (Woodson 2008).

In occupational therapy, the intervention focus is the human condition of the client to enable them to move from a situation of major disability to a situation of social participation through new, modified or recovered occupations. In order to do this, occupational therapists use clinical reasoning, which is a complex process of thinking and decision making, associated with professional action. Clinical reasoning underlies the intervention process and helps the therapist in specific contexts to obtain the necessary data, to cooperate with clients, to identify problems that need intervention, to set objectives, to plan sessions with clients and others, and to carry out and adapt treatment activities according to clients' feedback (Benamy 1996, Chapparo and Ranka 2000). In this process, different forms of clinical reasoning – some explicit, others tacit – have been demonstrated (Mattingly and Fleming 1994). Explicit reasoning is directed by theory but tacit thinking is more intuitive and based on common sense, personal or professional values and culture as it is taken for granted. The use of the different forms of reasoning varies according to therapists' experience and the characteristics of the tasks (Sinclair 2007).

Explicit forms of reasoning are used to assess and act upon while considering the client's health condition and the impact this condition has on performance and skills. Explicit forms of reasoning are practised on biomedical contents or contents belonging to the classical operative principle of occupational therapy. In Albert's case, explicit forms of reasoning are based on assessment which provides specific knowledge of Albert's motor, sensory and perceptual limitations due to stroke. This knowledge assists the therapist in choosing appropriate models, methods and techniques for Albert.

Explicit reasoning is sometimes called scientific reasoning (Tomlin 2008). 'Scientific' means that the therapists are guided by theory, think logically and use hypotheses, deduction and induction, and are able to give some rationality to their decisions (Rogers 1983, Rogers and Holm 1991). During the assessment, this reasoning goes through five stages: iterative: cue acquisition, hypothesis generation, cue interpretation and hypothesis evaluation (Rogers and Holm 1991). In the end, the therapist develops an understanding of the client's performance components and skill limitations. Scientific reasoning can also be deductive, comparative and inferential, and can be used in deciding on the intervention task, grading activity or environmental organization (Tomlin 2008). For instance, in Albert's case, the therapist assesses the motor function of Albert's left arm, and then analyzes the motor functions necessary to shuffle playing cards. He or she compares these functions to those Albert presently has and deduces how to implement the activity 'shuffling play cards'. The therapist decides that this activity has an interest according to treatment objectives and decides to offer this activity as an opportunity during a treatment session. This type of explicit reasoning is frequently held by novices.

Therapists who encounter novel situations process in a hypothetico-deductive manner, rather than the faster process of pattern recognition

(Higgs and Jones 2008). More experienced practitioners get a quick image of performance, function, skills limitations and their clients' assets by recognizing discreet signs that are particularly eloquent for them. They judge rapidly what action needs to be undertaken (Robertson 1996). In their case, assessment tools serve to document the case for others. Unfortunately, therapists who operate in this way are only partially able to explain what they do and how they arrive at decisions and they justify their decisions in a way not always congruent with the followed rules (Harries 2007). These therapists although typically more accurate can make errors due to, for instance, too few observations or an overestimation of some pieces of information (Tomlin 2008).

During assessment and intervention sessions, the expert therapists know how to subtly adjust their action to the client's response (Sinclair 2007). Usually the expert's reasoning is more intuitive than the novice's. Their clinical process mixes assessment and treatment moments and seems less logical when compared to a biomedical model. For some therapists, such expertise endows the process with more discernment. In a complex, uncertain and changing situation, they manage better than novices because they can consider all the parameters of a situation and know better how to reconcile motivational, volitional, functional and relational aspects relating to the client. Nevertheless, the expert therapist is partially unaware of his or her own mental process and can also forget important cues that would contradict his or her usual way of perceiving (Harries 2007).

Interactive knowledge (interpersonal knowledge)

Besides scientific or procedural reasoning, which is usually explicit, there are forms of reasoning that are qualified as anti-positivist because they concern reasoning that focuses on the understanding of the client as a person in a context. These forms of reasoning are intended to face the hazards of the therapeutic relationship. They give meaning to the intervention not in relation to the disease or disability but to illness as it is experienced by the person (Mattingly and Fleming 1994).

During sessions, occupational therapists are involved in interaction with clients not only from the rehabilitation and functional perspective but also from the perspective of clients' experience of illness, disability and emotions. They adjust their behaviours, discourses, rate of sessions, activity choices, verbal and non verbal feedback according to their perception of what is happening in the interaction (Fortmeier and Thanning 2002). This kind of thinking helps to engage clients in sessions, finely adapt objectives and therapeutic strategies and give to the person a feeling of self-confidence and trust in the occupational therapist's competences. Interactive reasoning in the interaction creates a shared language between therapists and clients

(Mattingly and Fleming 1994). With this reasoning, the occupational therapist can understand what Albert endures as he has lost his capacity to drive his truck and what he experiences while slowly recovering his capacities.

In parallel with the therapist's considerations of the interaction between the client and themselves, therapists are also thinking and talking to themselves about what is happening during the sessions and in the client's life. In relation to the context of the client, the occupational therapist reflects upon the client's human condition and imagines the person in their future life in order to lead the intervention towards the best possible outcome. For instance, the therapist asks him- or herself if it is desirable for Albert to continue to see his workmates in the pub and, if the answer is yes, how to adapt therapy to make that possible. Mattingly and Fleming (1994) describe this knowledge as implicit, but further research has found that this type of reasoning is probably less implicit than thought, with occupational therapists being able to manipulate reasoning through their own reflexive practice (Boyt Schell 2008). Client-centred practice or new frameworks, guide therapists to be more aware of what kind of experience and emotion they produce in clients during sessions.

Pragmatism and values

Occupational therapists' clinical reasoning and decisions are also influenced by their work context or even their personal context (Boyt Schell 2008). Personal or professional values also have an impact on treatment (Chapparo and Ranka 2000).

Occupational therapists think in a pragmatic way when they decide how to adapt an intervention to the context of an interdisciplinary team, the clients on their caseload, the duration of sessions or the entire process of rehabilitation, the available equipment in the unit, hospital norms, cost containment, and the national healthcare system. For instance, if Albert's therapist cannot visit his home, they cannot observe the environment and must discuss this issue with him and his family. They must imagine how it is, and ask appropriate questions and give advice without being able to see the actual context. Pragmatic reasoning has also to do with the occupational therapist's knowledge and expertise, because therapists can only use competences they possess. Pragmatic reasoning resembles conditional reasoning but it has more to do with the occupational therapists' internal and external context and not the client's context.

Occupational therapists as professionals and human beings in a specific culture have values that influence their intervention. For instance, occupational therapists value autonomy and independence, engagement, client-centred practice and equal access to healthcare. Perception of a situation or a person is also influenced by theses values. Reasoning held on the basis of such an ethical point of view is ethical reasoning (Meyer 2007). Ethical reasoning is intended to judge what it is that is 'good' to do in a situation (Schell 1998). It is possible that what is considered as 'good' for an occupational therapist may not or cannot be considered as 'good' in a hospital and that the therapist may have conflict with other professionals or face an ethical dilemma. Rogers, in 1983, stressed that the final decision about what ought to be done in an intervention is making an ethical decision. Things have not changed if evidence-based practice does not recognize that the final decision must take the client's opinion and expertise into account: clinical decisions must be based on ethical thinking.

Narrative thinking

Opposite to scientific reasoning, the occupational therapist guides their process through storytelling. They tell stories to themselves and to their colleagues. They build the story with the client. Narrative thinking helps therapists to capture a client's multiple dimensions and to organize them in time and space. Narrative thinking also assists in understanding complex situations and gives meaning to what happens during intervention. With narrative reasoning, therapy becomes a story taking place in time, with difficult and easier moments, with failure and victories, full of challenges (Mattingly 1998). In Albert's case, this form of reasoning helps to set goals, to understand how he might participate in society and manage after discharge.

Narrative reasoning is probably used with a mix of other forms of thinking to make understanding a situation more intelligible. Reflexive practice largely turns to narrative reasoning because it is through stories that we share our ideas, understanding much more than through scientific reasoning.

Blending knowledge and reasoning from physiotherapy and occupational therapy for shared care

In our example of Albert's rehabilitation journey following a stroke so far, we have separated our description of physiotherapy and occupational knowledge and reasoning. Although useful to illustrate the distinct aspects of these professions, this separation underrepresents the common and integrated nature of physiotherapy and occupational therapy practice in many areas of healthcare. By using the case study of Albert we have revealed that occupational therapists and physiotherapists use many types of knowledge and reasoning to manage their clinical work, be a team player, function as a member of a multidisciplinary organization and represent clients. Functioning in a team requires taking part in team development and being able to let go or accept particular roles (Antoniadis and Videlock 1991, Rush and Shelden 1996). This is particularly relevant when client-focused teamwork progresses from multidisciplinary (separate disciplinary treatment plans) to interdisciplinary (shared plan and monitoring of progress) or even transdisciplinary (crossing professional boundaries) modes of service delivery, particularly in small rural organizations that have limited resources.

Experience from our work as health professionals indicates, and as evident in the content of this chapter, physiotherapists and occupational therapists have much in common in relation to knowledge and ways of reasoning. As we focus on Albert and his story we can see that in practice this shared perspective supports a team approach to his management.

During his rehabilitation Albert received input from both the physiotherapist and occupational therapist. Formal team meetings were held in which these professionals shared the goals with each other and with the rest of the team, including social workers, medical practitioners and speech pathologists. The physiotherapist and occupational therapist agreed on goals of rehabilitation that focused on strategies to recover optimal function rather than on accommodating to his existing level of function. The physiotherapist and occupational therapist discussed Albert's needs at home and the strategies they were both using to achieve the goal of returning home. They organized joint therapy sessions where they could both work on transfers and mobility. They also negotiated the timing of their individual therapies to account for the goals they were trying to work towards on a particular day to avoid Albert experiencing excessive fatigue.

Sources of knowledge and strategies to enhance professional development

In physiotherapy and occupational therapy different sources of knowledge have been identified in the literature, including knowledge from reading and professional education, and from work colleagues, mentors, personal experience and critical reflection on one's clinical experience (Beeston and Simons 1996, Jensen 2000, Resnik and Jensen 2003). Patients are also considered 'a powerful, central, valued source of clinical knowledge' (Jensen 2000: 37).

Increasingly, the framework of evidence-based practice and clinical practice guidelines are being advocated as a primary means of accessing and applying knowledge. In the case of healthcare professionals working with Albert, resources such as Clinical Guidelines for Acute Stroke Management (National Stroke Foundation 2007) have been developed. This knowledge is formal and has a research base that provides an evidence-base for intervention (Woodson 2008).

In spite of this strong emphasis on research-based practice in the literature, findings from research studies are not readily integrated into clinical practice (Estabrooks 2001, Jette et al. 2003). Whereas knowledge acquired by health professionals at university represents a large body of knowledge brought to clinical practice, Smith found that much of the propositional knowledge subsequently gained was acquired sporadically and opportunistically when required in specific clinical instances. Specific effort was required by practitioners to increase their propositional knowledge following graduation, as they perceived that the nature of their workload did not allow time for building propositional knowledge during work hours. As a result, practitioners may seek out more contextually relevant sources of knowledge, such as other health professionals, particularly where insufficient time is available to engage in evidence-based practice (Jette et al. 2003).

Context-embedded practitioner knowledge, or professional craft knowledge, is knowledge that arises from the processing of experience. Non-propositional knowledge is contextual in nature, having been particularly constructed to enable practitioners to work in their particular work situations (Hedberg and Larrson 2004). This knowledge is largely related to practical skills, some of which are learned during academic education and others during clinical experience, for instance, how to physically facilitate an action, simplify a task, or move a wheelchair in order to access a bathtub. Smith found that non-propositional knowledge was derived from individual practitioners' experiences of success and failure and responses to decisions they had made in the past. Non-propositional knowledge was also acquired by asking other health professionals for knowledge and advice, observing and being taught or shown by others the usual ways of practice in context, and accessing written protocols that articulate ways of practice. Eraut (2004: 254), with particular reference to the notion of the social contexts of practice, notes that:

> The episodic memories of individuals are influenced both by the semiconscious socialization process through which norms, values, perspectives and interpretations of events are shaped by local workplace culture, and by their

conscious learning from others, and with others, as they engage in cooperative work and tackle challenging tasks.

This idea has been developed by Lave and Wenger (1991), who put forward the notion of communities of practice, and emphasized that learning in practice is a 'matter of acculturation, of joining a community of practice, rather than the application of skills or principles which operate independently of social context' (Cope 2000: 851). Learning occurs in a particular situation and therefore the contextual elements of the situation are acquired at the same time as other knowledge (Higgs 2004). Non-propositional knowledge is thus more appropriately considered as constructed rather than acquired. Higgs, Fish and Rothwell (2004: 93) proposed a view of knowledge that arises from a dynamic process of striving to construct or make sense of the world; of taking understandings, insights, observations and experiences and exploring them in relation to existing knowledge, in terms of the perceived realities of experience and other forms of evidence, such as logic and peer review, in order to construct a view of reality that makes sense to the knowledge maker.

Multiple sources of knowledge become blended, often through narrative reasoning and reflexive critique of this knowledge, resulting in a body of knowledge that uniquely informs an individual's practice. When used ethically, knowledge leads to 'good' decisions with the client.

So far, we have discussed experienced therapists who have gained knowledge and clinical reasoning through working with people such as Albert. New graduates may feel that they lack competence in different areas through lack of experience, contacts and/or knowledge (Lee and Mackenzie 2003, Steenbergen and Mackenzie 2004, Tryssenaar and Perkins 2001). Neistadt (1996) noted that once a new graduate became more confident in the clinical decision-making process, they were more confident in the services they provided to clients. They also experienced improved job satisfaction because they had greater understanding of the complexity of their work (Neistadt 1996). Post graduation strategies to help graduates achieve a state of competence in practice and increase practitioner confidence include continuing education courses and providing mentors (Tryssenaar and Perkins 2001).

Continuing professional development (CPD) for healthcare professionals involves life-long learning to improve and maintain competencies and standards of care (Hunter and Nicol 2002, Shillitoe 2002) to provide efficacious evidence-based intervention and to maximize quality of life (Sackett 1996). Findings of a recent systematic review of 32 studies (30 RCTs) demonstrated that lectures alone (that is, passive dissemination of information) were not sufficient to change clinical practice, but that interactive workshops had a moderately large effect (O'Brien et al. 2006). The effect size reported was

0.84 (95 per cent CI 0.51 to 1.17). Interactive learning is an important strategy used in adult learning, and has been used in continuing education (Schoo 2008) because allied health professionals prefer the format (Stagnitti 2005). Kirkpatrick (1994) described four levels of CE effect evaluation and Gusky (2000) five, and Schoo (2008) provided evidence of transfer of knowledge and skills (level two) and potential implementation of learning among the rural participants (level three). Although measuring improved clinical practice and patient outcomes was outside the scope of the latter study, some qualitative comments made reference to this level.

Principles that enhance the success of adult learning include perceived relevance, founded on and added to previous experience; active involvement and sharing; a problem-focus, fostering responsibility for self-learning; mixing activities and times for reflection or evaluation; and engendering trust and respect (Spencer and Jordan 1999). Extending one's knowledge also includes reflection upon one's practice, as well as perceiving, feeling or adapting one's behaviour to a situation (Mattingly and Fleming 1994).

In conclusion

Occupational therapists and physiotherapists share part of their knowledge, think with the same forms, and are in a good position to enhance their knowledge, both propositional and non-propositional, by working together. Moreover, they share the same context of practice where they face similar problems. These include difficulties in implementing evidence-based practice because of workload (and perhaps poor recognition from their hierarchy); the necessity of discussing formal knowledge learned in continuing education to change practice; and the need to reflect upon practice to enhance their competence. They also face the challenge of making their knowledge explicit so that it can be formalized and transmitted, so that they might be recognized as experts.

References

Antoniadis, A. and Videlock, J.L. 1991. In search of teamwork: a transactional approach to team functioning. *Infant-Todler Intervention: The Transdisciplinary Journal*, 1(1), 157–67.

Beeston, S. and Simons, H. 1996. Physiotherapy practice: practitioners' perspectives. *Physiotherapy Theory and Practice*, 12(4), 231–42.

Benamy, B. 1996. *Developing Clinical Reasoning Skills: Strategy for the Occupational Therapist*. San Antonio: Therapy Skills Builders.

Benner, P. and Tanner, C. 1987. Clinical judgement: how expert nurses use intuition. *American Journal of Nursing*, 87, 23–31.

Boyt Schell, B.A. 2008. Pragmatic reasoning, in *Clinical and Professional Reasoning in Occupational Therapy*, edited by B.A. Boyt Schell and J. Schell. Philadelphia: Lippincott, Williams and Wilkins, 169–87.

Chapparo, C. and Ranka, J. 2000. Clinical reasoning in occupational therapy, in *Clinical Reasoning in the Health Profession*, 2nd Edition, edited by J. Higgs and M.A. Jones. Oxford: Butterworth Heinemann, 128–37.

Cope, P. 2000. Situated learning in the practice placement. *Journal of Advanced Nursing*, 31, 850–6.

Crepeau, E. 2003. Analyzing occupation and activity. A way of thinking about occupational performance, in *Willard and Spackman's Occupational Therapy*, 10th Edition, edited by E. Crepeau, S. Cohn and B.A. Boyt Schell. Philadelphia: Lippincott, Williams and Wilkins, 203–7.

Edwards, I. 2004. Clinical reasoning strategies in physical therapy. *Physical Therapy*, 84(4), 312–35.

Edwards, I. and Jones, M. 2007. Clinical reasoning and expertise, in *Expertise in Physical Therapy Practice*, 2nd Edition, edited by G. Jensen, J. Gwyer, L.M. Hack and K.F. Shepard. Boston: Elsevier, 192–213.

Eraut, M. 2004. Practice-based Evidence, in *Evidence-Based Practice*, edited by G. Thomas and R. Pring. Milton Keynes: Open University Press, 80–91.

Estabrooks, C.A. 2001. Research utilization and qualitative research, in *The Nature of Qualitative Evidence*, edited by J.M. Morse, J.M. Swanson and A.J. Kuzel. Thousand Oaks: Sage, 275–98.

Fortmeier, S. and Thanning, G. 2002. *From the Patient's Point of View: An Activity Theory Approach to Occupational Theory*. Copenhagen: Ergoterapeutforeningen.

Gusky, T.R. 2000. *Evaluating Professional Development*. Thousand Oaks: Sage.

Harries, P. 2007. Knowing more than we can say, in *Contemporary Issues in Occupational Therapy: Reasoning and Reflection*, edited by J. Creek and A. Lawson-Porter. Chichester: J. Wiley, 161–88.

Hedberg, B. and Larrson, U.S. 2004. Environmental elements affecting the decision-making process in nursing practice. *Journal of Clinical Nursing*, 13, 316–24.

Higgs, J. 2004. Educational theory and principles related to learning clinical reasoning, in *Clinical Reasoning for Manual Therapists*, edited by M. Jones and D. Rivett. Oxford: Elsevier Butterworth Heinemann, 379–402.

Higgs, J., Fish, D. and Rothwell, R. 2004. Practice knowledge-critical appreciation, in *Developing Practice Knowledge for Health Professionals*, edited by J. Higgs, B. Richardson and M. Dahlgren. Oxford: Elsevier Butterworth Heinemann, 89–106,

Higgs, J. and Jones, M. 2008. Clinical decision making and multiple problem spaces, in *Clinical Reasoning for Health Professions*, 3rd Edition, edited by J. Higgs and M. Jones. Oxford: Elsevier Butterworth Heinemann, 3–17.

Higgs, J. and Titchen, A. 2001. Framing professional practice: knowing and doing in context, in *Professional Practice in Health, Education and Creative Arts*, 2nd Edition, edited by J. Higgs and A. Titchen. Oxford: Blackwell Publishing, 3–15.

Hunter, E. and Nicol, M. 2002. Systematic review: evidence of the value of continuing professional development to enhance recruitment and retention of occupational therapists in mental health. *British Journal of Occupational Therapy*, 65, 207–15.

Jensen, G. 2000. Expert practice in physical therapy. *Physical Therapy*, 80, 28–52.

Jette, D.U., Grover, L. and Keck, C.P. 2003. A qualitative study of clinical decision making in recommending discharge placement from the acute care setting. *Physical Therapy*, 83(3), 224–36.

Jones, M. 2008. Clinical reasoning in physiotherapy, in *Clinical Reasoning for the Health Professions*, 3rd Edition, edited by J. Higgs and M. Jones. Oxford: Elsevier Butterworth Heinemann, 245–56.

Kirkpatrick, D.L. 1994. *Evaluating Training Programs: The Four Levels*. San Francisco: Berett-Koehler.

Lave, J. and Wenger, E. 1991. *Situated Learning: Legitimate Peripheral Participation*. New York: Cambridge University Press.

Law, M. (ed.) 1998a. *Client-Centered Occupational Therapy*. Thorofare: Slack Incorporated.

Law, M. 1998b. *Canadian Occupational Performance Measure*. 3rd Edition. Ottawa: Canadian Association of Occupational Therapists.

Lee, S. and Mackenzie, L. 2003. Starting out in rural New South Wales: the experiences of new graduate occupational therapists. *Australian Journal Rural Health*, 11(1), 36–43.

Mattingly, C. 1998. *Healing Dramas and Clinical Plots: The Narrative Structure of Experience*. Cambridge: Cambridge University Press.

Mattingly, C. and Fleming, M. 1994. *Clinical Reasoning: Forms of Inquiry in a Therapeutic Practice*. Philadelphia: F.A. Davis.

Meyer, S. 2007. *Démarches et Raisonnements en Ergothérapie*. Lausanne: Haute école de travail social et de la santé.

National Stroke Foundation 2007. *Clinical guidelines for acute stroke management*. Available at: http://www.strokefoundation.com.au/images/stories/healthprofessionals/clinical%20guidelines%20for%20acute%20stroke%20management.pdf [accessed: 25 May 2009].

Neistadt, M.E. 1996. Teaching strategies for the development of clinical reasoning. *American Journal of Occupational Therapy*, 50(8), 676–84.

O'Brien M.A., Freemantle, N., Oxman, A.D. Wolf, F., Davis, D.A. and Herrin, J. 2006. Continuing education meetings and workshops: effects on professional practice and health care outcomes. *Cochrane Database of Systematic Reviews* 2006(4).

Polanyi, M. 1958. *Personal Knowledge: Towards a Post Critical Philosophy.* London: Routledge and Kegan Paul.

Resnik, L. and Jensen, G. 2003. Using clinical outcomes to explore the theory of expert practice in physical therapy. *Physical Therapy*, 83(12), 1090–106.

Robertson, L. 1996. Clinical reasoning, part 2: novice/expert differences. *British Journal of Occupational Therapy*, 59(5), 212–16.

Rogers, J. 1983. Eleonor Clarke Slagle Lectureship –1983: clinical reasoning: the ethics, science, and art. *American Journal of Occupational Therapy*, 37(9), 601–16.

Rogers, J. and Holm, M. 1991. Occupational therapy diagnostic reasoning: a component of clinical reasoning. *American Journal of Occupational Therapy*, 45(11), 1045–53.

Rush, D. and Shelden, M. 1996. On becoming a team: a view from the field. *Seminars in Speech and Language*, 17(2), 131–42.

Sackett, D.L. 1996. Evidenced based medicine: what it is and what it isn't. *British Medical Journal*, 312, 71–2.

Schell, B. 1998. Clinical reasoning : the basis of practice, in *Willard and Spacksman's Occupational Therapy*, 9th Edition, edited by M. Neistadt and E. Crepeau. Philadelphia: Lippincott Williams and Wilkins, 90–100.

Schell, B. 2003. Overview of the intervention, in *Willard and Spackman's Occupational Therapy*, 10th Edition, edited by E. Crepeau, S. Cohn and B.A. Boyt Schell. Philadelphia: Lippincott Williams and Wilkins, 455–90.

Schoo, A.M. 2008. The evolution of a state-wide continuing education programme for allied health professionals. *International Journal of Therapy and Rehabilitation*, 15(2), 60–6.

Shillitoe, R. 2002. Clinician, update thyself: assessing the value of local training courses. *British Journal of Therapy and Rehabilitation*, 9, 166–70.

Sinclair, K. 2007. Exploring the facets of clinical reasoning, in *Contemporary Issues in Occupational Therapy: Reasoning and Reflection*, edited by J. Creek and A. Lawson-Porter. Chichester: J. Wiley, 143–60.

Smith, M. 2006. Clinical decision making in acute care cardiopulmonary physiotherapy. Unpublished PhD thesis, The University of Sydney, Australia.

Smith, M., Higgs, J. and Ellis, E. 2007. Physiotherapy decision making in acute cardiorespiratory care is influenced by factors related to the physiotherapist and the nature and context of the decision: a qualitative study. *Australian Journal of Physiotherapy*, 53(4), 261–7.

Spencer, J.A. and Jordan, R.K. 1999. Learner centred approaches in medical education. *British Medical Journal*, 318, 1280–3.

Stagnitti, K. 2005. Access and attitude of rural allied health professionals to CPD and training. *International Journal of Therapy and Rehabilitation*, 12(8), 355–61.

Steenbergen, K. and Mackenzie, L. 2004. Professional support in rural New South Wales: perceptions of new graduate occupational therapists. *Australian Journal Rural Health*, 12, 160–5.

Titchen, A. and Errser, S. 2001. The nature of professional craft knowledge, in *Practice Knowledge and Expertise in the Health Professions*, edited by J. Higgs and A. Titchen. Oxford: Butterworth Heinemann, 35–41.

Tomlin, G. 2008. Scientific reasoning, in *Clinical and Professional Reasoning in Occupational Therapy*, edited by B.A. Boyt Schell and J. Schell. Philadelphia: Lippincott, Williams and Wilkins, 91–124.

Tryssenaar, J. and Perkins, J. 2001. From student to therapist: exploring the first year of practice. *American Journal of Occupational Therapy*, 55(1), 19–27.

Wilby, H. 2007. The importance of maintaining a focus on performance components in occupational therapy practice. *British Journal of Occupational Therapy*, 70(3), 129–32.

Woodson, A.W. 2008. Stroke, in *Occupational Therapy for Physical Dysfunction*, 6th Edition, edited by M.V. Radomski and C.A. Trombly. Philadelphia: Lippincott Williams and Wilkins, 38.

World Confederation of Physical Therapists (WCPT). 2009. *Description of physical therapy – what is physical therapy?* Available at: http://www.wcpt.org/node/29599 [accessed 29 June 2009].

World Federation of Occupational Therapists (WFOT). 2008. *Text of the WFOT pamphlet*. Available at: http://www.wfot.org/office_files/ABOUT%20 OCCUPATIONAL%20THERAPY%282%29.pdf [accessed: 10 April 2008].

11 Using knowledge in the practice of dealing with addiction: an ideal worth aiming for

Peter Miller

Addiction, excessive consumptions, Alcohol and Other Drug (AOD) problems, dependence: whatever the name used to describe the range of behaviours involved when people become almost solely focused on a single behaviour or substance, the behaviours span all levels of society and touch virtually every caring profession. Addiction-related practice and theory constitute a unique and fascinating area of theory and practice because of its truly pan-disciplinary nature. The behaviour is impacted upon, and impacts on, economic factors, political imperatives, social factors (gender, class and ethnicity), psychological factors, physiology, psychopharmacology, neuropsychology and, according to some, even genetics. The convergence of this wide range of bodies and types of knowledge means that there is great debate within the different sectors and many issues of professional competition for dominance. It is one of the few areas in modern society where most policy works in direct opposition to the vast body of research and expert opinion.

Despite a massive evidence base, the most popular conceptions of AOD use still revolve around 'addiction', the disease model and rational choice. All of these conceptualizations fail to explain the majority of AOD problems and have been roundly disproved, yet their influence remains. This chapter will briefly cover some of the major debates in the field and demonstrate how different bodies of knowledge (combined with professional self-interest) have contributed to the field, ending with a discussion of where clinical practice and research are heading in the search for more effective interventions for addiction-related problems.

Defining drugs, addiction and treatment

In such a broad field of human behaviour, it is wise to define what we are talking about and choose a number of specific instances to discuss. Within the field there are many behaviours, substances and debates. The greatest of these is what to call the range of behaviours, which begins with pleasure seeking and ends with life-destroying dependence, huge social issues and for many, death.

Addiction, dependence and excessive or dangerous consumptions

Within the realm of 'addiction' there are a great many debates about terminology, definition and what behaviours fall within such terminology. While addiction is the term most commonly known to refer to this set of behaviours, many believe it is an inaccurate and misleading concept (Moore 1992), a view I personally subscribe to. Unfortunately, it is a concept with almost universal currency and one which needs almost no explanation. Experience internationally has shown that there is little point debating the issue beyond acknowledging that better terms are available and that the concept of addiction is inherently flawed. The concept of addiction moves beyond the realm of substances and covers behaviours such as gambling. For these reasons, and in the interests of parsimony, I will most commonly refer to 'addiction' and addiction-related problems.

Of course there have been many attempts to define addiction (Babor and Hall 2007). In one of the most highly cited and regarded attempts, Edwards and Gross (1976) outlined seven diagnostic criteria for alcohol dependence: narrowing of behavioural repertoire, salience of alcohol use, increased tolerance, repeated withdrawal symptoms, relief from or avoidance of withdrawal symptoms through further alcohol use, subjective awareness of a compulsion to drink, and reinstatement after abstinence. Key features included the notion of 'impaired control' and a recurring withdrawal/relief drinking cycle. Social, cultural and economic factors were also recognized as important in shaping how the syndrome might 'look' within different cultures and contexts. However, Moore (1992) points out that beneath such surface idiosyncrasies there existed a psychobiological core – based on tolerance, withdrawal and relief drinking – that was essentially the same wherever the syndrome manifested itself. Once triggered, psychobiology explained how dependence was maintained. Possibly the most controversial element of the dependence syndrome was that at a certain point in their drinking, individuals crossed an objective divide, regardless of social labels, and became 'dependent' (Edwards and Gross 1976). In the words of Edwards (1980: 24):

> A man starts to drink for many reasons and when he is dependent, many of these reasons will still pertain; they are not wiped out because of the superadded fact of the dependence. But the dependence now provides reasons for drinking which are truly superadded, and which may dominate the many preceding reasons for drinking and heavy drinking. Dependence becomes a self-perpetuating behaviour.

A second school of thought was 'the continuum model', which viewed dependence on any activity or substance as normal human behaviour (e.g. Orford 1985). Individuals could be placed on the continuum of dependence, which ranged from 'nil' through to 'severe'. For those espousing this more psychological perspective (Moore 1992), dependence was a question of variation rather than a change in state.

Despite the differences between the two theories, both maintain a focus on the individual, although they pay lip-service to factors outside the individual's control, such as social, cultural and economic factors. 'Dependence' was thought to provide a new, more flexible way of identifying, understanding and responding to a particular type of alcohol-related problem and was considered a major advance, both theoretically and practically, on 'alcoholism' and 'addiction'. The World Health Organization adopted such a definition in the ninth edition of its International Classification of Diseases, and it was also incorporated into the DSM-III-R. However, the term 'dependence' failed to gain universal appeal, and today all labels are used somewhat interchangeably, although the use of a certain term is often interpreted as reflecting an individual's conception of the nature of the syndrome. The biggest problem with talk of dependence or addiction is that all such terms fail to deal with the reality that most problems associated with such behaviours come from the general population who have neither, but engage in sporadic behaviour which is harmful (that is, problematic substance use or dangerous consumptions). This new terminology, while quick to catch on in Australia, is not well understood in the United Kingdom or the United States.

Theoretical models used in the intervention of 'addiction'

Theories have been constantly developed which incorporate individual psychological (e.g. West 2006), cultural (e.g. Eckersley 2005), social (e.g. Moore 1993) and societal (e.g. Zinberg 1984) factors that go a very long way towards addressing most of the factors involved in an individual developing addiction-related behaviours. Sadly, this is not the case, and globally the two dominant ways of thinking about addiction treatment (the 12 step and 'stages of change' models) have been roundly disproved.[1] In both cases, there are elements which hold a clear attraction, particularly from a clinical point of view, and both have an easy logic about them.

The 12 step model

The 12 step model (Alcoholics Anonymous [AA], Narcotics Anonymous [NA]) is the best known and most influential model of addiction treatment. However, it is in fact a model of mutual support, most commonly enacted through 'meetings'. The model had its beginnings in 1935 in Akron, Ohio, as the outcome of a meeting between two former alcoholics, and is a non-alcoholic fellowship that emphasizes universal spiritual values in daily living. The 12 step model simply acts to bring people with AOD problems together in a non-judgemental environment where they can discuss their problems, hear the stories of others and gain support. It works on replacing negative social groupings with positive ones focused on abstinence. Aside from meetings, the 12 step model also encourages new members to take on a 'mentor' who commits to always being available should the person need help or someone to talk with. A clinical model which purports to be based on the 12 step model called the Minnesota Model has also been developed and forms the basis of many residential rehabilitation facilities globally. However, the model is not aligned with the original AA model and has essentially none of its strengths (such as peer support and new social groupings), but is mostly focused on the 12 steps theory. This theoretical model has been comprehensively demonstrated to be ineffective (Ferri et al. 2006). Critiques abound pointing out how none of the steps has ever been validated, or any of the assumptions ever supported by research (such as someone being an addict forever more), that the organization is cult-like in both its goals and practice (Valverde and White-Mair 1999), and that the inclusion of a 'higher power' excludes most people who have addiction-related problems.

On the other hand, saying 12 steps does not work would also misrepresent the situation. There is a significant body of research that demonstrates the usefulness of AA and NA as adjunct therapies to other treatment modalities

---

1   It should be noted here that neither of these theories are dominant in Australia, although both have some devotees and US and UK interest groups occasionally try to encourage greater uptake of such therapies. This was particularly the case under US President George W. Bush's 'President's Emergency Plan for AIDS Relief' (PEPFAR) programme to encourage faith-based and abstinence-focused interventions. Naturally, this was in direct conflict with the research evidence of the day.

(e.g. Gossop et al. 2003; Project MATCH Research Group 1997). Based simply on the ubiquitous nature of such 12 step groups, they have undeniably helped many millions of people worldwide to deal with their addictions.

The Transtheoretical Model of behaviour change or Stages of Change (SOC) model

The Transtheoretical Model of behaviour change, known to many as the Stages of Change (SOC) model, states that chronic behaviour patterns such as smoking can be characterized as belonging to one of five or six 'stages' (Prochaska and DiClemente 1982, 1986). Stage definitions vary from behaviour to behaviour and across different versions of the model, but the general model consists of 'precontemplation', 'contemplation', 'preparation', 'action' and 'maintenance'. The model further proposes that individuals progress through stages sequentially but usually revert to prior stages before achieving maintenance and then termination (West 2005). However, there are serious problems with the model, many of which have been well articulated (e.g. Bunton et al. 2000, Etter and Perneger 1999, Whitelaw et al. 2000). Despite the fact that it has been argued that the problems with this model are so serious that it has held back advances in the field of health promotion (West 2005), its popularity continues largely unabated. Even in the absence of a new theory, simply reverting to the common sense approach that was used prior to the Transtheoretical Model would be better than staying with the model. In that approach people were asked simply about desire to change and ability to change and it was recognized that these were affected by a range of personal and situational factors including addiction (West 2005). In essence, the dominance of this model, in spite of the overwhelming scientific evidence, acts as an effective marker of a lack of knowledge being used in practice.

Other models

Naturally, there are many other theoretical models used in the area of addiction and its treatment. However, these have been almost singularly unsuccessful in making their way into treatment service systems on any significant scale. What is most commonly seen in most professional treatment services, certainly outside the United State, with its 12 step dominance, is the use of atheoretical models, where most clinicians simply have little addiction-specific training and use the skills and theories taught to them in their basic disciplinary training, whether that be medicine, psychology, social work, nursing or sociology. This leads to the interesting phenomenon of there being services where many staff hold very divergent views about how people develop addictive behaviours and, consequently, the best way to treat them. In these settings, treatment ends up being a conglomeration (some say eclectic collection) of therapies, such as Cognitive Behavioural Therapy (CBT) and Motivational Interviewing (MI), without a great deal of theoretical underpinning, although some of the more traditional residential rehabilitation models (such as therapeutic communities) claim to be different and work from a general theoretical principle. Sadly they have been found to be exceedingly expensive (Gossop et al. 2002), mostly ineffective and often dangerous for most clients who relapse and have a three-fold risk of overdose death (Darke and Hall 2003).

Within the Australian context, one of the most commonly adopted and conceptually sound models in use is the 'Drug, set and setting' model proposed by Norman Zinberg (Zinberg 1984). Zinberg proposed that 'an exclusive focus on drug pharmacology ("drug") and individual psychology ("set") was not sufficient to understand the drug experience without reference to a third interactive component – the "setting" or social context' (Moore 1993: 413). The multifocused approach of such a framework allows for the many considerations which exist in the drug-using event. As such, it encourages a holistic view of drug use, realizing that while pharmacology and psychology play important roles in drug use, equal weighting should be given to understanding the contexts in which we use drugs and how the usually impact on both psychopharmacology and psychology. For Zinberg, 'setting' referred to both the immediate social situation in which drug use occurs and the wider beliefs, sanctions and values brought to drug use by particular social groups. Naturally such beliefs vary across cultures and sub-cultures. As our understanding of psychopharmacology increases, we are beginning to understand how a person's reaction to social situations can influence the levels of different hormones in their system and, consequently, the way in which the drugs might affect them. Zinberg's important insights led, amongst other things, to people thinking about the ways in which the environment in which drug use occurs can be made less harmful, embodied to a degree in the philosophy of harm reduction (see below).

Such an understanding of addiction and substance use also highlights the need for a multidisciplinary approach. Like few other fields, the treatment of addiction-related problems involves a vast array of professional groups. At the policy and academic level, economists and criminologists work in the same field (and sometimes with the same individuals) as psychiatrists, social workers and genetic scientists. At the treatment end of the field, the reality is that people with addiction-related problems present with a long list of problems, some that contributed to the issues to start with and some that have developed as a consequence of their subsequent behaviours. This multidisciplinarity inevitably results in many varied and interesting collaborations and, of course, the occasional turf war. In a standard course of treatment, a heroin user can expect to work with GPs, nurses, psychologists, social workers, 'counsellors', housing workers and often psychiatrists (depending on the country and its treatment structure). More common consequences of different types of addiction lead to other problems, ranging from HIV and hepatitis C, through financial problems to legal problems. None of the disciplines has absolute mastery as each brings its own specialist knowledge to the table, although there is a fairly standard hierarchy within the medically focused services. For instance, there seems little point in supplying a person with counselling for their alcoholism if they are homeless. Different conceptions of drug use, its causes and the best treatment abound within each of the disciplines involved, but in the end it is rare to see a service (and seldom a good one) that is run by a single professional group.

Interventions

Harm reduction

The most recent change in dealing with addiction-related problems has been the harm reduction philosophy. Harm reduction (or harm minimization) is not exactly a theory of addiction; it is rather a treatment philosophy. It can fit within most theories of addiction as a philosophy, though it sits uncomfortably with some more than others. Hamilton et al. describe harm minimization as 'an evolving approach to drug use [that] attempts to reduce … the harmful consequences that arise from the use of drugs' (Hamilton et al. 1998: 136). Rumbold and Hamilton identify the major advantages of harm minimization as: a value-neutral view of drug use; a value-neutral view of users; a focus on problems or harmful consequences resulting from use; an acceptance that abstinence is irrelevant; and a belief that the user has and should continue to have an active role in making choices and taking action about their drug use (Rumbold and Hamilton 1998: 137). Harm reduction is most commonly seen in initiatives such as needle and syringe programmes, opiate substitution programmes (methadone is by far the most common), party-safe initiatives and controlled drinking or usage programmes. The tenets of harm minimization are based on a number of promising propositions in comparison with previous Australian prohibitionist drug policy approaches, although some have identified a number of minor shortcomings (Miller 2001: 168).

Effectiveness of interventional strategies

An essay on knowledge-in-practice would be of little value without looking at what the literature says about which interventions are most effective for the treatment of addiction-related problems. The immense breadth of behaviours and substances included within the field makes a comprehensive review untenable, even within a single book. However, a number of individuals and groups have tried to collate the evidence into some form of meaningful comparisons. The most commonly referred to types of comparison are the Cochrane collaborations, which come from the medical tradition of comparing different treatment options, seeing the randomized control trial as the 'gold standard' (see http://www.cochrane. org/reviews/en/topics/59_reviews.html). Another attempt was the Mesa Grande project by Miller and colleagues (Miller 1992, Miller and Wilbourne 2002).

Pharmacology

Without delving into this literature too deeply, it is perhaps unsurprising that the use of pharmacotherapies has proved most successful for alcohol, tobacco and heroin dependence (e.g. Mattick et al. 2003). By far the greatest amount of evidence surrounding the treatment of addiction-related problems comes from the development and trialling of different medical and pharmacological treatments. This applies primarily to the treatment of opiate dependence (methadone, buprenorphine, LAAM and naltrexone) and nicotine dependence (nicotine replacement therapies [NRTs] and others such as Zyban and varenicline). Medication is generally improved by the use of psychosocial interventions (most usually CBT and MI), though these are not effective as stand-alone treatments. However, these findings reflect clinical trial data and there is currently great debate (and some significant doubt) about whether these benefits are seen in the context of 'everyday treatment' – an issue which will be discussed in greater depth later in this chapter.

Motivation enhancing interventions

Miller et al. (2002) found that 'brief interventions' head the list of evidence-based treatment methods, even with brief motivational enhancement approaches removed to a separate category. Brief interventions are basically a set of techniques that typically involve a screening or assessment process, feedback, client engagement, simple advice or brief counselling, goal setting and follow up. They have relied heavily on concepts and techniques borrowed from Behavioural Self-Control Training (BSCT) or CBT. There is a strong evidence base for these because of the large number of studies conducted and the fact that brief interventions are often compared with a true no-treatment control (Miller and Wilbourne 2002). Behavioural skill training approaches continue to dominate the remainder of the 'Top 10' list of treatment methods supported by controlled trials. Three of these pay particular attention to the client's social support network: social skills training, the community reinforcement approach and behavioural marital therapy.

There is also an emphasis on the client's motivation for change, whether through intrinsic motivational enhancement, specific behaviour contracting, or the rearrangement of social contingencies to favour change. Attention to the person's social context and support system is prominent among several of the most supported approaches. It is also instructive to consider what does not appear among well-supported treatment methods, but instead is found at the bottom of the list. Here one finds methods designed to educate, confront, shock or foster insight regarding the nature and causes of addiction. Also found at the bottom are relaxation training, milieu therapy and mandatory A.A. attendance, along with poorly specified alcoholism counselling and standard treatment-as-usual. However, a number of recent studies are pointing out that much of the effect seen in such trials may be related to an 'assessment effect', similar in some ways to the Hawthorne effect (where people's behaviour changes following any new or increased attention). These studies have found that intensive assessment typical of research trials appears to have a beneficial treatment effect in and of itself and control subjects show similar improvements in drug use to those receiving motivational interviewing (McCambridge and Strang 2005). While this research is in its infancy, it has some significant implications for the claimed effect sizes of a number of behavioural therapies.

'Positively focused interventions'

The other group of interventions that I have identified is what I call 'real world interventions'. These interventions reflect thinking around Maslow's (1943) 'hierarchy of needs', specifically that, in order to help someone with a social disorder such as addiction, look at what 'normal' people do, and if it is missing in the addict's life, include it in programmes which help them to re-integrate as a productive social member. The three major areas in which interventions have been focused are work (vocational therapies), family and exercise.

Vocational therapies

Despite the chronic nature of addiction, most treatments are brief by design and seem designed to treat an acute problem, even though we know people will be in treatment for almost ten years (Mattick et al. 1993). However, research in the last decade has begun to focus on longer term treatments that revolve around people in treatment getting support to conduct as normal lives as possible while in recovery, thereby learning the skills and habits necessary for life as 'normal'. Naturally, they require a great deal of time, patience and support. Essentially, vocational therapies work on the same principle as the paid employment most of us are used to. Service users contribute labour and learn skills and in return gain some form of compensation. Different models have different philosophies around whether that reward will be of the tangible (monetary) type (Silverman et al. 2002) or less tangible (positive praise and the reward of rehabilitation) (Blankertz et al. 2004). Some link abstinence with greater reward whereas others work with the individual wherever they are at. This dynamic usually reflects cultural biases, with abstinence-focused programmes usually found in the United States. While relapse is common, as in other treatments, the long-term focus of this type of intervention and added bonus of people in treatment learning skills and contributing to the economy has major individual and community advantages (Silverman et al. 2005).

Family therapies

Another area which has often been seen as an adjunct is family-based intervention. However, for some people, dealing with family is one of the major factors in the development of their drug use and in their recovery. Families can play an important role in people's motivations around both drug use and recovery (Bammer and Weekes 1994). The influence of sexual partners on a person's risk behaviour is substantial (Rhodes and Cusick 2000). The most common response regarding the role of the family is that it can act as a deterrent to risky behaviour. For example:

> Charlene, 19 yrs, I'm not afraid of dying from heroin, but I look at my family and I can't put them through hell, so I watch my ways. I should care about myself, but if I die, I die. I live by 'one day at a time' and I try to put a smile on my face everyday. I don't want my family or my loved ones stressing or going through hell. (Miller 2002)

However, this relationship is seldom straightforward, and the narrative below points to the complex nature of the impact of an individual's family on their heroin use, and vice versa.

Caroline, 28 yrs … I've got a beautiful mother and grandmother who really care about me. They're scared to death about my drug use. Always scared that I'll go back to it. But, they're very pushy about it is well. All they want is the best for me, but they don't trust me. I understand the trust not being there. Because of things I've done in the past. But they don't seem to let go. They think you should be able to just give up like that. Everything is them, them, them putting a guilt trip on to me. The guilt trip they put on to me, they don't think about the fact that it's making me go back and use more. To cover up the hurt that I've put onto them. It goes round and round. (Miller, 2002)

The importance of including families wherever possible has been increasingly recognized. While many of the therapies are still in the development stage in terms of large-scale clinical trials, results suggest that working with the families of addicts is a vital element of an evidence-based model of treatment and may, in some instances, be enough of an intervention in its own right (Liddle 2004).

Diet and exercise

As a part of the Mesa Grande project mentioned earlier, Miller and colleagues found exercise to be more effective than many psychosocial interventions, including psychotherapy, 12 step facilitation, relaxation therapy and family therapy (Miller and Wilbourne 2002). Oddly, much of the data relating to exercise comes from it being used as a control condition in other clinical trials, usually in conjunction with improving people's diets. This simple intervention, the most common and successful for the overall health of most Western nations, shows promising results when applied to in-treatment populations and reflects the overall value of using 'positive psychology' principles for addiction treatment (Seligman 2002).

Knowledge-in-practice in 'positively focused interventions'

The above interventions are almost antithetical to most addiction treatments, in part because there is no one professional group that could claim ownership. Yet they demonstrate greater efficacy than many of the most common forms of 'treatment'. Certainly, in most services that cater for addiction-related problems, the idea that you could prescribe an individual exercise, work and some family time would be scoffed at – particularly if it was claimed at the same time that such an intervention was far more likely to have a long-term beneficial effect.

'Complementary' therapies

In contrast to positively focused interventions and the motivation enhancing therapies discussed above, some complementary or alternative medicines (CAM) are widely used in the treatment of addiction-related problems, despite a broad evidence base that shows their ineffectiveness. For example, a 2005 US national survey of substance misuse services found that 4.4 per cent of them offered acupuncture to their clients (US Substance Abuse and Mental Health Services Administration 2006). In the United Kingdom, just over 50 per cent of drug services listed in a national directory of services offer complementary therapies to clients (Drugscope 2007). Acupuncture is by far the most widely used and investigated CAM used in drug misuse treatment. A Cochrane review of acupuncture for opioid dependence concluded that research findings did not support the efficacy of acupuncture for opiate detoxification (Ter Riet et al. 1990) or cocaine dependence (Gates et al. 2006). Studies into the effectiveness of auricular acupuncture for alcohol treatment have also found no positive effects on drinking levels or craving for drink over placebo treatments, and more of the acupuncture patients dropped out of treatment during this period (Bullock et al. 1999). Similarly, the small number of randomized trials conducted so far have failed to find a benefit for auricular acupuncture in the treatment of symptoms associated within inpatient settings (Trumpler et al. 2003).

Knowledge-in-practice in complementary 'therapies'

Reviews of CAM suggest that while they are under-researched there is little realistic promise of effective interventions being identified (Gates et al. 2006). Of particular interest to this book is the reality that many of these therapies remain extremely popular with both therapists and clients. This is despite the overwhelming evidence that they do not work. Whilst the literature describes the popularity of these interventions amongst clinicians, it fails to describe the degree to which they are wed to these practices. In treatment settings from the United Kingdom, Australia and the United States, clinicians strongly defend the use of such therapies, particularly acupuncture, and simply choose to disagree with the research. It does not reflect what they see – or choose to see – in daily practice.

This highlights what is often seen as the difference between empirically supported treatments and clinically popular treatments. Within AOD treatment, effectiveness is generally quite low in terms of absolute recovery (usually, though not necessarily, defined as abstinence). Addiction can most closely be likened to a chronic, recurring disease such as diabetes (see McLellan et al. 2000). This means that treatment effectiveness is generally low, particularly when moved into the clinical setting, as distinct from the world of clinical trials. In this world, clinicians often see service users on a long-term basis, with little obvious progress – a phenomenon labelled the 'clinical fallacy' (Gossop 2008). A 'treatment career' (as opposed to their 'drug using career') most often begins in a person's late twenties, almost ten years after they first start using drugs regularly, and lasts for over ten years, with an average of nine major treatment episodes and many more informal attempts and frustrations (Ross et al. 2005). Many service users die before reaching the end of their treatment journey and the overall experience is dominated by successive failures and few successes (McLellan et al. 2000). Service users are often frustrated people with low self-esteem and many complex behavioural problems and generally have poor self-expression and low levels of self-control. This makes for a very difficult therapeutic environment where 'normal' treatment seldom has little obvious immediate benefit or symptom relief.

In this context, complementary therapies – where the service user is able to get one-on-one attention and have something that feels therapeutic done to them – leaves them feeling happier than when they walked through the door. This effect has consistently been found to equate to a placebo effect. That is, sham treatments do just as well, but researchers have failed to note that in the context of most AOD treatment settings globally, even a placebo effect is seen as beneficial.

Employing empirically supported therapies (EST)

Treatment efficacy research in the addictions has been successful by some standards (Carroll and Rounsaville 2007). A growing number of well-conducted multi-centre clinical trials have provided moderate support for a number of behavioural therapies (e.g. Project MATCH Research Group 1997, UKATT Research Team 2005). A number of recent very large studies of AOD treatment have highlighted the need to move towards different models of understanding what constitutes good treatment (Project MATCH Research Group, 1997, UKATT Research Team 2005). Based on these trial results, the new model emphasizes factors such as client commitment, therapist allegiance and the client–therapist alliance. Positive changes are also viewed as being influenced by an array of interrelated factors promoting or constraining positive change (Carroll and Rounsaville 2007).

What is meant to happen and what actually happens in treatment

Unfortunately, even with the evidence from these large trials identifying which treatments are more effective and what factors are most likely to improve treatment outcomes, the gap between research knowledge and clinical practice is both persistent and formidable (Fals-Stewart et al. 2004). Certainly, the majority of treatment programmes in the United States and the United Kingdom remain grounded in traditional counselling models that have been found ineffective (Carroll and Rounsaville 2007). In addition, many AOD treatment programmes, particularly in the United States, persist in their use of interventions and strategies that may be harmful to some populations (for example, group treatments for antisocial adolescents) (Carroll and Rounsaville 2007, Dishion et al. 1999).

When clinicians are asked why they are reluctant to implement EST, they report two common reservations. Firstly, the experimental conditions of a randomized trial seldom reflect real life practices. Clinicians in trials are usually well trained and closely monitored and may also be treatment manual guided. This results in more homogenous and higher quality clinical practice than is attainable in the real world (Carroll and Rounsaville 2007). Thus, controlled trials will most likely overstate how much of a difference following clinical practice guidelines can make in everyday practice. Secondly, most addiction treatment trials have eligibility criteria that can prevent enrolment of the most severely troubled patients (Humphreys et al. 2008). Thus, clinicians might reasonably conclude that the results of clinical trials do not represent the majority of their patients who, for example, are homeless or have serious psychiatric co-morbidities.

Incorporating knowledge into practice does work

While many scientists believe that clinical practice should be guided by the findings of well-controlled clinical trials, many clinicians believe that everyday practice is too variable and that real-world patients are too diverse for practice to be based on efficacy studies conducted under ideal conditions (Humphreys et al. 2008, Kernick 1998). For example, while rigorous randomized trials have shown that the optimum dose for methadone substitution treatment for heroin dependence is around 100mg (Strang 1997), most frontline clinicians continue to prescribe 30mg as a standard dose. This undermines the effectiveness of the best-supported treatment for opiate dependence available in the community setting (Strang et al. 1996). This occurs for many reasons, including middle-class beliefs about dependence, lack of graduate and undergraduate training for GPs and a lack of clinical supervision on prescriber practices for treatment for opiate dependence (Strang and Sheridan 1998, 2003). Recent evidence from trials such as the Multisite Opiate Substitution Treatment (MOST) study has shown that Opiate Substitution Treatment (OST) clinical practices found efficacious in clinical trials and incorporated into practice guidelines (dosing in the recommended range and providing psychosocial services) improve the outcomes of typical opiate-dependent patients seen in everyday practice (Humphreys et al. 2008). This research constitutes the beginning of a body of work that will improve the relationship between knowledge and practice.

Training versus 'craft knowledge'

Standard training approaches (the most common of which are brief workshops) have been shown to be of limited effectiveness in imparting key skills and competence to experienced clinicians (Barlow et al. 1999, Davis et al. 1992, Fals-Stewart et al. 2004, VandeCreek et al. 1990). A number of studies in the United States have demonstrated that workshop training fails to adequately impart key skills for both motivational interviewing and CBT (Rubel et al. 2000). Only training conditions that offered intensive didactic training plus performance-based supervision and feedback enabled clinicians to reach acceptable standards. Naturally, such intensive training is expensive, time-consuming and drains the resources of small service providers, without little obvious difference to clinicians or management (Carroll and Rounsaville 2007). Certainly, it appears that clinicians who are strongly wedded to a particular clinical approach are unlikely to attain competence in all clinical approaches (Weissman et al. 1982). In a similar vein, clinicians who have only 'on-the-job' training lack basic clinical skills, and it is not clear how these basic skills should be taught, or even whether they can be taught (Sholomskas et al. 2005). Another problem seen arising from poorly trained staff is treatment staff 'telling' service users what they need, negating ownership and further disenfranchising vulnerable people (Pill et al. 1999).

These findings hold a number of serious implications for the notion of 'craft knowledge' in the treatment of addiction-related problems. First and foremost, it is implicit from the research findings discussed above that craft knowledge in the addictions is at best an acronym for unprofessional and ineffective behaviour. When asked, most clinicians will report competency in a wide array of psychosocial interventions and that they conform to best practice standards – most often under the smokescreen of being 'eclectic' (Best and Day n.d., Best et al. 2008). Yet current research suggests they are more 'jacks of all trades – masters of none'. Second, the craft knowledge that is in use is ineffective. While there may be settings where craft knowledge surpasses that of research and theory, generic treatment provided within most settings is only marginally effective. Third, if there is any craft knowledge in the treatment of addictions, it points to major themes (such as social support and positive psychology) rather than specific interventions.

Expanding on this third point, there is some evidence for craft knowledge in the treatment of addictions, although the domains in which it exist are probably better served by solid backgrounds in understanding the aetiology of addiction and what factors help to make people function. The main type of craft knowledge is displayed through some of the more effective elements of both the SOC and 12 step models. As mentioned earlier, much of this can be explained from a consideration of Maslow's (1943) hierarchy of needs and what lay people, or untrained workers might perceive as gaps in a person's well-being (Seligman 2002). In essence, these can be characterized as being: 1) support when and where it is needed (unlikely to reach the world of professional treatment) and 2) a simple progression of treatment that is attractive to clinicians and addicts alike. While there is no evidence that such a progression works, and much to the contrary, the ability to spell out a model and progression through treatment appears very attractive to people entering treatment and to those supplying it. However, it should be noted that the examples of craft knowledge are not passed down or consciously valued by practitioners in the field. Rather, they are most usually seen as an intuitive direction in which clinicians point people when they seek assistance for their problems.

Practice based on knowledge

The question remains, of course: What would a treatment system for addiction based on the accumulated knowledge look like? A big question. But the above review suggests a number of fundamental elements. Such a model would have a vast array of interventions, varying in level of intervention, theoretical background and desired outcome. This would address the knowledge that 'addiction' is a set of behaviours that varies with each person and that the best intervention is ultimately the one which suits them and allows them to reach their potential. The system would have at its front end an understanding of reducing harm wherever possible and at its end a goal of re-integrating people into society to a level at which they can achieve their best. It would use social support and supported self-help as a major tool and give people a stepped treatment plan which gives them an idea of the direction they can head in. But it would only do this after listening to their story and working with them to determine what steps suit them best, because the most important knowledge we keep getting from research about addiction is that treatment works best when the service user shares their goals.

What direction for knowledge in practice in addiction treatment?

In this chapter I have critically reviewed the most up-to-date research on the treatment of addiction-related problems. I have specifically not discussed other areas such as service systems, national or global policy or even treatment philosophies, though it is safe to say that practice is in fact far less influenced in these other fields than has just been described in the treatment field.

In the process of this review it was difficult to conclude anything other than, at a global level, knowledge has very little to do with practice in the treatment of addiction-related disorders. However, there is also evidence that a number of clinical research groups in the United Kingdom and the United States are moving to identify the causes of this problem and improve the uptake of ESTs. In this exceptionally multidisciplinary field, it is also worth noting that the majority of this push is coming from medical and psychological disciplines, though support is building from sociology and nursing.

From the evidence reviewed in this chapter, it was also clear that 'craft knowledge' within the treatment of addiction-related disorders is neither desirable nor effective, and in many instances has been shown to both dangerous for the addict and often driven by the ideological or financial goals of unprofessional service providers. This cannot be stated too lightly in this context as many damaged and vulnerable people are further harmed constantly by people claiming some form of craft knowledge.

References

Babor, T.F. and Hall, W. 2007. Standardizing terminology in addiction science: to achieve the impossible dream. *Addiction*, 102: 1015–18.

Bammer, G. and Weekes, S. 1994. Becoming an ex-user: insights into the process and implications for treatment and policy. *Drug and Alcohol Review*, 13, 285–92.

Barlow, D.H., Levitt, J.T. and Bufka, L.F. 1999. The dissemination of empirically supported treatments: a view to the future. *Behaviour Research and Therapy*, 37: S147–62.

Best, D. and Day, E. n.d. What treatment means in practice: an analysis of the therapeutic activity provided in criminal justice drug treatment services in Birmingham, England. *Addiction Research and Theory*. Unpublished paper.

Best, D., Day, E., McCarthy, T., Darlington, I., and Pinchbeck, K. 2008. Editorial: The hierarchy of needs and care planning in addiction services: what Maslow can tell us about addressing competing priorities. *Addiction Research and Theory*, 16(4), 305–7.

Blankertz, L., Magura, S., Staines, G.L., Madison, E.M., Spinelli, M., Horowitz, E. et al. 2004. A new work placement model for unemployed methadone maintenance patients. *Substance Use Misuse*, 39, 2239–60.

Bullock, M.L., Kiresuk, T.J., Pheley, A.M., Culliton, P.D. and Lenz, S.K. 1999. Auricular acupuncture in the treatment of cocaine abuse: a study of efficacy and dosing. *Journal of Substance Abuse Treatment*, 16, 31–8.

Bunton, R., Baldwin, S., Flynn, D. and Whitelaw, S. 2000. The 'stages of change' model in health promotion: science and ideology. *Critical Public Health*,10, 55–70.

Carroll, K.M. and Rounsaville, B.J. 2007. A vision of the next generation of behavioral therapies research in the addictions. *Addiction,* 102(6), 850–69.

Darke, S. and Hall, W. 2003. Heroin overdose: research and evidence-based intervention. *Journal of Urban Health*, 80, 189–200.

Davis, D.A., Thomson, M.A., Oxman, A.D. and Haynes, R.B. 1992. Evidence for the effectiveness of CME: a review of 50 randomized controlled trials. *Journal of the American Medical Assocaition*, 268, 1111–17.

Dishion, T.J., McCord, J. and Poulin, F. 1999. When interventions harm: peer groups and problem behavior. *American Psychologist*, 54, 755–64.

Drugscope 2007. Available at: http://www.drugscope.org.uk/resources/databases/helpfinder.html [accessed 21 January 2008].

Eckersley, R.M. 2005. 'Cultural fraud': the role of culture in drug abuse. *Drug and Alcohol Review*, 24, 157–63.

Edwards, G. 1980. Alcoholism treatment: between guesswork and certainty, in *Alcoholism Treatment in Transition,* edited by G. Edwards and M. Grant. London: Croom Helm, 307–20.

Edwards, G. and Gross, M.M. 1976. Alcohol dependence: provisional description of a clinical syndrome. *British Medical Journal*, 300, 1058–61.

Etter, J.F. and Perneger, T.V. 1999. A comparison of two measures of stage of change for smoking cessation. *Addiction*, 94, 1881–9.

Fals-Stewart, W., Logsdon, T. and Birchler, G.R. 2004. Diffusion of an empirically supported treatment for substance abuse: an organizational autopsy of technology transfer success and failure. *Clinical Psychology: Science and Practice,* 11, 177–82.

Ferri, M.M.F., Amato, L. and Davoli, M. 2006. *Alcoholics Anonymous and other 12-step programmes for alcohol dependence.* Cochrane Database of Systematic Reviews, issue 3, article number: CD005032. DOI: 10.1002/14651858. CD005032.pub2.

Gates, S., Smith, L.A. and Foxcroft, D.R. 2006. *Auricular acupuncture for cocaine dependence.* Cochrane Database of Systematic Reviews, issue 1, article number: CD005192. DOI: 10.1002/14651858.CD005192.pub2).

Gossop, M. 2008. The clinical fallacy and treatment outcome. *Addiction*, 103, 89–90.

Gossop, M., Harris, J., Best, D., Man, L.H., Manning, V., Marshall, J. and Strang, J. 2003. Is attendance at alcoholics anonymous meetings after inpatient treatment related to improved outcomes? A 6-month follow-up study. *Alcohol and Alcoholism*, 38(5), 421–6.

Gossop, M., Marsden, J., Stewart, D. and Treacy, S. 2002. Change and stability of change after treatment of drug misuse; 2-year outcomes from the National Treatment Outcome Research Study (UK). *Addictive Behaviors*, 27, 155–66.

Hamilton, M., Kellehear, A. and Rumbold, G. 1998. *Drug Use in Australia: A Harm Minimisation Approach.* Melbourne: Oxford University Press.

Humphreys, K., Trafton, J.A. and Oliva, E.M. 2008. Does following research-derived practice guidelines improve opiate-dependent patients' outcomes under everyday practice conditions? Results of the multisite opiate substitution treatment study. *Journal of Substance Abuse Treatment*, 34: 173–9.

Kernick, D.P. 1998. Lies, damned lies, and evidence-based medicine. *The Lancet*, 351, 1824.

Liddle, H.A. 2004. Family-based therapies for adolescent alcohol and drug use: research contributions and future research needs. *Addiction*, 99(S2), 76–92.

Maslow, A.H. 1943. A Theory of Human Motivation. *Psychological Review*, 50, 370–96.

Mattick, R.P., Breen, C., Kimber, J. and Davoli, M. 2003. Methadone maintenance therapy versus no opioid replacement therapy for opioid dependence. Cochrane Database System Review, issue 2, article number: CD002209. DOI: 10.1002/14651858.CD002209.

Mattick, R.P.M., Baillie, A., Grenyer, B., Hall, W., Hando, J., Jarvis, T.,Ward, J. and Webster, P. 1993. *A Treatment Outline for Approaches to Opioid Dependence: Quality Assurance in the Treatment of Drug Dependence Project*, National Drug Strategy Monograph Series, 21. Canberra: Australian Government Publishing Service.

McCambridge, J. and Strang, J. 2005. Deterioration over time in effect of motivational interviewing in reducing drug consumption and related risk among young people. *Addiction*, 100, 470–78.

McLellan, A.T., Lewis, D.C., O'Brien, C.P. and Kleber, H.D. 2000. Drug dependence, a chronic medical illness: Implications for treatment, insurance, and outcomes evaluation. *Journal of the American Medical Association*, 284, 1689–95.

Miller, P.G. 2001. A critical review of the harm minimisation ideology in Australia. *Critical Public Health*, 11, 167–78.

Miller, P.G. 2002. Dancing with Death: Risk, Health Promotion and Injecting Drug Users. Unpublished PhD thesis, Deakin University, Geelong.

Miller, W.R. 1992. The effectiveness of treatment for substance abuse. Reasons for optimism. *Journal of Substance Abuse Treatment*, 9, 93–102.

Miller, W.R. and Wilbourne, P.L. 2002. Mesa grande: a methodological analysis of clinical trials of treatments for alcohol use disorders. *Addiction*, 97, 265–77.

Moore, D. 1992. Deconstructing 'dependence': an ethnographic critique of an influential concept. *Contemporary Drug Problems*, 19, 459–90.

Moore, D. 1993. Beyond Zinberg's 'social setting': the processural view of illicit drug use. *Drug and Alcohol Review*, 12, 413–21.

Orford, J. 1985. *Excessive Appetites: A Psychological View of Addictions*. Chichester and New York: John Wiley and Sons.

Pill, R., Rees, M.E., Stott, N.C.H. and Rollnick, S.R. 1999. Can nurses learn to let go? Issues arising from an intervention designed to improve patients' involvement in their own care. *Journal of Advanced Nursing*, 29(6), 1492–9.

Prochaska, J.O. and DiClemente, C.C. 1982. Transtheoretical therapy toward a more integrative model of change. *Psychotherapy: Theory, Research and Practice*, 19, 276–87.

Prochaska, J.O. and DiClemente, C.C. 1986. Toward a comprehensive model of change, in *Treating Addictive Behaviours: Process of Change*, edited by W.R. Miller and N. Heather. New York: Plenum Press, 3–27.

Project MATCH Research Group 1997. Matching alcoholism treatments to client heterogeneity: project MATCH posttreatment drinking outcomes. *Journal of Substance Abuse Treatment*, 58, 7–29.

Rhodes, T. and Cusick, L. 2000. Love and intimacy in relationship risk management: HIV positive people and their sexual partners. *Sociology of Health and Illness*, 22, 1–26.

Ross, J., Teesson, M., Darke, S., Lynskey, M., Ali, R., Ritter, A. and Cooke, R. 2005. The characteristics of heroin users entering treatment: findings from the Australian treatment outcome study (ATOS). *Drug and Alcohol Review*, 24, 411–18.

Rubel, E.C., Sobell, L.C. and Miller, W.R. 2000. Do continuing education workshops improve participants' skills? Effects of a motivational interviewing workshop on substance-abuse counselors' skills and knowledge. *The Behavior Therapist*, 23, 73–7.

Rumbold, G. and Hamilton, M. 1998. Addressing drug problems: the case for harm minimisation, in *Drug Use in Australia: A Harm Minimisation Approach*, edited by M.A. Hamilton, A. Kellehear and G.R. Rumbold. Melbourne: Oxford University Press, 130–45.

Seligman, M.E.P. 2002. Positive psychology, positive prevention, and positive therapy, in *Handbook of Positive Psychology*, edited by C.R. Snyder and S.J. Lopez. New York: Oxford University Press, 3–12.

Sholomskas, D.E., Syracuse-Siewert, G., Rounsaville, B.J., Ball, S.A., Nuro, K.F. and Carroll, K.M. 2005. We don't train in vain: a dissemination trial of three strategies for training clinicians in cognitive behavioral therapy. *Journal of Consulting and Clinical Psychology*, 73(1), 106–15.

Silverman, K., Wong, C.J., Grabinski, M.J., Hampton, J., Sylvest, C.E., Dillon, E.M. and Wentland, R.D. 2005. A web-based therapeutic workplace for the treatment of drug addiction and chronic unemployment. *Behavior Modification*, 29(2), 417.

Silverman, K., Wong, C.J., Wentland, R.D., Svikis, D., Stitzer, M.L. and Bigelow, G.E. 2002. The therapeutic workplace business: a long-term treatment for drug addiction and chronic unemployment. *Drug and Alcohol Dependence*, 66(S165).

Strang, J. 1997. *Drug Misuse and Dependence: Guidelines on Clinical Management*. London: The Stationery Office.

Strang, J. and Sheridan, J. 1998. Effect of government recommendations on methadone prescribing in south east England: comparison of 1995 and 1997 surveys. *British Medical Journal*, 317, 1489–90.

Strang, J. and Sheridan, J. 2003. Effect of national guidelines on prescription of methadone: analysis of NHS prescription data, England 1990–2001. *British Medical Journal*, 327, 32–2.

Strang, J., Sheridan, J. and Barber, N. 1996. Prescribing injectable and oral methadone to opiate addicts: results from the 1995 national postal survey of community pharmacies in England and Wales. *British Medical Journal*, 313, 270–72.

Ter Riet, G., Kleijnen, J. and Knipschild, P. 1990. A meta-analysis of studies into the effect of acupuncture on addiction. *British Journal of General Practice*, 40, 379–82.

Trumpler, F., Oez, S., Stahli, P., Brenner, H.D. and Juni, P. 2003. Acupuncture for alcohol withdrawal: a randomized controlled trial. *Alcohol and Alcoholism*, 38(4), 369–75.

UKATT Research Team 2005. Effectiveness of treatment for alcohol problems: findings of the randomised UK alcohol treatment trial (UKATT). *British Medical Journal*, 331, 541.

US Department of Health and Human Services, Substance Abuse and Mental Health Services Administration 2006. *National Survey of Substance Abuse Treatment Services (N-SSATS): 2005*.

Valverde, M. and White-Mair, K. 1999. 'One day at a time' and other slogans for everyday life: the ethical practices of Alcoholics Anonymous. *Sociology*, 33, 391–3.

VandeCreek, L., Knapp, S. and Brace, K. 1990. Mandatory continuing education for licensed psychologists: its rationale and current implications. *Professional Psychology: Research and Practice*, 21, 135–40.

Weissman, M.M., Rounsaville, B.J. and Chevron, E. 1982. Training psychotherapists to participate in psychotherapy outcome studies. *American Journal of Psychiatry*, 139, 1442–6.

West, R. 2005. Time for a change: putting the Transtheoretical (Stages of Change) Model to rest. *Addiction*, 100, 1036–9.

West, R. 2006. *Theory of Addiction*. Oxford: Blackwell Publishing.

Whitelaw, S., Baldwin, S., Bunton, R. and Flynn, D. 2000. The status of evidence and outcomes in Stages of Change research. *Health Education Research*, 15, 707–18.

Zinberg, N.E. 1984. *Drug, Set, and Setting*. New Haven: Yale University Press.

Conclusions: Knowledge-in-practice in the caring professions: reflections on commonalities and differences

Heather D'Cruz, Struan Jacobs and Adrian Schoo

This book has taken up the theme of knowledge-in-practice in the caring professions, drawing on multidisciplinary perspectives. As outlined in the Introduction, we have approached this project by soliciting contributions from representatives of different disciplines and professions involved with caring for individuals, groups and communities. Our approach differs from the more usual approaches, which discuss knowledge-in-practice from the perspective of a particular profession or discipline, while promoting and encouraging multidisciplinary professional practice as a reflection of practice realities, organizational demands and the complexities of problems presented by client groups.

The book has been designed to contribute to this professional imperative of multidisciplinary team work and collaboration, exploring what knowledge-in-practice means for different caring professions. The intention is to increase awareness of and prompt reflection on the factors that inhibit, and those that promote, multidisciplinary practice, and also to propose appropriate approaches. As editors we have not been prescriptive in our guidelines to authors regarding how they should respond to the central aims of the book. Each chapter has been conceptualized by the individual contributor/s as their response to the task. The contributors would not necessarily claim to represent their profession in how they have approached their task. The editors wanted to make visible some of the ways in which professionals may conceptualize 'knowledge', 'practice' and 'knowledge-in-practice', questioning expectations of consensus or homogeneity within professions.

It is unusual to construct a text that places the different professions together with the aim of offering an opportunity for readers (educators and practitioners) to compare and contrast what knowledge-in-practice may mean for different professions, how members of different professions may envisage 'knowledge' and 'practice' as separate entities and, more particularly, how they connect these as knowledge-in-practice. It is hoped that readers have engaged with all or most chapters in the way that the editors have intended, as positioned readers in relation to the text (Barthes 1972: 109–31, Sarup 1993, 32–57, Rosenau 1992: 34–41), reading in a personal way, interpreting the meanings of the text in light of their own professional paradigms and nuanced understandings. The project has assumed a view of authors and audience as possessing valued attributes for contemporary professionals (Gordon 2003, Jacobson et al. 2006, Papadimos 2009, Cirocco 2007, Shaw 2007). Among these attributes are recognition of the self as a positioned and reflective subject, being open-minded and critically aware, having intellectual resources to recognize similarities and differences between perspectives, whether these be represented in texts or by colleagues, and having one's own understandings of 'knowledge', 'practice' and 'knowledge-in-practice'. It is easy to engage with what is familiar and comfortable; it is less easy when one is challenged by strangeness and differences. However, we believe that to foster appropriate and effective multidisciplinary practice, it is necessary to engage with the fundamental differences that underpin resistance by professional bodies and individuals to do more than aspire to such practice.

In certain respects the approach taken in this book is contentious, but at the same time it offers insights into contemporary professional practice questions of what knowledge-in-practice means as both concept and application, whereby professionals are expected to exercise and apply knowledge in specific situations constituting practice in the caring professions. The book also questions what 'knowledge' and 'practice' mean as separate concepts in professional education and when working with clients. In this conclusion, in keeping with our espoused aims of providing a somewhat unorthodox approach in this book, we might ask what are to be counted among the likely benefits. In approaching this question, we have engaged with authors' contributions as their interpretation of knowledge-in-practice from particular professional perspectives that implicitly or explicitly express awareness of multidisciplinarity. Our approach in this conclusion, as we tentatively theorize possible meanings of knowledge-in-practice and their implications for multidisciplinarity, may be described as 'emergent', in keeping with our non-prescriptive brief to contributors.

As editors reading all the chapters, our overall sense has been one of participating in a multidisciplinary team meeting, albeit in textual form. In this textual multidisciplinary team meeting, we encounter different languages and forms of representation of professional knowledge and particular professional aims and preoccupations in relation to clients, how clients' needs are assessed, what forms of intervention are appropriate, and what constitutes evidence to support such decisions. As editors, but also professionals and academics positioned within particular disciplines, we expect we have shared similar challenges with the readers of this text who are simultaneously practitioners, academics and educators. We have had to overcome our own preferences for representational styles, engage with unfamiliar vocabulary and concepts, and be open-minded about professional concerns that differ significantly from our own. For us, the process of reading has been illuminating through the challenges that have sensitized us to different ways of knowing and doing in a range of caring professions.

In what follows, the editors draw readers' attention to several salient features of the book. We indicate how the book may contribute to improving professional education and practice, recognizing multidisciplinarity as a means to move towards interdisciplinarity and transdisciplinarity.

Writing as representation

The most obvious feature of the text is the different approaches taken by authors encapsulated in their writing style, where writing is a representation of knowledge (Richardson 1994). While such a feature is normally unremarkable and unremarked in professional scholarly texts, being accepted as simply an artefact of the writing process, we wish to draw attention to it. Each author's writing style, we would point out, captures what is generally normative for the profession represented by the author, which is not to say that all representatives of that profession write in exactly the same way. Some chapters are written more introspectively and subjectively, while others are written prescriptively and in fairly technical language. The writing styles and readers' familiarity with them, according to particular professional styles, will likely encourage engagement with the content that unfamiliarity and its challenges will not. Assumptions and expectations of professional scholarly writing as representative of trustworthy knowledge offer opportunities for readers to critically reflect on norms about what valid and trustworthy knowledge is and how it ought to be represented.

An example of such expectations is in the differences between the more subjective and introspective chapters in this text, by Norton, Chaffey and D'Cruz. Norton and Chaffey do not cite 'evidence' in support of their experiences and intuitive claims, while D'Cruz cites extensively to develop an argument for the interconnections between knowledge, professional purpose, ethics and skills in knowledge-in-practice. Issues related to the legitimate representation of knowledge have also been discussed in this book by Hutchinson and Bucknall, and Sheean and Cameron, in relation to the contested knowledges in medical care. In interprofessional 'turf wars', preferences are often expressed for written over oral traditions, and for 'science' over 'non-science', as ways of knowing, with gatekeeping of technologies that entrench these divisions. These distinctions have been associated with gender stratification in (and between) professions such as medicine, general nursing and midwifery. Similar distinctions are drawn, and debates occur, in social work between knowledge associated with the academy (and writing) and knowledge in the field of practitioners (with preferred oral traditions) that D'Cruz discusses, and this situation may have resonances for other professions where academic education is necessary for professional practice.

The next feature of the style of each chapter is the language and concepts that will be familiar to readers from the profession represented, but which are mostly unfamiliar (and possibly challenging) to readers from other professions. These linguistic and conceptual features encapsulate fundamental differences between professions as each possesses its own body of disciplinary knowledge. While a reader from one profession is not expected to learn another profession's paradigms and concepts, exposure to these differences in texts can serve to replicate the everyday experiences of practitioners working in multidisciplinary teams where each team member's knowledge base is not fully known or appreciated, or is dismissed as irrelevant or strange. Linguistic and stylistic differences that are normative in one profession may not be fully appreciated or understood in another, especially as such differences may be demonstrated in what is said in team meetings or in how such knowledge is practised. These features of the structure of each chapter are likely to engender impatience with the author, due to readers' discomfort with the style, including features such as introspective, subjective, prescriptive, objectivist, using or avoiding use of statistics, different forms of expression and specialized vocabulary.

Knowledge-for- and -in-practice

The section above discussed how professional knowledge may be represented as legitimate through vocabulary and style. This section presents an overview of the similarities and differences in what knowledge-for- and -in-practice is from the perspectives of contributors. All the authors in the book allude to the politics of knowledge associated with debates about the relationship between epistemology, methodology and evidence that is represented as valid for effective practice. Some authors discuss the distinction between knowledge as empiricist/realist and as relativist, with relativism being a feature of professional practice, accounting for different ways of knowing (including that of the client). For most contributors, these paradigm debates occur within their profession and also between professions. For example, Miller discusses interventions related to addictions that are informed by research evidence into 'what works', and interventions that are ineffective but which continue to be supported purely for ideological reasons. Such paradigm debates are further complicated by the ethical and practical necessity for clients' participation that includes their perspective on the problem and possible interventions.

These complications include expectations of professional expertise and related duty of care, and legal liability for the processes and outcomes of professional practice, which may differ across professions. Holmes' discussion of the politics of multidisciplinary teams in psychiatry highlights the place of the psychiatrist as the team leader who carries legal responsibilities for the care of the patient, while at the same time being respectful of the contributions of all team members.

Expectations of professional expertise and duty of care may also vary according to assumptions concerning degrees of certainty related to knowledge within professions. While most contributors explicitly comment on the tentative nature of professional knowledge, there are differences associated with how knowledge-for-practice is generated and what knowledge-in-practice is. These implicit differences between assumptions about expertise underpin professional hierarchies and roles, and skills and resources, perhaps best encapsulated by Sheean and Cameron's discussion of the place of midwives in obstetric care and the struggles against obstetricians in seeking an equal place in the care of pregnant women. These differences reflect the nature of presenting problems and professional purpose and roles.

Knowledge-in-practice: problem identification and professional role

Those writing in, and for, particular professions capture differences in what their profession's problems are, how they can be known, which problems their profession is competent to solve, and which problems lie beyond their jurisdiction. There are professional differences in the purpose of engagement and urgency of action. Norton's description of the necessity of 'waiting', in her work as a psychotherapist, to ascertain 'knowing' what 'the problem' is and what her role may be, emphasizes how differently problems, urgency of response and professional roles may be seen or expected in other professional fields, such as medicine or nursing.

Presenting problems may range from ones that are easily identified and described, with a sensory basis in 'facts', to the unknown, the obscure and the intangible, for example, Norton discussing psychotherapy and Holmes discussing psychiatry. Norton is able to engage through psychotherapy with a problem that the client is unable to name, spending a considerable time in 'the space between knowing and not knowing', 'waiting', and being willing and able to live with challenges to her expertise. This approach may be contrasted to other contributors to this book writing about medicine (Greenberg), general nursing (Hutchinson and Bucknall), midwifery (Sheean and Cameron), and physiotherapy and occupational therapy (Smith, Meyer, Stagnitti and Schoo). In these professions, problems are typically known to the senses: problems of the physical body are associated with knowledge derived from research into clinical and randomized controlled trials into interventions. In these professions, practice can make direct links between a presenting problem, technical forms of intervention, such as medication, instruments and equipment, and between outcomes – these direct links strengthening claims for efficacy. On the other hand, in professions like social work, psychotherapy and, to some extent, psychiatry, the problem is often less clearly defined, with professional purpose, related knowledge and forms of intervention – the self as instrument in counselling, dialogue/active interviews – being restricted to problems that are relatively invisible and more open to contestation as to their form and cause. In these cases, it is often difficult to directly connect interventions with outcomes.

These professional differences influence perceptions of the validity of knowledge and claims of effectiveness, that become incorporated into politics of multidisciplinary practice. For example, how does a practitioner of one of those professions that is described as an 'invisible trade' (Pithouse 1987) justify to another what role is performed and why it is necessary? Access to resources, particularly funding, staffing, infrastructure or equipment, becomes associated with professional territories and hierarchies, as pointed out by Sheean and Cameron in their contrasting of midwifery to obstetric care, and by Hutchinson and Cameron in general nursing.

The politics of multidisciplinary knowledge includes clients' perspectives of professional expertise and the claims and counter-claims that different professions make as regards their prowess in solving problems. The professional knowledge of biomedicine can only be interpreted by those with a specialised training, with clients necessarily reliant on the professional as expert (Greenberg). In the profession of social work, drawing from knowledge of the life world and concerning problems of living, issues are less clear-cut, knowledge of 'what works' is more equivocal, and the claims of professionals are more susceptible of being challenged by clients and other professionals. Psychiatry is an example of a profession that bridges the divide between professions whose presenting problems are clearly visible and whose interventions able to be concretized into a cause-effect relationship, and professions whose focus and scope are more diffuse. Holmes' discussion of the role of the psychiatrist that includes dialogue with the client in establishing the nature of the problem as perceived by the client, also accommodates more direct and concrete interventions, including medications and hospitalization, that may have particular outcomes and claims as to effectiveness.

Most contributors to this book recognize the links between research and theory that inform the knowledge-for-practice that is transmitted in professional education. Some contributors present an argument for practice-generated knowledge as complementing research-based knowledge (Hutchinson and Bucknall), and/or as a legitimate site for researching knowledge-in- and -for-practice (D'Cruz). Writing in the text about biomedical knowledge as the commonly affirmed gold standard for evidence against which all other professions are found wanting, Greenberg comments on the loose connections between 'evidence' and 'efficacy', arguing that a 'lack of scientific evidence does not necessarily mean lack of efficacy, but rather that efficacy has not yet been conclusively confirmed or denied'. Contributors to the book recognize that knowledge-for-practice is not to be revered or blindly followed but is tentative, to be made sense of in interaction with clients, with some contributors writing in a reflective style about how knowledge-in-practice is accomplished in their own practice. Greenberg defines this awareness of the tentativeness of knowledge and the uncertainty of practice as 'wisdom' – 'that breadth of the spirit which makes the difference between the first rate healer and the capable technician' (citing Davies 1984).

The dialectical relationship between theory and practice is acknowledged by several contributors to this volume and is variously interpreted, including questions of 'what should happen between an analyst and a client' (Norton); what is appropriate knowledge for practice with people, each of whom is a unique individual; and what can research contribute to such knowledge (Hutchinson and Bucknall; D'Cruz). Obviously, knowledge and skills are presented in training for practice but, of itself, this approach does not educate for how to practise with actual clients – what Lawn and Battersby refer to as 'practical tools for implementation'. In psychotherapy and psychiatry 'theories are not articles of faith, they are instruments of knowledge' (Norton, citing Jung 1945), and practice involves testing hypotheses in relation to and with the client (Holmes, Norton). Some contributors use case studies to examine the connections between knowledge and practice, explicating 'clinical reasoning' (Smith, Meyer, Stagnitti and Schoo; Hutchinson and Bucknall; Sheean and Cameron; Chaffey), 'narrative thinking' and 'ethical reasoning'. To similar effect, an interview is 'deconstructed' to show the complexity of knowledge as theories, ethics and skills, being the situated micro-practices familiar to each profession (D'Cruz). Contributors emphasize knowledge as generated in their practice, note how it complements formal knowledge generated by research, and envisage it as a site for research about knowledge-in-practice – perspectives that reflect the concepts of 'tacit knowing' and 'craft knowledge' (Polanyi 1967) as discussed in Jacobs' overview of professional knowledge-in-practice. An exception is Miller who disputes the relevance of the category of craft knowledge in working with addictions, suggesting the concept is ideologically driven or based on untested assumptions of 'what works'. Miller writes as a scholar and researcher who has studied a particular social problem (addictions), and who now uses this knowledge in his practice with people with addictions. This is unlike the contributors who have been educated into particular professions and whose professional qualifications may allow them to practise in diverse fields regarding a range of individual or social problems. These practice interests also happen to influence their scholarship and research into particular problems. The professional as practitioner may complicate the academic expectation of disinterested engagement with research evidence, while at the same time contesting what constitutes research evidence. This awareness of paradigm differences within and across professions may be complicated by professional demarcation disputes ('turf wars'), the effect of which is to exclude competitors. These political dimensions introduce barriers that need to be surmounted to achieve cooperative practice.

Knowledge-for- and -in-practice: clients' participation

Knowledge is envisaged as having contextual relevance for clients. Most contributors to this book acknowledge the importance of clients' participation in the helping process, without which the effectiveness of services can be compromised. The participation of the client has been variously discussed, depending on the professional role. What is emphasized by authors in this book is the importance of the relationship between practitioner and client. In professions whose problems can be identified in concrete ways, and whose interventions are designed to resolve clearly defined problems, emphasis is given to the importance of an appropriate relationship with clients, including their participation in the process, as we see described by Hutchinson and Bucknall for general nursing, and Sheean and Cameron for midwifery and obstetric care.

In professions where the nature of problems presented may be less tangible and open to debate, it is essential that the client be actively engaged with, and by, the practitioner in deciding the problem that needs attention and how it may be addressed. There is greater opportunity for this form of partnership in psychotherapy, as described in by Norton, and to a lesser extent in psychiatry where Holmes indicates clients can be involved in decisions about their medication and hospitalization. In social work, clients' participation is as much an expression of professional values as it is related to professional efficacy (D'Cruz). Chaffey provides a unique insight into being both a professional occupational therapist and a client with a disability, underscoring the importance of client participation and partnership in achieving effective outcomes.

Implicit in most of the contributors' perspectives on clients' participation is the thought that the client is an *individual* who seeks help as opposed to groups whose members have common problems, or communities whose disadvantages contribute to substantial problems amongst individual members. Miller does discuss group approaches to helping clients with addictions, but he is unconvinced as to their effectiveness compared with individually tailored interventions that combine pharmacology and psychosocial services. The dominant conceptualization of 'the client' as a unique individual is encapsulated in Norton's description of the helping relationship as 'a form of sensitive engagement with clients that may have a generalized character but needs to emerge *de novo* within each, unique, analytic encounter' (Norton). Similarly, in biomedicine, Greenberg comments that the differences between individuals' healthcare needs must be the first consideration. He goes on to note that consumers' choice and willingness to take medications also needs to be considered on the balance of probabilities where the predicted result of the medications, while never certain, 'is towards the higher end of the efficacy spectrum'.

Participatory practice with clients may be complicated by clients' expectations of professional knowledge and what can be achieved, particularly if clients are hostile to practitioners due to their histories with service providers, and for a myriad of other reasons. The recent emergence of participatory professional practice simultaneously legitimizes clients' knowledge about their own problems and challenges or destabilizes the expertise of professionals who may have to acknowledge that their knowledge is partial and incomplete (Norton).

The complicated relationship between clients (re-designated in recent years as 'consumers' [Ife 1997: 49–56]), practitioners and knowledge differs between professions. For example, clients using the Internet may be able to access some or all of the information available to medical practitioners, but may 'lack relevant "background" information, the more sophisticated skills needed to question this and the additional skills to then pose specific questions and find the knowledge they seek' (Greenberg). As discussed above, there may also be differences between professions regarding the nature of the relationship with clients in attending to presenting problems. It can be argued that in professions whose knowledge is more diffuse, complicated or disputed, there are more opportunities for both collaboration and contestation between clients and practitioners concerning what is legitimate for, and in, practice. In these professions, expertise has less to do with technological interventions and more to do with dialogue with the client about his/her life experiences, circumstances and what is meaningful in resolving problems of a personal nature. In the chapters of this book, the relationship between theory and practice often appears to involve skills and tools having to be negotiated, with the process sometimes being as important as the outcome. These uncertainties can impact on the legal liabilities for duty of care that professionals face, with the issue hinging on clients' expectations about satisfactory outcomes. Greenberg poses fundamental questions that arise from expectations of clients' participation that assume increased satisfaction. Does consumer satisfaction indicate effectiveness? Is satisfaction related to agreement on the interventions provided or on participation in decisions about such processes, even if the professional ultimately may have to intervene in ways the client may not agree with? Does a client's inability to attribute problem resolution to professional intervention necessarily mean that the professional's role has been irrelevant or ineffective? Can such outcomes be controlled? Regarding the question of integrating consumers' perspectives into evidence-based practice, Greenberg asks, 'Should consumer satisfaction be the sole criterion, or should clinical processes and outcome be considered as well?'

Finally, in a rarely acknowledged perspective on the reciprocity and mutuality of the relationship between clients and professionals beyond the immediate problem, Holmes and Norton each discuss the importance of professionals recognizing their feelings towards the client that may influence the helping relationship as a process and outcome. They also recognize the influence of the patient (client) on the doctor (professional) (Norton, cites Jung 1931), which may profoundly affect the professional in unexpected ways.

Multidisciplinarity and interdisciplinarity

While most of the contributors to this book are representatives of particular professions, the few who are not write about practice in a particular field or problem area that requires interdisciplinary knowledge. Miller, writing on addictions, focuses on a particular social problem, arguing that the knowledge required for effective interventions is not associated with particular professions, but emerges from evaluation research that is relatively unaffected by professional agendas. He considers that the necessary knowledge and skills can be learnt by practitioners from a range of caring professions involved with people with substance addictions. Being problem-based, this approach differs from professionally focused approaches associated with particular aims, values and ethics, knowledge and practices.

Lawn and Battersby also illustrate ways in which a problem-based approach crosses professional boundaries in their study of 'person-centred care', which requires a collaborative, multidisciplinary approach and generalist skills taught to all health and allied health practitioners. Through their problem-based approach to professional knowledge-in-practice, highlighting how multidisciplinary perspectives may become interdisciplinary through a focus on a problem and research-derived knowledge of 'what works', Miller, and Lawn and Battersby also suggest questions about the nature of professions and whether separate professions are needed where the same knowledge-for- and -in-practice can be taught to any practitioner working with clients who experience a given problem.

Smith, Meyer, Stagnitti and Schoo intimate an alternative approach to multidisciplinarity as knowledge-in-practice, focusing on approaches to a single problem (stroke) by separate professions – physiotherapy and occupational therapy. These professions have 'shared and distinctive elements ... [there being a] close relationship between [these] two professions ... [that] maintain defined and separate roles in health practice', with the aim of better outcomes for patients through complementarity of interventions. Smith and her co-authors discuss concepts of 'shared care' and the 'blending of knowledge' through 'client-focused teamwork [that] progresses from multidisciplinary (separate disciplinary treatment plans) to interdisciplinary (shared plan and monitoring of progress) or even transdisciplinary (crossing professional boundaries)'. Using an approach that proposes greater introspection by practitioners about what knowledge-in-practice may mean, D'Cruz reflects on a social work research interview that was offered as a starting point for discussion between social workers and others in the 'caring' professions where interviews form an indispensable practice for assessing problems and negotiating interventions.

Multidisciplinarity is clearly a concern for many authors in this book, and in some cases it appears as fundamental to conflicts over the validity of professional knowledge and professional roles, this being underscored by Sheean and Cameron in relation to midwives and obstetricians. In psychiatry, Holmes acknowledges the 'team processes' that are essential to effective service provision, with the qualification that they can 'impair the functioning of any group, giving rise to tensions around autonomy, authority, responsibility and perceived value within the team'.

Even in cases that blur professional demarcations through shared research-derived knowledge and skills, in Miller's discussion of addiction, for example, pharmacological interventions have to be complemented by what might be described as 'social work', the object being to assist clients with broader problems which, left unresolved, would vitiate the more direct pharmacological interventions. Miller raises questions about skills for practitioners as he describes approaches for 'practice based on knowledge' that are recognizably social work practice approaches.

Multidisciplinarity in professional education and professional practice

This book indicates skills and approaches that are called for in effective multidisciplinary practice. They include an awareness of the need for interprofessional practice that is based on engaging with different forms of professional knowledge and different roles. A dynamic relationship is envisaged, involving deliberations over how problems are defined and which interventions are most appropriate. Professional values and ethics intersect with professional knowledge. Our reflections in this Conclusion on the similarities and differences between knowledge-in-practice from multidisciplinary perspectives suggest that a salutary awareness has been developing in some professions regarding the need for subjective knowledge, intuition, introspection and an honest confronting of the fact that sometimes, as professionals, we just do not know how to help our clients. To be sure, there are important differences between professions in this regard, influenced by their assumptions about knowledge and professional expertise.

Awareness of participatory practice that is inclusive of clients is an ethical and political concern for many professions, additional to the universal concern for efficacy. The differences between professions in terms of whether clients' participation is encouraged, and how this participation is constrained by professional knowledge, roles and expectations combine to suggest the value of dialogue between professionals on teams so that the differences that could lead to disrespect or conflict can instead be grasped as opportunities for understanding and building better teams through the complementarity of knowledge, roles and practice. Engaging in such practices in professional education would demonstrate constructive multidisciplinary practice.

The process of reading the chapters in this book, which encapsulate different professional preoccupations, has no doubt posed challenges related to such differences. It is hoped that readers who have persevered with the challenge have become aware of the need for open-mindedness, reflexivity (Taylor and White 2000, 2001) and critical reflection (Fook 1996, 1999) as part of the engagement with the text. We hope that this approach to reading as a relationship between reader and text may encourage readers to extend such practices towards members of their multidisciplinary teams in workplaces, because as we indicated at the outset of this Conclusion, the process of reading a multidisciplinary text has parallels with actual professional practice in teams.

Indeed, dialogue about different ways of knowing can lead us beyond reflexive and critical engagement with differences. Beginning with reading texts by those outside our professional circles, and attending to the challenges that are posed by having to deal with what is alien and different, we may increase the chances and opportunities for improved multidisciplinary practice. This can come about through understanding why and how each profession does what it does; and how professions differ in purpose, paradigms, ontology, epistemology, values and ethics, and in their relationship with clients. Shaw (2007), for example, in writing about social work research and claims to its distinctiveness, challenges the claims of 'special character' associated with the profession. In particular, he challenges the 'belief that social work has a basic value position that has greater merit/greater human authenticity/is more whole-person oriented, etc. than any other professions' (Shaw 2007: 662). Instead, he argues 'it will make us disinclined to listen to the voices of colleagues in other disciplines and professions' (Shaw 2007: 663).

In addition to the particular professional perspectives on knowledge-in-practice, this book enhances the understanding of knowledge-in-practice in the caring professions through the examples it furnishes of problem-based, as opposed to professionally focused, practices, such as working with people with addictions, necessitating interdisciplinary practice, or in aiming to achieve a common professional aim, as with 'person-centred care'. These problem-based approaches that appear to transcend professional boundaries raise questions about professions, demarcated forms of knowledge and generally qualified professionals whose on-the-job learning leads to specializations (for example, in mental health, addictions, criminal justice). Is it better to educate professionals to work in specific fields of practice associated with particular problems, which, it is claimed, is a more effective way of responding to 'industry' needs and gaining political recognition and funding, as it is currently argued in the case of Australian social work and with regard to the accreditation of mental health social workers under Medicare (AASW 2008a, 8; AASW 2008b; Medicare and AASW Accredited Social Workers, 2008)? Or is the downside of specialist knowledge the increasing likelihood of clients being treated in fragmented ways, with their problems not seen as interconnected?

References

AASW March 2008a. *Australian Social Work Education and Accreditation Standards*. Canberra: Australian Association of Social Workers. Available at:

http://www.aasw.asn.au/becomeamember/becomingasw/AASWEdn AccredStandards1108.pdf.

AASW May 2008b. *Australian Social Work Education and Accreditation Standards: Statement of Specific Mental Health Curriculum Content for Social Work Qualifying Courses.* Canberra: Australian Association of Social Workers. Available at: http://www.aasw.asn/becomeamember/ becomingasw/IMHStatementofCurriculumContent.pdf.

Barthes, R. 1972. *Mythologies.* London: Vintage Press.

Beresford, P. 2000. Service users' knowledge and social work theory: conflict or collaboration? *British Journal of Social Work,* 30(4), 489–503.

Cirocco, M. 2007. How reflective practice improves nurses' critical thinking ability. *Gastroenterology Nursing,* 30(6), 405–13.

Davies, R. 1984. *Can a Doctor be a Humanist?* The David Coit Gillman Lecture, Johns Hopkins Medical School, in Davies, R. 1996. *The Merry Heart.* New York: Viking Press.

Fook, J. (ed.) 1996. *The Reflective Researcher.* St Leonards: Allen and Unwin.

Fook, J. 1999. Critical reflectivity in education and practice, in *Transforming Social Work Practice: Postmodern Critical Perspectives,* edited by B. Pease and Jan Fook. St Leonards: Allen and Unwin, 195–208.

Gordon, J. 2003. Clinical review: ABC of learning and teaching in medicine – one to one teaching and feedback. *British Medical Journal,* 326(7388), 543–5.

Ife, J. 1997. *Rethinking Social Work: Towards Critical Practice.* Melbourne: Longman.

Jacobson, L., Hawthorne, K. and Wood, F. 2006. The 'Mensch' factor in general practice: a role to demonstrate professionalism to students. *British Journal of General Practice,* 56(533), 976–9.

Jung, C. 1985 [1945]. The psychology of the transference, in *The Collected Works of C.G. Jung,* volume 16. Princeton: Princeton University Press.

Medicare and AASW Accredited Social Workers, May 2008. Available at: http://www.aasw.asn.au/medicare.html.

Papadimos, T. 2009. Reflective thinking and medical students: some thoughtful distillations regarding John Dewey and Hannah Arendt. *Philosophy, Ethics, and Humanities in Medicine,* 4(5), doi:10.1186/1747-5341-4-5. Available at:http://www.peh.med.com/content/4/1/5 [accessed 25 May 2009].

Pithouse, A. 1987. *Social Work: The Social Organisation of an Invisible Trade.* Aldershot: Avebury.

Polanyi, M. 1967. *The Tacit Dimension.* New York: Anchor Books.

Richardson, L. 1994. Writing: a method of inquiry, in *Handbook of Qualitative Research,* edited by N. Denzin and Y. Lincoln. 2nd Edition. Newbury Park: Sage, 516–29.

Rosenau, P. 1992. *Postmodernism and the Social Sciences: Insights, Inroads and Intrusions.* Princeton: Princeton University Press.

Sarup, M. 1993. *An Introductory Guide to Post-Structuralism and Postmodernism.* 2nd Edition. London: Harvester Wheatsheaf.

Shaw, I. 2007. Is social work research distinctive? *Social Work Education,* 26(7), 659–69.

Taylor, C. and White, S. 2000. *Practising Reflexivity in Health and Welfare: Making Knowledge.* Buckingham: Open University Press.

Taylor, C. and White, S. 2001. Knowledge, truth and reflexivity: the problem of judgement in social work. *Journal of Social Work,* 1(1), 37–59.

Index

251